LIVING LANGUAGE®

ESSENTIAL

SPANISH

FOR

LAW ENFORCEMENT

D0027532

THE LIVING LANGUAGE® SERIES

Living Language Basic Courses, Revised & Updated
Spanish*	*Japanese**	*Portuguese (Brazilian)*
French*	*Russian*	*Portuguese (Continental)*
German*	*Italian**	*Inglés/English for Spanish Speakers*

Living Language Intermediate Courses
Spanish 2	*French 2*
German 2	*Italian 2*

Living Language Advanced Courses, Revised & Updated
Spanish 3	*French 3*

Living Language All the Way™ (Ultimate™)
Spanish*	*Japanese**	*Russian 2** *(1998)*
French*	*Spanish 2**	*Japanese 2** *(1998)*
German*	*French 2**	*Inglés/English for Spanish Speakers**
Italian*	*German 2**	*Inglés/English for Spanish Speakers 2**
Russian* *(1998)*	*Italian 2**	*Chinese (1999)*

Living Language Children's Courses
Spanish	*French*

Living Language Conversational English
for Chinese Speakers	*for Korean Speakers*
for Japanese Speakers	*for Spanish Speakers*
for Russian Speakers	

Living Language Essential Language Guides
Essential Spanish for Healthcare
Essential Spanish for Law Enforcement

Living Language Fast & Easy™
Spanish	*Italian*	*Portuguese*
French	*Russian*	*Czech*
German	*Polish*	*Hungarian*
Japanese	*Korean*	*Mandarin (Chinese)*
Arabic	*Hebrew*	*Inglés/English for Spanish Speakers*

Living Language All-Audio
Spanish	*Italian*
French	*German*

Living Language Speak Up!® Accent Elimination Courses
Spanish   American Regional
Asian, Indian and Middle Eastern

Fodor's Languages for Travelers
Spanish	*Italian*
French	*German*

LIVING LANGUAGE MULTIMEDIA™ TriplePlay *Plus!*
Spanish	*English*	*Hebrew*
French	*Italian*	
German	*Japanese*	

LIVING LANGUAGE MULTIMEDIA™ Your Way 2.0
Spanish	*French*	*Inglés/English for Spanish Speakers*

LIVING LANGUAGE MULTIMEDIA™ Let's Talk
Spanish	*French*	*English*
Italian	*German*	

*Available on Cassette and Compact Disc.

LIVING LANGUAGE®

ESSENTIAL

SPANISH

FOR

LAW ENFORCEMENT

Written by
Ana Novas
Director, Spanish Adventures in Learning

Consultant
P. J. Guido
Training Officer, Santa Monica Police Department

Edited by
Helga Schier, Ph.D.

Living Language, A Random House Company
New York

Published by Living Language, a division of Crown Publishers, Inc.,
201 East 50th Street, New York, New York, 10022. Member of the
Crown Publishing Group.

Random House, Inc. New York, Toronto, London, Sydney, Auckland
http://www.livinglanguage.com/

Living Language is a registered trademark of Crown Publishers, Inc.

Printed in the United States of America

Designed by Cynthia Dunne

Library of Congress Cataloging in Publication Data is available
upon request.

ISBN 0-609-80137-6

10 9 8 7 6 5 4 3 2 1

First Edition

ACKNOWLEDGMENTS

Many thanks to the Living Language® staff: Helga Schier, Kathryn Mintz, Lisa Alpert, Ana Suffredini, Christopher Warnasch, Liana Parry, Lenny Henderson, Cynthia Dunne, and Erin Bekowies. Special thanks also to Elinor Jackson, James Len and Harold Engold from the Haledon Police Department, Paul Baca at the Denver Police Department, and the following individuals at the Lakewood Police Department: Captain Alan Youngs, Sgt. Jeff Cohn, Sharon Swafford, Viola Herron, Lynn Dicus, Diana Rose, Kevin Paletta, Stan Connally, and Vincent Barrera. Thanks also go to Javier Galvan and Ana Sofía Ramirez-Gelpí. Without their help and patience, this program would never have been possible.

CONTENTS

INTRODUCTION

Living Language® Essential Spanish for Law Enforcement offers a fast, efficient, and cost-effective way to learn the Spanish skills you'll need on the job. The program gives you *only* the vocabulary and phrases relevant to police work. The phrasebook format lets you speak and understand Spanish immediately, without hours of serious study. The notes on vocabulary, grammar, and culture that you'll find throughout the book will help you use the language and interact with Spanish speakers more effectively.

Essential Spanish for Law Enforcement takes you through the most typical situations in which successful communication is a potentially life-saving skill. You'll learn how to interview witnesses, Mirandize and book suspects, conduct DUI procedures, and communicate during domestic abuse situations or gang-related crimes, all in Spanish. Unlike any other program, *Living Language® Essential Spanish for Law Enforcement* features *realistic* language, including slang and street language that will help you handle almost any situation.

The complete program consists of this text and three hours of recordings. However, if you are already comfortable with your Spanish pronunciation, this manual may also be used on its own.

Course Materials

• THE MANUAL •

Living Language® Essential Spanish for Law Enforcement consists of eight sections, six of which deal with different aspects of law enforcement: *The Field Notebook, In Case of an Emergency, On the Road, Administrative Services, Crimes and*

Misdemeanors, and *Community Service.* Each section includes several dialogues about specific on-the-job situations related to the general topic. For example, *Crimes and Misdemeanors* provides dialogues on issues such as *Homicide* and *Drug-Related Crimes; Administrative Services* highlights issues such as *Report Release* and *Booking a Suspect;* and *Community Service* features *Missing Persons* and *Dealing with the Homeless.* The dialogues branch out in several directions to account for the most likely outcomes of each situation.

Communication is not a one-way street. Therefore, speaking skills *and* comprehension skills are taught to guarantee that you can ask the questions *and* understand the answers. Therefore, culture notes address different customs in the Spanish speaking community that will help you do your job better. And vocabulary and grammar notes, will improve your ability to speak Spanish.

The other two sections in the manual include our introductory section, *The Bare Essentials,* which provides an overview of the Spanish language and culture, and our *Reference* section in the back includes a concise grammar summary, a two-way glossary, and an easy-to-use index.

• THE REFERENCE GUIDE •

The pocket reference guide is designed to be used on the job. It features the most important words, phrases, and sentences from the manual, including helpful phrases for emergency situations. In addition, the reference guide serves as a transcript for the recordings. All of the material in **boldface** and ***boldface italics*** can be found on the two ninety-minute cassettes included in this package.

• THE RECORDINGS (two ninety-minute cassettes) •

The cassettes feature the most important words and phrases in the manual. You'll hear the Spanish phrases with their English translations, and pauses are provided for you to repeat after the native Spanish speakers. The recordings can be used without the manual or the reference guide—perfect for learning and practicing on the go.

And one last note...

Living Language® Essential Spanish for Law Enforcement is an indispensable tool for anyone working in law enforcement. However, the skills that are required to deal with potentially life-threatening situations safely and effectively go well beyond the linguistic realm. This program is not meant to override the training you received or the strategies you developed. *Living Language® Essential Spanish for Law Enforcement* is a valuable source for the Spanish language skills you'll need on the job—no more and no less—and is, thus, not a replacement but a crucial supplement to your training as a law enforcement officer.

LIVING LANGUAGE®

ESSENTIAL
SPANISH
FOR
LAW ENFORCEMENT

THE BARE ESSENTIALS

1. The Spanish Alphabet

a	ah
b	beh
c	seh
ch	cheh
d	deh
e	eh
f	EH-feh
g	heh
h	AH-cheh
i	ee
j	HOH-tah
k	kah
l	EH-leh
ll	EH-yeh
m	EH-meh
n	EH-neh
ñ	EH-nyeh
o	oh
p	peh
q	koo
r	EH-reh

rr	EH-rreh
s	EH-seh
t	tehh
u	oo
v	veh
w	doh-bleh-OO
x	EH-kees
y	ee-gree-EH-gah
z	SEH-tah

2. Pronunciation Chart

• VOWELS •

SPANISH SOUND	APPROXIMATE SOUND IN ENGLISH	EXAMPLE
a	(f<u>a</u>ther)	*trabajar* (to work)
e	(<u>a</u>ce, but cut off sharply)	*señor* (mister)
i	(f<u>ee</u>)	*día* (day)
o	(n<u>o</u>te)	*pistola* (pistol)
u	(r<u>u</u>le)	*mucho* (much)
y	(f<u>ee</u>t)	*y* (and) [only a vowel when standing alone]

• DIPHTHONGS •

SPANISH SOUND	APPROXIMATE SOUND IN ENGLISH	EXAMPLE
ai/ay	(<u>a</u>isle)	*bailar* (to dance)
		hay (there is, there are)
au	(n<u>ow</u>)	*auto* (car)
ei	(may)	*peine* (comb)
ia	(yarn)	*gracias* (thanks)
ie	(yet)	*siempre* (always)
io	(yodel)	*adiós* (bye)
iu	(you)	*ciudad* (city)
oi/oy	(oy)	*estoy* (I am)
ua	(<u>wa</u>nd)	*cuando* (when)
ue	(<u>we</u>t)	*bueno* (good)
ui/uy	(s<u>wee</u>t)	*cuidado* (care)
		muy (very)

• CONSONANTS •

The letters *k* and *w* appear in Spanish in foreign words like *kilowatt, kilometer*. In some countries, the *k* is spelled with the Spanish equivalent, *qu: quilómetro*. The *w* in Spanish sounds like an English *v: kilowatt*.

SPANISH SOUND	APPROXIMATE SOUND IN ENGLISH	EXAMPLE
l/m/n/p/s/t	similar to English	
b	at the beginning of a word or after *m*, similar to English	*bueno* (good)
	elsewhere, similar to English, but softer, allowing air to pass between lips, like *v*	*cabeza* (head)
c* (before *e/i*)	s (<u>c</u>ertain)	*cena* (dinner)
d	similar to English, but softer, allowing air to pass between lips, like th (<u>the</u>)	*verdad* (truth)
	after *n*, as in English: d (<u>d</u>o)	*corriendo* (running)
c (before *a/o/u*)	k (<u>c</u>atch)	*como* (how)
cc	cks (a<u>cc</u>ent)	*acción* (action)
ch	ch (<u>ch</u>urch)	*mucho* (much)
g (before *a/o/u*)	hard g (<u>g</u>o)	*gasolina* (gas)
g (before *e/i*)	hard h (<u>h</u>e)	*gente* (people)
h	always silent	*alcohol* (alcohol)
j	hard h (<u>h</u>e)	*jefe* (boss)
ll	In Latin America: ** y (yet); in Spain: lli (mi<u>lli</u>on)	*llamar* (to call)
ñ	ny (ca<u>ny</u>on)	*niño* (child)
qu	k (<u>k</u>ite)	*que* (that)
r	in middle of word, single trill (th<u>r</u>ow)	*pero* (but)

* In some regions of Latin America: *s* (vision).
** In certain Latin American countries, initial *ll* is pronounced with more friction, like *s* in vision, or *j* in judge.

r	at beginning of word, double trill	*ropa* (clothes)
rr	double trill	*carro* (car)
v	v (<u>v</u>ote, but softer, allowing air to pass between lips)	*viernes* (Friday)
x	cks (ro<u>cks</u>)	*taxi* (cab)
y	y (yet)	*yo* (I)
z *	s	*zona* (zone)

3. The Spanish Language

Although Spanish is a language different from English, there are many rules, which are identical between the two. Just like in English, the basic word order of Spanish is subject-verb-object.

This man stole my car.   *Este hombre robó mi coche.*

The subject is the word referring to the agent (*este hombre*), the one who performs the action. The verb describes the action (*robó*), and the object is the word referring to the thing or person receiving the action (*mi coche*).

Just like the English verb, the Spanish verb can have different tenses and thus specify whether the action is performed in the present, past, or future. The "moods" of the verb express whether an action is really happening (indicative), may happen (conditional), or is hypothetical (subjunctive and potential).

Spanish verbs have different endings depending on whether the subject is singular or plural, you, me, he, we, or they.

You have a tattoo.   *Usted tiene un tatuaje.*
They have drugs.   *Ellas tienen drogas.*

Since the verb ending can indicate what or who the subject is, you don't always have to make explicit reference to the subject of the verb.

* In parts of Spain, *z*—and also *c* before *e* or *i*—is pronounced like English *th*. Examples: *zona, cera, cinco.*

[I] am a police officer.	*Soy policía.*		
[We] are going to the police station.	*Vamos a la estación de policía.*		

All Spanish nouns have a gender, i.e., they are either masculine or feminine. In some cases, the gender is obvious: a man is masculine, and a woman is feminine.

the man	*el hombre*	the woman	*la mujer*
a man	*un hombre*	a woman	*una mujer*

In most cases, however, gender and meaning are unrelated, and it is the ending of the noun that determines the gender. The adjective, a word that describes the noun, always has to agree with the gender and number of the noun it describes. That means that the adjective endings have to be either masculine or feminine, singular or plural, just like the noun it describes.

the black man	*el hombre negro*	the black woman	*la mujer negra*
the black men	*los hombres negros*	the black women	*las mujeres negras*

So, it makes quite a difference whether you're speaking about or to a woman or a man.

Are you hurt? (addressing a male)	*¿Está usted herido?*		
(addressing a female)	*¿Está usted herida?*		

In this book we will list both whenever necessary:

Are you hurt?	*¿Está usted herido/a?*

It is important to remember that, unlike English, Spanish has two different forms of address, depending on how well you know a person. *Tú* is the familiar form of address used with family members, friends, children, and pets. *Usted* is the polite form of address used towards everyone else. Using *tú* with someone you are not on familiar terms with is considered inappropriate and disrespectful. Therefore, it is best to always use *usted* on the job, unless you are dealing with children. Similarly, it is uncommon to use a person's first name in Spanish unless you are very well acquainted. For this reason, it is best to address everyone, witnesses and suspects alike, by their last name and with the polite form of address, again unless you are dealing with children.

Spanish uses accent marks on written words. Sometimes, words that look alike have different meanings depending on whether they have an accent mark or not.

you	*tú*	your	*tu*
is	*está*	this	*ésta*
I know	*sé*	yourself, himself, herself, itself, to him, to her, to you, to them	*se*
you, give!	*dé*	of, from	*de*

If you remember these few rules, there's no need to worry about grammatical details. The phrases and sentences in this book are written for you to use them as printed. All you have to do is familiarize yourself with them, and you're ready to go. Should you be curious, however, please refer to the grammar notes throughout the book, and to the grammar summary in the appendix.

4. The Latino Culture

A. A QUICK OVERVIEW OF THE HISTORY OF MODERN IMMIGRATION

By the year 2000, Americans of Hispanic and/or Latino descent will comprise the largest minority living in the U.S., and by the year 2050 they are expected to make up between 10 and 22 percent of the entire U.S. population. Their contributions span all areas of public life: from agricultural fields to the political arena; from science, education, literature, and art to the world of business. Terms such as "Latino" and "Hispanic" have emerged only recently to describe the ethnic background of a group of Americans with various cultural and national backgrounds. Because the word "Hispanic" often carries an association with Spain and the negative implications of the conquest and colonization of America, the term "Latino" is often preferred by the Spanish-speaking people of this continent. However, many

Latinos and Hispanics don't think about themselves as such, but refer to themselves as Mexican-American, Tejano, Puerto Rican, Colombian, or other cultural and national designators describing any of the Spanish-speaking countries from which they or their ancestors may have come. In fact, the terms "Hispanic" and "Latino" at times seem to be nothing but an attempt to simplify a very complex cultural phenomenon, similar to classifying Englishmen and New Zealanders within the same ethnic category just because both speak English. Therefore, the most respectful and neutral approach is to allow people to classify and name themselves.

The Hispanics and Latinos living in the U.S. are comprised of the following main groups: Cubans and Cuban-Americans, Puerto Ricans, Mexicans and Mexican-Americans, Central Americans, Spaniards, and South Americans.

Cubans have been living in the U.S. since the eighteenth century. Today, there are three generations of Cuban-Americans living in the U.S. Most of them—more than half a million—live in Florida. Cuban immigration was mainly motivated by politics and began around 1959 with the communist revolution in Cuba. Immediately after Fidel Castro came to power, a huge number of Cubans fled to the U.S. A second major wave of immigration took place in 1976, when Castro opened his jails and put 125,000 political prisoners in boats and sent them to the U.S., where they were accepted by the Carter administration.

Puerto Rico is an American protectorate, and Puerto Ricans are U.S. citizens. Exposure to mainland prosperity after serving in the U.S. military in World War II, coupled with the population explosion on the island, caused many Puerto Ricans to move to the mainland, seeking better economic opportunities. One-third of all Puerto Ricans—2.3 million—live in one of the fifty U.S. states. In New York City alone there are 900,000. Drugs, crime, and an alarming lack of educational opportunities in New York City's *El Barrio* are some of the reasons why the population of this area has become one of the most socially disadvantaged Latino group.

Mexicans and Mexican-Americans represent the largest and culturally most complex group—20 million people. Their cultural heritage dates back centuries. Originally, the American Southwest was a Spanish colony that was incorporated into Mexico and was settled by Spaniards and "mestizos," who had a mixture of Spanish or Mexican and Indian ethnicity. In 1848, this territory was lost to the U.S. Although the resulting treaty of Guadalupe Hidalgo assigned land rights to Mexicans who homesteaded in Texas, many Americans ignored these rights and subjected Mexicans to abuse and cultural or racial discrimination. The Spanish language was banned from schools, the Mexican culture looked down upon, and the American English language and culture became dominant. Today, many Americans of Latino background are mistakenly taken for Mexicans, no matter what their national origin.

As a result of past discrimination and abuse, some Mexican-Americans may be sensitive to identity issues. Many were raised with the belief that abandoning their Mexican roots would lead to a brighter future in Anglo-American society. Therefore, many may have grown up hearing the Spanish language at home but do not speak it themselves. They may consider themselves Mexican when talking to Anglo-Americans, but American when talking to Mexican nationals.

Americans with Mexican-Indian roots refer to themselves as Chicanos. Inspired by the Civil Rights movement in the 1960's, the Chicano movement—which is political, social, cultural, and intellectual by nature—emerged to protest the discrimination against Mexican-Americans and to restore their cultural identity.

Central Americans and South Americans started entering the United States in greater numbers in the late 1970's and continued in the 1980's and 1990's. Economic hardship in the Dominican Republic, Colombia, and Peru, as well as political persecution in countries such as Nicaragua, El Salvador, and Guatemala, brought many new citizens to this country. New York has the world's second-largest Dominican population— about 800,000—and about 500,000 Salvadorans live in Los Angeles. There are also thousands of Argentinians, Panamanians, and Ecuadorians who come to this country today to work and make a better life for themselves and their families, just like millions of people from Europe did many years ago.

Spaniards have immigrated into the U.S. for centuries, ever since Cristopher Columbus "discovered" America in 1492. Spaniards came as explorers, *conquistadores,* missionaries, refugees, and as individuals attracted by the riches of the "land of opportunity."

B. DEALING WITH CULTURAL STEREOTYPES

The United States is a multicultural society. As a police officer, you meet and communicate with people from a variety of cultural and national backgrounds on a daily basis. An awareness of the stereotypes many non-Hispanic Americans may have about the Latino culture, and vice versa, will increase your cultural sensitivity, and will make your encounters with the Latino community easier, more cordial, and successful.

Stereotypes are strategies to help us make sense of actions, customs, and beliefs that seem foreign and strange to us. Some stereotypes may be partially true in a general sense, but are usually not true at all when dealing with a particular individual face to face. For example, a widespread stereotype is that Americans drink beer only out of cans, chew gum at all times, and often carry a gun. Without a doubt, everyone would agree that this is a rather simplistic view of American culture, recognize this as a stereotype that needs explanation, or even dismiss it as nonsense. Nonetheless, similarly simplistic views of Latino culture are taken rather seriously.

Latinos don't like to work, take siestas all the time, and are in this country illegally. Sound familiar? Without a proper explanation, nothing could be further from the truth. While it is true that the work day is divided by a siesta time in southern regions of the globe to escape the midday heat, it is not true that Latinos don't like to work. Instead, a typical work day in Latin American countries and Spain is extended far into the evening hours. The long break at midday is used to share the biggest meal of the day with family, friends, or associates the way Americans do at dinner time. And while it is true that there are illegal immigrants in the U.S., it is also true that most Latinos are either legal aliens or American citizens, contributing to the gross national product and paying taxes as much as American citizens of other backgrounds. Only a very small percentage of both legal and undocumented Latinos takes advantage of the welfare programs this country offers—5 percent uses free medical care and 1 percent lives on food stamps.

Stereotypes are a fact of life. They will probably always exist, but that doesn't mean that they have a place in law enforcement. On the contrary, stereotypes contribute to misunderstandings and inappropriate behavior in situations that call for objectivity and fairness. Cultural differences don't make one group better or worse than another, just different. Armed with this open-minded attitude, your work among Latinos in your community may become easier, more enjoyable, and rewarding.

5. Essential Phrases

Hello!	¡Hola!	¡OH-lah!
Good morning.	Buenos días.	BWEH-nohs dyahs.
Good afternoon.	Buenas tardes.	BWEH-nahs TAHR-dehs.
Good evening.	Buenas noches.	BWEH-nahs NOH-chehs.
Good-bye.	Adiós.	Ah-DYOHS.
Have a good day!	¡Qué le vaya bien!	¡Keh leh VAH-yah byehn!
What's your name?	¿Cómo se llama?	¿KOH-moh seh YAH-mah?
Do you speak English?	¿Habla usted inglés?	¿AH-blah oos-TEHD een-GLEHS?
Do you need an interpreter?	¿Necesita un intérprete?	¿Neh-seh-SEE-tah oon een-TEHR-preh-teh?

| An interpreter will be here any minute. | Un intérprete llegará en cualquier momento. | Oon een-TEHR-preh-teh yeh-gah-RAH ehn kwahl-KYEHR moh-MEHN-toh. |

| Sign here, please. | Firme aquí, por favor. | FEER-meh ah-KEE, pohr fah-VOHR. |

| May I ask you a few questions? | ¿Puedo hacerle unas preguntas? | ¿PWEH-doh ah-SEHR-leh OO-nahs preh-GOON-tahs? |

| Give me the information. | Déme la información. | DEH-meh lah een-fohr-een-fohr-mah-SYOHN. |

| Tell me. | Dígame. | DEE-gah-meh. |

| Listen to me. | Escúcheme. | Ehs-KOO-cheh-meh. |

| Thank you. | Gracias. | GRAH-syahs. |

| You are welcome. | De nada. | Deh NAH-dah. |

| I'm sorry. | Lo siento. | Loh SYEHN-toh. |

| Are you... | ¿Está usted... | ¿Ehs-TAH oos-TEHD... |

| • okay? | • bien? | • byehn? |

| • hurt? | • herido/a? | • eh-REE-doh/dah? |

| Where does it hurt? | ¿Dónde le duele? | ¿Dohn-deh leh DWEH-leh? |

| Do you need... | ¿Necesita... | ¿Neh-seh-SEE-tah... |

| • an ambulance? | • una ambulancia? | • oo-nah ahm-boo-LAHN-syah? |

| • help? | • ayuda? | • ah-YOO-dah? |

| Do you have medical insurance? | ¿Tiene seguro médico? | ¿TYEH-neh seh-GOO-roh MEH-dee-koh? |

| How may I help you? | ¿En qué puedo ayudarle? | ¿Ehn keh PWEH-doh ah-yoo-DAHR-leh? |

| Can I take you somewhere? | ¿Puedo llevarlo/a a alguna parte? | ¿PWEH-doh yeh-VAHR-loh/lah ah ahl-GOO-nah PAHR-teh? |

| What's your date of birth? | ¿Cuál es su fecha de nacimiento? | ¿Kwahl ehs soo FEH-chah deh nah-see-MYEHN-toh? |

How old are you?	¿Cuántos años tiene?	¿KWAHN-tohs AH-nyohs TYEH-neh?
Do you have proof of insurance?	¿Tiene prueba del seguro?	¿TYEH-neh PRWEH-bah dehl seh-GOO-roh?
May I see the registration for this car?	¿Puedo ver el registro de este carro?	¿PWEH-doh vehr ehl reh-HEES-troh deh ehs-teh KAH-rroh?
Where is your driver's license?	¿Dónde está su licencia de manejar?	¿DOHN-deh ehs-TAH soo lee-sehn-SYAH deh mah-neh-HAHR?
Repeat slowly, please.	Repita más despacio, por favor.	Reh-PEE-tah mahs dehs-PAH-syoh pohr fah-VOHR.
What's your phone number?	¿Cuál es su número de teléfono?	¿Kwahl ehs soo NOO-meh-roh deh teh-LEH-foh-noh?
Your phone number at work?	¿Su número de teléfono en el trabajo?	¿Soo NOO-meh-roh deh teh-LEH-foh-noh ehn ehl trah-BAH-hoh?
Number by number, please.	Número por número, por favor.	NOO-meh-roh pohr NOO-meh-roh, pohr fah-VOHR.
Your name and last name/s?	¿Su nombre y apellido/s?	¿Soo NOHM-breh ee ah-peh-YEE-doh/dohs?
Where are you going?	¿Adónde va?	¿Ah-DOHN-deh vah?
Where...	¿Dónde...	¿DOHN-deh...
• do you live?	• vive?	• VEE-veh?
• do you work?	• trabaja?	• trah-BAH-hah?
Get out of the car.	Salga del carro.	SAHL-gah dehl KAH-rroh.
Stay in the car.	Quédese en el carro.	KEH-deh-seh ehn ehl KAH-rroh.
Get in the car.	Suba al carro.	Soo-bah ahl KAH-rroh.
Don't move.	No se mueva.	Noh seh MWEH-vah.
Follow me.	Sígame.	SEE-gah-meh.
Go over there.	Vaya allí.	VAH-yah ah-YEE.
Come over here.	Venga aquí.	VEHN-gah ah-KEE.

Stop!	¡Alto! ¡Párese!	¡AHL-toh! ¡PAH-reh-seh!
Drop the gun.	Suelte la pistola.	SWEHL-teh lah pees-TOH-lah.
Put your hands up!	¡Manos arriba!	¡MAH-nohs ah-RREE-bah!
Now!	¡Ahora!	¡Ah-OH-rah!
Stand up.	Levántese.	Leh-VAHN-teh-seh.
Sit down.	Siéntese.	SYEHN-teh-seh.
Don't talk.	No hable.	Noh AH-bleh.
Lie on the ground.	Échese en el suelo.	EH-cheh-seh ehn ehl SWEH-loh.
Put one hand behind your back.	Ponga una mano detrás de la espalda.	POHN-gah OO-nah MAH-noh deh-TRAHS deh lah ehs-pahl-dah.
Now the next hand.	Ahora la otra mano.	ah-OH-rah lah oh-trah MAH-no.
You are under arrest.	Está arrestado/a.	ehs-TAH ah-rehs-TAH-doh/ah.
Shut up!	¡Cállese!	¡KAH-yeh-seh!
Calm down!	¡Cálmese!	¡KAHL-meh-seh!
Everything will be okay.	No le pasará nada.	Noh leh pah-sah-RAH NAH-dah.

6. Numbers

A. CARDINAL NUMBERS

zero	cero	SEH-roh
one	uno	OO-noh
two	dos	dohs
three	tres	trehs
four	cuatro	KWAH-troh
five	cinco	SEEN-koh
six	seis	says
seven	siete	SYEH-teh

eight	*ocho*	OH-choh
nine	*nueve*	NWEH-veh
ten	*diez*	dyes
eleven	*once*	OHN-seh
twelve	*doce*	DOH-seh
thirteen	*trece*	TREH-seh
fourteen	*catorce*	kah-TOHR-seh
fifteen	*quince*	KEEN-seh
sixteen	*dieciséis*	dyeh-see-says
seventeen	*diecisiete*	dyeh-see-SYEH-teh
eighteen	*dieciocho*	dyeh-see-OH-choh
nineteen	*diecinueve*	dyeh-see-NWEH-veh
twenty	*veinte*	VAYN-teh
twenty-one	*veintiuno*	vayn-tee-OO-noh
twenty-two	*veintidós*	vayn-tee-DOHS
twenty-three...	*veintitrés...*	vayn-tee-TREHS...
thirty	*treinta*	TRAYN-tah
forty	*cuarenta*	kwah-REHN-tah
fifty	*cincuenta*	seen-KWEN-tah
sixty	*sesenta*	seh-SEHN-tah
seventy	*setenta*	seh-TEHN-tah
eighty	*ochenta*	oh-CHEHN-tah
ninety	*noventa*	noh-VEHN-tah
one hundred	*cien*	SYEHN
one hundred one	*ciento uno*	SYEHN-toh OO-noh
one hundred two...	*ciento dos...*	SYEHN-toh dohs...
one hundred twenty...	*ciento veinte...*	SYEHN-toh VAYN-teh...
one hundred thirty...	*ciento treinta...*	SYEHN-toh TRAYN-tah...
two hundred	*doscientos/as*	dohs-SYEHN-tohs/tahs
three hundred	*trescientos/as*	trehs-SYEHN-tohs/tahs

four hundred	*cuatrocientos/as*	kwah-troh-SYEHN-tohs/tahs
five hundred	*quinientos/as*	kee-NYEHN-tohs/tahs
six hundred	*seiscientos/as*	says-SYEHN-tohs/tahs
seven hundred	*setecientos/as*	seh-teh-SYEHN-tohs/tahs
eight hundred	*ochocientos/as*	oh-choh-SYEHN-tohs/tahs
nine hundred	*novecientos/as*	noh-veh-SYEHN-tohs/tas
one thousand	*mil*	meel
two thousand	*dos mil*	dohs meel
three thousand...	*tres mil...*	trehs meel...
one million	*un millón*	oon mee-YOHN
two million...	*dos millones...*	dohs mee-YOH-nehs...

B. ORDINAL NUMBERS

first	*primero*	pree-MEH-roh
	primer/a	pree-MEHR/MEHR-ah
second	*segundo/a*	seh-GOON-doh/dah
third	*tercero*	tehr-SEH-roh
	tercer/a	tehr-SEHR/SEH-rah
fourth	*cuarto/a*	KWAHR-toh/tah
fifth	*quinto/a*	KEEN-toh/tah
sixth	*sexto/a*	SEHKS-toh/tah
seventh	*séptimo/a*	SEHP-tee-moh/mah
eighth	*octavo/a*	ohk-TAH-voh/vah
ninth	*noveno/a*	noh-VEH-noh/nah
tenth	*décimo/a*	DEH-see-moh/mah

THE FIELD NOTEBOOK

1. Information Gathering

CULTURE NOTE ••••

POLITENESS Latinos tend to give detailed explanations before answering a question with a simple "yes" or "no." This is considered a sign of politeness. Explaining why one agrees or disagrees is a matter of showing courtesy and respect. Courtesy phrases such as *por favor* (please), *es un placer* (it's my pleasure), and *perdón* (excuse me) should be used freely, and commands should always be softened with *por favor* (please).

A. ESTABLISHING THE EVENT

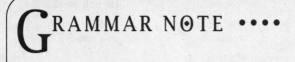

GRAMMAR NOTE ••••

ASKING QUESTIONS To ask questions in Spanish, reverse the order of verb and subject.

| You have... | Usted tiene... |
| Do you have...? | *¿Tiene usted...?* |

Just like English, Spanish uses question words such as *¿qué?* (what?).

| *¿Qué tiene usted?* | What do you have? |

Here's a list of important question words:

What?	*¿Qué?*
Of what?	*¿De qué?*
Which?	*¿Cuál?*
How?	*¿Cómo?*
Where?	*¿Dónde?*
From where?	*¿De dónde?*
To where?	*¿Adónde?*
When?	*¿Cuándo?*
How much?	*¿Cuánto?*
How many?	*¿Cuántos/as?*
Why?	*¿Por qué?*
Who?	*¿Quién?*
With whom?	*¿Con quién?*
To whom?	*¿A quién?*
Whose?	*¿De quién?*

It is also possible to just allow your voice to rise in the end of the sentence as you would in English.

| You have...? | *¿Usted tiene...?* |

In writing, use question marks at the beginning and at the end (*¿...?*). Please note that there is no equivalent for the auxiliary "do/does/did."

| Did you witness the accident? | *¿Vio el accidente?* |

OFFICER	AGENTE	
Who called the police?	¿Quién llamó a la policía?	¿Kyehn yah-MOH ah lah poh-lee-SEE-ah?
Can anyone translate for me?	¿Puede alguien traducirme?	¿PWEH-deh ahl-gyehn trah-doo-SEER-meh?
WITNESS	**TESTIGO**	
I...	Yo...	Yoh...
• called.	• llamé.	• yah-MEH.
• don't know.	• no sé.	• noh seh.
My...	Mi...	Mee...
• husband.	• esposo.	• ehs-POH-soh.
• wife.	• esposa.	• ehs-POH-sah.
• daughter.	• hija.	• EE-hah.
• son.	• hijo.	• EE-hoh.
• neighbor.	• vecino/a	• veh-SEE-noh/nah.
A relative.	Un pariente.	Oon pah-RYEHN-teh.
OFFICER	**AGENTE**	
What happened?	¿Qué pasó?	¿Keh-pah-SOH?
WITNESS	**TESTIGO**	
Somebody...	Alguien...	AHL-gyehn...
• broke into my house.	• entró en mi casa.	• ehn-TROH ehn mee KAH-sah.
• stole my car.	• se llevó mi carro.	• seh yeh-VOH mee KAH-rroh.
• fired shots.	• disparó.	• dees-pah-ROH.
• threatened me with a knife.	• me amenazó con un cuchillo.	• meh ah-meh-nah-SOH kohn oon koo-CHEE-yoh.
OFFICER	**AGENTE**	
Is anybody hurt?	¿Hay heridos?	¿Ahy eh-REE-dohs?
Take me there.	Lléveme allí.	YEH-veh-meh ah-YEE.
How many people are hurt?	¿Cuántos heridos hay?	¿KWAHN-tohs eh-REE-dohs ahy?

Where is/are the injured person/people?	¿Dónde está/están la persona herida/las personas heridas?	¿DOHN-deh ehs-TAH/ehs-TAHN lah pehr-SOH-nah eh-REE-dah/lahs pehr-SOH-nahs eh-REE-dahs?
WITNESS	TESTIGO	
Someone has been...	Han...a alguien.	Ahn...ah AHL-gyehn.
• shot.	• disparado	• dees-pah-RAH-doh
• stabbed.	• apuñalado	• ah-poo-nyah-LAH-doh
• beaten up.	• pegado	• peh-GAH-doh
• robbed.	• robado	• roh-BAH-doh
• kidnapped.	• secuestrado	• seh-kwehs-TRAH-doh
• assaulted.	• asaltado	• ah-sahl-TAH-doh
• raped.	• violado	• vee-oh-LAH-doh
Someone has been hit by...	Alguien ha sido atropellado por...	AHL-gyehn ah see-doh ah-troh-peh-YAH-doh pohr...
• a car.	• un carro.	• oon KAH-rroh.
• a motorcycle.	• una moto.	• oonah MOH-toh.
Several people got hurt.	Varias personas han sido heridas.	VAH-ryahs pehr-SOH-nahs ahn SEE-doh eh-REE-dahs.
Nobody got hurt.	Nadie resultó herido.	NAH-dyeh reh-sool-TOH eh-REE-doh.
OFFICER	AGENTE	
Did you call...	¿Llamó...	¿Yah-MOH...
• an ambulance?	• una ambulancia?	• OO-nah ahm-boo-LAHN-syah?
• a doctor?	• a un médico?	• ah OON MEH-dee-koh?
• the paramedics?	• a los paramédicos?	• ah lohs pah-rah-MEH-dee-kohs?
WITNESS	TESTIGO	
Yes, I did.	Sí, la/lo/los llamé.	See, lah/loh/lohs yah-MEH.

English	Spanish	Pronunciation
No, I didn't.	*No, no la/lo/los llamé.*	Noh, noh lah/loh/lohs yah-MEH.
Someone else called an ambulance.	*Alguien llamó una ambulancia.*	AHL-gyhen yah-MOH OO-nah ahm-boo-LAHN-syah.

OFFICER / *AGENTE*

| Do you know who did it? | *¿Sabe quién lo hizo?* | ¿SAH-beh kyehn loh EE-soh? |

WITNESS / *TESTIGO*

• A bunch of people...	• *Un grupo de gente...*	• Oon GROO-poh deh HEHN-teh...
• Only one person...	• *Solo una persona...*	• SOH-lah OO-nah pehr-SOH-nah...
• I don't know who...	• *No sé quién lo hizo...*	• Noh seh kyehn loh EE-soh...
• Two or three people...	• *Dos o tres personas...*	• Dohs oh trehs pehr-SOH-nahs...
• My son...	• *Mi hijo...*	• Mee EE-hoh...
• A neighbor...	• *Un/a vecino/a...*	• Oon/oo-nah veh-SEE-noh/nah...
• A stranger...	• *Un/a desconocido/a...*	• Oon/oo-nah dehs-koh-noh-SEE-doh/dah...
• The kids...	• *Los niños...*	• Lohs NEE-nyohs...
• I...	• *Yo...*	• Yoh...
...did it.	*...lo hice/lo hicieron.*	...loh EE-seh/loh ee-SYEH-rohn.

OFFICER / *AGENTE*

| When did this happen? | *¿Cuándo ocurrió esto?* | ¿KWAHN-doh oh-koo-RYOH EHS-toh? |

WITNESS / *TESTIGO*

It happened...	*Ocurrió...*	Oh-koo-RYOH...
• one hour ago.	• *hace una hora.*	• AH-seh OO-nah OH-rah.
• a few minutes ago.	• *hace unos minutos.*	• AH-seh OO-nohs mee-NOO-tohs.

- a while ago.
- *hace un momento.*
- AH-seh OON moh-MEHN-toh.

- this morning.
- *esta mañana.*
- EHS-tah mah-NYAH-nah.

- this afternoon.
- *esta tarde.*
- EHS-tah TAHR-deh.

- this evening.
- *esta noche.*
- EHS-tah NOH-cheh.

- last night.
- *anoche.*
- ah-NOH-cheh.

- yesterday.
- *ayer.*
- ah-YEHR.

B. FINDING WITNESSES

GRAMMAR NOTE ••••

SUBJECT PRONOUNS

I	*yo*
you (inf.)	*tú*
you (form.)	*usted*
he/she	*él/ella*
we	*nosotros/as*
you all (pl.)	*ustedes*
they	*ellos/ellas*
I work.	*Yo trabajo.*
I am working.	*Yo trabajo./Yo estoy trabajando.*

OFFICER	AGENTE	
Are there any witnesses?	*¿Hay testigos?*	¿Ahy tehs-TEE-gohs?

WITNESS	TESTIGO	
I saw/he/she saw...	*Yo vi/él/ella vio...*	Yoh vee/ehl/EH-yah VEE-oh...
• what happened.	• *lo que pasó.*	• loh keh pah-SOH.
• everything.	• *todo.*	• TOH-doh.

- I'm/he/she is a/we are...

- Yes, there are several...

- No, there are no...

...witness(es).

- *Yo soy/él, ella es/ nosotros somos...*

- *Sí, hay varios...*

- *No, no hay...*

...*testigo/s(a/s).*

- Yoh soy/ehl, ehl-ah ehs/noh-soh-trohs soh-mohs...

- See, ay VAH-ryohs...

- Noh, noh ay...

...tehs-TEE-goh/s (ah/s)

C. ESTABLISHING DETAILS OF THE EVENT

CULTURE NOTE ••••

THE CONCEPT OF TIME   In the United States, time is money, and thus, the way of life is much more fast paced than in Latino countries. "Time flies" *(el tiempo vuela)*, whereas for Latinos it merely "passes" *(el tiempo pasa).* A clock "runs" *(corre)* in American English, whereas in Spanish it "walks" *(anda).* Time is just not quite as important to Latinos as it is to most non-Hispanic Americans. Therefore, don't be surprised if a witness is not able to tell you the exact time of an event. The question *¿Cuándo ocurrió esto?* (When did this happen?) may often be answered with a rather vague *Entre las cuatro y las seis* (between four and six) or even something like *No sé...durante la noche* (I don't know...during the night).

Since Latinos seem to have a more relaxed concept of time, punctuality is less important, as well. Arriving ten or fifteen minutes late for an appointment is not considered rude at all. Similarly, if you are kept waiting for a little while, this is not meant as an insult, but is supposed to give you time to relax and collect your thoughts.

OFFICER	AGENTE	
What did you see?	¿Qué vio?	¿Keh VEE-oh?
Did the suspect/s...	¿El/los sospechoso/s...	¿Ehl/Los sohs-peh-CHOCH-soh/sohs...
• threaten the victim?	• amenazó/amenazaron a la víctima?	• ah-meh-nah-SOH/ah-meh-nah-SAH-rohn ah la VEEK-tee-mah?
• threaten you?	• lo amenazó/amenazaron a usted?	• loh ah-meh-nah-SOH/ah-meh-nah-SAH-rohn ah oos-TEHD?
• use force?	• usó/usaron fuerza?	• oos-OH/oos-AH-rohn FWEHR-sah?
• have...	• tenía/tenían...	• teh-NEE-ah/teh-NEE-ahn...
• a weapon?	• un arma?	• oon AHR-mah?
• a gun?	• una pistola?	• OO-nah pees-TOH-lah?
• a knife?	• un cuchillo?	• oon koo-CHEE yoh?
• cause physical harm with...	• le causó/le causaron daño físico con...	• leh kow-SOH/leh kow-SAH-rohn DAH-nyoh FEE-see-koh kohn...
• their hands?	• las manos?	• lahs MAH-nohs?
• a weapon?	• un arma?	• oon AHR-mah?
What did he/she/they do?	¿Qué hizo/hicieron?	¿Keh EE-soh/ee-SYEHR-rohn?
WITNESS	TESTIGO	
He/she didn't...	Él/ella no...	Ehl/EH-yah noh...
• see me.	• me vio.	• meh VEE-oh.
• threaten me.	• me amenazó.	• meh ah-meh-nah-SOH.
He/she yelled...	Él/ella...	Ehl/EH-yah...
• at me.	• me gritó.	• meh gree-TOH.
• at the victim.	• le gritó a la víctima.	• leh gree-TOH ah lah VEEK-tee-mah.
He/she...the victim/me.	Él/ella le/me...a la víctima/a mí.	Ehl/EH-yah leh/meh... ah lah VEEK-tee-mah/ah mee.

• punched	• *dio puñetazos*	• DEE-oh poo-nyeh-TAH-sohs
• kicked	• *dio patadas*	• DEE-oh pah-TAH-dahs
• pushed	• *empujó*	• ehm-poo-HOH
• hit	• *pegó*	• peh-GOH
He/she...	*Él/ella...*	Ehl/EH-yah...
• made obscene remarks.	• *dijo obscenidades.*	• DEE-hoh ohbs-seh-nee-DAH-dehs.
• gave me the middle finger.	• *hizo un gesto obsceno.*	• EE-soh oon HEHS-toh ohbs-SEH-noh.
• pointed the gun at me.	• *me apuntó con la pistola.*	• meh ah-poon-TOH kohn lah pees-TOH-lah.
OFFICER	*AGENTE*	
What did he/she/they take?	*¿Qué robó/robaron?*	¿Keh roh-BOH/roh-BAH-rohn?
Did he/she/they steal...	*¿Él/ella/ellos robaron...*	¿Ehl/EH-yah/EH-yohs roh-BAH-rohn...
• money?	• *dinero?*	• dee-NEH-roh?
• a TV?	• *un televisor?*	• oon teh-leh-vee-SOHR?
• a VCR?	• *un VCR?*	• oon Veh Seh Eh-rreh?
• a computer?	• *una computadora?*	• OO-nah kohm-poo-tah-DOH-rah?
• a car?	• *un carro?*	• oon KAH-rroh?
• jewelry?	• *joyas?*	• HOH-yahs?
How did/he/she/they get in?	*¿Cómo entró él/ella/ entraron ellos?*	¿KOH-moh ehn-TROH ehl/EH-yah/ehn-TRAH-rohn EH-yohs?
Did he/she/they come in through...	*¿Él/ella entró/ellos entraron por...*	¿Ehl/EH-yah ehn-TROH/EH-yohs ehn-TRAH-rohn pohr...
• a window?	• *una ventana?*	• OO-nah vehn-TAH-nah?
• the back door?	• *la puerta de atrás?*	• lah PWEHR-tah deh ah-TRAHS?
• the front door?	• *la puerta de adelante?*	• lah PWEHR-tah deh ah-deh-LAHN-teh?

WITNESS	TESTIGO	
It happened very fast.	*Ocurrió muy rápido.*	Oh-koo-RYOH mwee RAH-pee-doh.
I don't know.	*No sé.*	Noh seh.

OFFICER	AGENTE	
Did the suspect/s leave...	*¿El/los sospechoso/s se fue/fueron...*	¿Ehl/lohs sohs-peh-CHOH-soh/sohs seh FWEH-rohn...
• on foot?	• *a pie?*	• ah pyeh?
• in a vehicle?	• *en un vehículo?*	• ehn oon veh-EE-koo-loh?
What direction did the suspects take?	*¿En qué dirección se fueron los sospechosos?*	¿Ehn keh dee-REHK-SYOHN seh FWEH-rohn lohs sohs-peh-CHOH-sohs?

WITNESS	TESTIGO	
He/she/they left in a car.	*Se fue/fueron en un carro.*	Seh FWEH/FWEH-rohn ehn oon KAH-rroh.
He/she/they ran.	*Se fue/fueron corriendo.*	Seh FWEH/FWEH-rohn koh-RYEHN-doh.
He/she/they went...	*Se fue/fueron hacia...*	Seh FWEH/FWEH-rohn AH-syah...
• north.	• *el norte.*	• ehl NOHR-teh.
• south.	• *el sur.*	• ehl soor.
• east.	• *el este.*	• ehl EHS-teh.
• west.	• *el oeste.*	• ehl oh-EHS-teh.
• that way.	• *en esa dirección.*	• ehn eh-sah dee-rehk-SYOHN.
• down the street.	• *calle abajo.*	• KAH-yeh ah-BAH-hoh.
• up the street.	• *calle arriba.*	• KAH-yeh ah-REE-bah.
• left.	• *a la izquierda.*	• ah lah ees-KYEHR-dah.
• right.	• *a la derecha.*	• ah lah deh-REH-chah.
• straight.	• *derecho.*	• deh-REH-choh.
I don't know where he/she/they went.	*No sé por dónde se fue/fueron.*	Noh seh pohr DOHN-deh seh fweh/FWEH-rohn.

VOCABULARY ••••

DIRECTIONS

north	norte	NOHR-teh
south	sur	soor
east	este	EHS-teh
west	oeste	oh-EHS-teh
right	a la derecha	ah lah deh-REH-chah
left	a la izquierda	ah lah ees-KYEHR-dah
up	arriba	ah-RREE-bah
down	abajo	ah-BAH-hoh
under	debajo	deh-BAH-hoh
on top	encima	ehn-SEE-mah
behind	detrás	deh-TRAHS
straight	derecho	deh-REH-choh
front	enfrente	ehn-FREHN-teh
outside	afuera	ah-FWEH-rah
inside	adentro	ah-DEHN-troh
to turn	doblar	doh-BLAHR
block	bloque, cuadra, manzana	BLOH-keh, KWAH-drah, mahn-SAH-nah
mile	milla	MEE-yah
one-half mile	media-milla	MEH-dyah MEE-yah

D. DESCRIPTION OF SUSPECTS

V⊙CABULARY ••••

PHYSICAL DESCRIPTION

boy	*niño*	NEE-nyoh
girl	*niña*	NEE-nyah
young man	*muchacho*	moo-CHAH-choh
young woman	*muchacha*	moo-CHAH-chah
young person	*jóven*	HOH-vehn
man	*hombre*	OHM-breh
woman	*mujer*	moo-HEHR
old man	*viejo*	VYEH-hoh
old woman	*vieja*	VYEH-hah
tall	*alto/a*	AHL-toh/tah
short	*bajo/a*	BAH-hoh/jah
long	*largo/a*	LAHR-goh/ah
straight	*lacio/a*	LAH-syoh/ah
curly	*rizado/a*	ree-SAH-doh/ah
fat	*gordo/a*	GOHR-doh/dah
skinny	*delgado/a*	dehl-GAH-doh/dah
small	*pequeño/a*	peh-KEH-nyoh/nyah
average	*mediano/a*	meh-DYAH-noh/nah
big	*grande*	GRAHN-deh
light	*claro/a*	KLAH-roh/rah
light skinned	*güero/a*	WEH-roh/ah
dark	*oscuro/a*	OHS-KOO-roh/rah
dark skinned	*moreno/a*	moh-REH-noh/nah

(cont'd.)

Physical Description *(cont'd.)*

freckled	*pecoso/a*	peh-KOH-soh/sah
blonde	*rubio/a*	ROO-byoh/byah
black	*negro/a*	NEH-groh/ah
white	*blanco/a*	BLAHN-koh-ah
brown	*castaño/a*	kahs-TAH-nyoh/ah
green	*verde*	VEHR-deh
blue	*azul*	ah-SOOL
hair	*el pelo*	ehl PEH-loh
eye	*el ojo*	ehl OH-hoh
Latino	*latino/a*	lah-TEE-noh/ah
Hispanic	*hispano/a*	ees-PAH-noh/ah
Asian	*asiático/a*	ah-SYAH-tee-koh/ah
Japanese	*japonés/a*	hah-poh-NEHS/ah
Chinese	*chino/a*	CHEE-noh/ah

OFFICER	**AGENTE**	
Describe the suspect/s.	*Describa al/a los sospechoso/s.*	Dehs-KREE-bah ahl/ah los sohs-peh-CHOH-soh/sohs.
Were they male or female?	*¿Era/eran hombre/s o mujer/es?*	¿EH-rah/EH-rahn OHM-breh/brehs oh moo-HEHR/rehs?
What did he/she/they look like?	*¿Cómo era/eran?*	¿KOH-moh EH-rah/EH-rahn?
Do you know them?	*¿Los/las conoce?*	¿Lohs/lahs koh-NOH-seh?
What are their names?	*¿Cómo se llaman?*	¿KOH-moh seh YAH-mahn?
Where do they live?	*¿Dónde viven?*	¿DOHN-deh VEE-vehn?
Can you point them out?	*¿Puede señalarlos/las?*	¿PWEH-deh seh-nya-lahr-los/lahs?

GRAMMAR NOTE ····

DESCRIBING SOMEONE   The following three verbs are important for suspect descriptions.

TO BE *SER:*

He/she is, you (form.) are intelligent.	*Es inteligente.*
They/you (pl.) are big.	*Son grandes.*
I/he/she was, you (form.) were, it was thin.	*Era delgado/a.*
They/you (pl.) were thin.	*Eran delgados/as.*

TO WEAR, TO CARRY *LLEVAR:*

He/she is, you are wearing light clothes.	*Lleva ropa clara.*
They/you (pl.) are wearing dark clothes.	*Llevan ropa oscura.*
I/he/she was, you were wearing baggy pants.	*Llevaba unos pantalones flojos.*
They/you (pl.) were wearing a white shirt.	*Llevaban una camisa blanca.*

TO HAVE *TENER:*

He/she has, you have a tattoo.	*Tiene un tatuaje.*
They/you (pl.) have freckles.	*Tienen pecas.*
I/he/she had a tattoo.	*Tenía un tatuaje.*
They/you (pl.) had freckles.	*Tenían pecas.*

WITNESS	TESTIGO	
The suspect/s was/were...	*El/los sospechoso/s era/eran...*	Ehl/lohs sohs-peh-CHOH-soh/sohs EH-rah/EH-rahn...
• a man/men.	• *un hombre/hombres.*	• oon OHM-breh/OHM-brehs.
• a woman/women.	• *una mujer/mujeres.*	• OO-nah moo-HEHR/moo-HEH-rehs.
• short.	• *bajo/a/os/as.*	• BAH-hoh/ah/ohs/ahs.
• tall.	• *alto/a/os/as.*	• AHL-toh/ah/ohs/ahs.

• bald.	• *calvo/a/os/as.*	• KAHL-voh/ah/ ohs/ahs.
• fat.	• *gordo/a/os/as.*	• GOHR-doh/ah/ ohs/ahs.
• skinny.	• *delgado/a/os/as.*	• dehl-GAH-doh/ah/ ohs/ahs.
• old.	• *viejo/a/os/as.*	• VYEH-hoh/ah/ohs/ ahs.
• teenagers.	• *adolescentes.*	• ah-doh-lehs-SEHN- tehs.
• dark skinned/light skinned.	• *moreno/a/os/as/ güero/a/os/as.*	• moh-REH-noh/ah/ ohs/ahs/WEH-roh/ah /ohs/ahs.
• black/white/Asian/ Latino.	• *negro/a/os/as/ gringo/a/os/as/ asiático/a/os/as/ latino/a/os/as.*	• NEH-groh/ah/ohs/ahs/ GREEN-goh/ah/oh/ ahs/ah-SYAH-tee- koh/ah/ahs/ohs/lah- TEE-noh/ah/ohs/ahs.
He/she/they had…	*Él/ella tenía/ellos tenían…*	Ehl/EH-yah teh-NEE- ah/EH-yohs teh-NEE- ahn…
• freckles.	• *pecas.*	• PEH-kahs.
• a scar.	• *una cicatriz.*	• OO-nah see-kah- TREES.
• a tattoo.	• *un tatuaje.*	• oon tah-TWAH-heh.
• long hair.	• *pelo largo.*	• PEH-loh LAHR-goh.
• short hair.	• *pelo corto.*	• PEH-loh KOHR-toh.
• straight hair.	• *pelo lacio.*	• PEH-loh LAH-syoh.
• curly hair.	• *pelo rizado.*	• PEH-loh ree-SAH- doh.
• a moustache.	• *un bigote.*	• oon bee-GOH-teh.
• a beard.	• *una barba.*	• OO-nah BAHR-bah.
• a big nose.	• *una nariz grande.*	• OO-nah nah-REES GRAHN-deh.
• a hook nose.	• *una nariz aguileña.*	• OO-nah nah-REES ah-gwee-LEH-nyah.

• blue eyes.	• *ojos azules.*	• OH-hohs ah-SOO-lehs.
• hazel eyes.	• *ojos avellanos.*	• OH-hohs ah-veh-YAH-nohs.
• brown eyes.	• *ojos castaños.*	• OH-hohs kahs-TAH-nyohs.
• gold teeth.	• *dientes de oro.*	• DYEHN-tehs deh OH-roh.
• dirty teeth.	• *dientes sucios.*	• DYEHN-tehs SOO-syohs.
• irregular teeth.	• *dientes irregulares.*	• DYEHN-tehs ee-rreh-goo-LAH-rehs.
• pimples.	• *granos.*	• GRAH-nohs.
Some teeth were missing.	*Le faltaban dientes.*	Leh fahl-TAH-bahn DYEHN-tehs.
He/she was/they were wearing…	*Él/ella llevaba/ ellos llevaban…*	Ehl/EH-yah yeh-VAH-bah/EH-yohs yeh-VAH-bahn…
• a baseball hat.	• *una gorra de béisbol.*	• OO-nah GOH-rrah deh BEHS-bohl.
• a striped shirt.	• *una camisa de rayas.*	• OO-nah kah-MEE-sah deh RAH-yahs.
• a checkered shirt.	• *una camisa de cuadros.*	• OO-nah kah-MEE-sah deh KWAH-drohs.
• jeans.	• *vaqueros.*	• vah-KEH-rohs.
• baggy pants.	• *pantalones muy flojos.*	• pahn-tah-LOH-nehs mwee FLOH-hohs.
• a big jacket.	• *una chaqueta grande.*	• OO-nah chah-KEH-tah GRAHN-deh.
• glasses.	• *lentes.*	• LEHN-tehs.
• shorts.	• *pantalones cortos.*	• pahn-tah-LOH-nehs KOHR-tohs.
• a brown sweater.	•*un suéter castaño.*	• oon SWEH-tehr kahs-TAH-nyoh.
• gloves.	• *guantes.*	• GWAHN-tehs.

- a mask.
- *una máscara.*
- OO-nah MAHS-kah-rah.

- dirty tennis shoes.
- *zapatos de tenis sucios.*
- sah-PAH-tohs deh TEH-nees SOO-syohs.

- blue sneakers.
- *alpargatas azules.*
- ahl-pahr-GAH-tahs ah-SOO-lehs.

He/she was barefoot.
Él/ella iba/ellos iban descalzo/descalzos.
Eh/EH-yah iba/EH-yohs EE-bahn dehs-KAHL-soh/desh-KAHL-sohs.

OFFICER
AGENTE

Was he/she/ were they...
¿Era/él/ella/ eran ellos...
¿EH-rah/ehl/EH-yah/ EH-rahn EH-yohs...

- medium built?
- *de mediana estatura?*
- deh meh-DYAH-nah ehs-tah-TOO-rah?

- lightweight?
- *de ligera estatura?*
- deh lee-HEH-rah ehs-tah-TOO-rah?

- heavy?
- *de estatura pesada?*
- deh ehs-tah-TOO-rah peh-SAH-dah?

What about his/her/ their height?
¿Cuanto medía/ medían?
KWAHN-toh meh-DEE-ah/meh-DEE-ahn?

WITNESS
TESTIGO

He/she/they were...
Él/ella era/ellos eran...
Ehl/EH-yah/EH-rah/ EH-yos EH-rahn...

- of light build.
- *de peso ligero.*
- deh PEH-soh lee-HEH-roh.

- of medium build.
- *de peso mediano.*
- deh PEH-soh meh-DYAH-noh.

- heavy looking.
- *pesado/s.*
- peh-SAH-doh/dohs.

- muscular.
- *musculoso/a/os/as.*
- moos-koo-LOH-soh/ sah/sohs/sahs.

- average.
- *de apariencia normal.*
- deh ah-pah-RYEN-syah norh-MAHL.

- thin.
- *delgado/a/os/as.*
- dehl-GAH-doh/dah/ dohs/dahs.

- obese.
- *gordo/a/os/as.*
- GOHR-doh/dah/ dohs/dahs.

He/she was/they were...	*Él/ella/ellos...*	Ehl/EH-yah/EH-yohs...
• less than 5'6" tall.	• *medía/medían menos de cinco pies y seis pulgadas.*	• meh-DEE-ah/meh-DEE-ahn MEH-nohs deh SEEN-koh pyes ee says pool-GAH-dahs.
• average.	• *era/eran de estatura mediana.*	• EH-rah/EH-rahn deh ehs-tah-TOO-rah meh-DYAH-nah.
• tall.	• *era/eran alto/a/os/as.*	• EH-rah/EH-rahn AHL-toh/tah/ tohs/tahs.

VOCABULARY ••••

CLOTHING

clothes	*ropa*	RROH-pah
belt	*cinturón*	seen-too-ROHN
skirt	*falda*	FAHL-dah
pants	*pantalones*	pahn-tah-LOH-nehs
blue jeans	*vaqueros*	vah-KEH-rohs
shirt	*camisa*	kah-MEE-sah
T-shirt	*camiseta*	kah-mee-SEH-tah
blouse	*blusa*	BLOO-sah
hat	*sombrero*	sohm-BREHR-roh
cap	*gorra*	GOH-rrah
dress	*vestido*	vehs-TEE-doh
coat	*abrigo*	ah-BREE-goh
pocket	*bolsillo/bolsa*	bohl-SEE-yoh/BOHL-sah
shoes	*zapatos*	sah-PAH-tohs

(cont'd.)

Clothing *(cont'd.)*

socks	*calcetines*	kal-seh-TEE-nehs
jacket	*chaqueta*	chah-KEH-tah
glove	*guante*	GWAHN-teh
boots	*botas*	BOH-tahs
stockings	*medias*	MEH-dyahs
glasses	*lentes*	LEHN-tehs
ring	*anillo*	ah-NEE-yoh
necklace	*collar*	koh-YAHR
earrings	*aretes*	ah-REH-tehs

E. DESCRIPTION OF VEHICLES

VOCABULARY ••••

COLORS

black	*negro*	NEH-groh
brown	*café*	kah-FEH
blue	*azul*	ah-SOOL
orange	*anaranjado*	ah-nah-rahn-HAH-doh
grey	*gris*	grees
green	*verde*	VEHR-deh
maroon	*morado*	moh-RAH-doh
red	*rojo*	RROH-hoh
yellow	*amarillo*	ah-mah-REE-yoh
pink	*rosa*	RROH-sah
white	*blanco*	BLAHN-koh

GRAMMAR NOTE ••••

THE GENDER AND NUMBER OF NOUNS In Spanish, every noun has a gender. In some cases, as with people, the gender is obvious: man, brother, father, etc., are masculine, while mother, sister, woman, etc., are feminine. However, with most other nouns, the gender and meaning are unrelated. Nouns ending in -*o,* most words ending in -*e* or in a consonant other than -*d* are masculine:

> *el libro* (book), *el profesor* (professor), *el árbol* (tree), *el aire* (air).
> exception: *el día* (day), *el mapa* (map), *el problema* (problem), *el sistema* (system).

Nouns ending in -*a, -d, -ción, -sión,* and many that end in -*e* are feminine.

> *la casa* (house), *la ciudad* (city), *la pared* (wall), *la situación* (situation),
> *la leche* (milk), *la televisión* (television).
> exception: *la mano* (hand).

In order to form the plural of nouns and adjectives add -*es* if the word ends in a consonant:

> the blue uniform   *el uniforme azul*
> the blue uniforms   *los uniformes azules*

Add -*s* if the noun or adjective ends in a vowel:

> the black gun   *la pistola negra*
> the black guns   *las pistolas negras*

El (the) and *un* (a/an) are the definite and indefinite articles for masculine nouns. *La* (the) and *una* (a/an) are the definite and indefinite articles for feminine nouns. The plural of *el/la* is *los/las.* The plural of *un/una* is *unos/unas.*

OFFICER	AGENTE	
Describe the vehicle.	*Describa el vehículo.*	Dehs-KREE-beh ehl veh-EE-koo-loh.
Was it two-door or four-door?	*¿Era de dos o cuatro puertas?*	¿EH-rah deh dohs oh KWAH-troh deh PWEHR-tahs?
Did it have any damage?	*¿Estaba dañado?*	¿Eh-STAH-bah dah-NYAH-doh?
Where?	*¿Dónde?*	¿DOHN-deh?
Was it old or new?	*¿Era nuevo o viejo?*	¿EH-rah NOOEH-voh oh vee-EH-hoh?

WITNESS	TESTIGO	
It was...	*Era...*	EH-rah...
• a car.	• *un carro.*	• oon KAH-roh.
• a pick-up truck.	• *una camioneta.*	• OO-nah kah-myohn-NEH-tah.
• a van.	• *un camión.*	• oon kah-MYOHN.
• a bicycle.	• *una bicicleta.*	• OO-nah bee-see-KLEH-tah.
• a motorcycle.	• *una moto.*	• OO-nah mo-toh.
I don't know the make.	*No sé que marca.*	Noh seh keh MAHR-kah.
I don't know what year.	*No sé de que año.*	Noh seh deh keh AH-nyoh.
It was a...	*Era...*	EH-rah...
• Chevy.	• *un Chevy.*	• oon Chevy.
• four-door Nissan.	• *un Nissan de cuatro puertas.*	• oon Nissan deh KWAH-troh PWEHR tahs.
• Toyota wagon.	• *una camioneta Toyota.*	• OO-nah kah-myohn-NEH-tahToyota.
• 60's Oldsmobile.	• *un Oldsmobile del sesenta.*	• oon Oldsmobile dehl seh-SEHN-tah.
It was a...car.	*Era un carro...*	EH-rah oon KAH-rroh...
• new	• *nuevo*	• NWEH-voh

- black
- blue
- grey
- green
- brown
- white
- red
- metallic

- *negro*
- *azul*
- *gris*
- *verde*
- *café*
- *blanco*
- *rojo*
- *metálico*

- NEH-groh
- ah-SOOL
- grees
- VEHR-deh
- kah-FEH
- BLAHN-koh
- ROH-ho
- meh-TAH-lee-koh

OFFICER

AGENTE

Was there anything unusual or special about the car?

¿Había algo diferente o especial acerca del carro?

¿Ah-BEE-ah AHL-goh dee-feh-REHN-teh oh eh-speh-SYAHL ah-SEHR-kah dehl KAH-rroh?

How many people were in the car?

¿Cuántas personas habia en el coche?

¿KWAHN-tahs pehr-soh-nahs ah-BEE-ah ehn ehl KOH-cheh?

WITNESS

TESTIGO

It had...

Tenía...

Teh-NEE-ah...

- a dent on the passenger's door.

- *un golpe en la puerta del pasajero.*

- oohn GOHL-peh ehn lah PWEHR-tah dehl pah-sah-HEH-roh.

- wide tires.

- *llantas/gomas muy anchas.*

- YAHN-tahs/GOH-mahs mwee AHN-chahs.

- bumper stickers all over...

- *calcomanías por toda/o...*

- Kahl-koh-mah-NEE-ahs pohr TOH-dah/doh...

  - the back window.

  - *la ventana de atrás.*

  - lah vehn-TAH-nah deh AH-trahs.

  - the bumper.

  - *la defensa/el parachoques.*

  - la deh-FEHN-sah/ehl pah-rah-CHOH-kehs.

It was...

Estaba...

Ehs-TAH-bah...

- rusty.

- *oxidado.*

- ohk-see-DAH-doh.

• scratched all over.	• *rayado por todas partes.*	• rah-YAH-doh pohr TOH-dahs PAHR-tehs.
• in good condition.	• *en buena condición.*	• ehn BWEH-nah kohn-dee-SYOHN.

OFFICER / *AGENTE*

Did you see the license plate?	*¿Vio usted el número de la placa?*	¿VEE-oh oos-TEHD ehl NOO-meh-roh de lah PLAH-kah?
What color was the plate?	*¿De qué color era la placa?*	¿Deh keh koh-LOHR EH-rah la PLAH-kah?
What was the plate number?	*¿Cuál era el número de placa?*	¿Kwahl EH-rah ehl NOO-meh-roh deh PLAH-kah?

WITNESS / *TESTIGO*

It was a car from…	*Era un carro de…*	Eh-rah oon KAH-rroh deh…
• VA.	• *Virginia.*	• Veer-GEE-nyah.
• CO.	• *Colorado.*	• Koh-loh-RAH-doh.
• CA.	• *California.*	• Kah-lee-FOHR-nyah.
No, I didn't see it.	*No, no lo vi.*	Noh, noh loh vee.

OFFICER / *AGENTE*

Thank you for your…	*Gracias por su…*	GRAH-syahs pohr soo…
• cooperation.	• *cooperación.*	• koh-oh-peh-rah-SYOHN.
• help.	• *ayuda.*	• ah-YOO-dah.
Please give me…	*Por favor deme…*	Pohr fah-VOHR DEH-meh…
• your name.	• *su nombre.*	• soo NOHM-breh.
• your address.	• *su dirección.*	• soo dee-rehk-SYOHN.
• your phone number.	• *su número de teléfono.*	• soo NOO-meh-roh deh teh-LEH-foh-noh.

CULTURE NOTE ••••

NAMES AND LAST NAMES Latinos use two surnames called *apellidos:* the father's and the mother's last name. If only one single last name is reported, it is most likely in order to adapt to American customs. In these cases usually the father's last name is used.

Juan Antonio Pérez García	*Pérez* is the father's name. *García* is the mother's name. *Antonio* is not abbreviated, as it is often done with middle names in English.
María Elena Ríos Fuentes de Pérez	*de Pérez* is Maria Elena's married name. *Rios* is her father's name. *Fuentes* is her mother's name.

If Juan Antonio and María Elena have a son named José María, his full name would be:

José María Pérez Ríos.

WITNESS	TESTIGO	
My name is ___.	*Me llamo* ___.	Meh YAH-moh___.
My address is ___.	*Mi dirección es* ___.	Mee dee-rehk-SYOHN ehs ___.
My phone number is ___.	*Mi número de teléfono es* ___.	Mee NOO-meh-roh de teh-LEH-foh-noh ehs ___.

OFFICER	AGENTE	
Please repeat number by number.	*Por favor, repita número por número.*	Pohr fah-VOHR reh-PEE-tah NOO-meh-roh pohr NOO-meh-roh.
Sign here, please.	*Firme aquí, por favor.*	FEER-meh ah-KEE, pohr fah-VOHR.

If you see or hear anything, please contact me at _____.	*Si ve algo o escucha algo, por favor, llámeme al _____.*	See veh AHL-goh oh ehs-KOO-chah AHL-go, pohr fah-VOHR, YAH-meh-meh ahl _____.
Thank you.	*Gracias.*	GRAH-syahs.
Good-bye.	*Adiós.*	Ah-dyohs.

2. Admonishments

A. WITNESS ADMONITION

OFFICER	AGENTE	
The fact that this subject is in custody should not influence your judgment.	*El hecho de que este sujeto esté bajo custodia no debe influenciar su juicio.*	Ehl EH-choh deh keh EHS-teh soo-HEH-toh ehs-TEH BAH-hoh koos-TOH-dyah noh DEH-beh een-floo-ehn-SYAHR soo JOO-syoh.
No implications should be drawn from the fact that a subject is in custody.	*No tiene que sacar conclusiones sólo porque el sujeto esté bajo custodia.*	Noh TYEH-neh khe sah-KAHR kohn-kloo-SYOH-nehs SOH-loh pohr-KEH ehl soo-HEH-toh ehs-TEH BAH-hoh koos-TOH-dyah.
There is no obligation for you to identify anyone.	*No tiene la obligación de identificar a nadie.*	Noh TYEH-neh lah oh-blee-gah-SYOHN deh ee-dehn-tee-fee-KAHR ah NAH-dyeh.
It is as important that you exonerate the subject as it is that you implicate him/her.	*Es tan importante que usted disculpe al sujeto como es que lo/la implique.*	Ehs tahn eem-pohr-TAHN-teh keh oos-TEHD dees-KOOL-peh ahl soo-HEH-toh KOH-moh ehs keh loh/lah eem-PLEE-keh.
If the subject is not responsible for the crime, the police	*Si el sujeto en custodia no es responsable del*	See ehl soo-HEH-toh ehn koos-TOH-dyah noh ehs rehs-pohn-

will continue searching for the suspect.	*crimen, la policía continuará buscando al sospechoso.*	SAH-bleh dehl KREE-mehn, lah poh-lee-SEE-ah kohn-TEEN-oo-ah-RAH boos-KAHN-doh ahl sohs-peh-CHOH-soh.

Culture Note ••••

FORMS OF ADDRESS Even though the word *señora* (Ma'am) is traditionally reserved for married women, it has recently become more common to use *señora* toward unmarried women as well. *Señorita* should only be used toward teenagers. If in doubt, simply ask: *¿Señora?/¿Señorita?* The word *señor* (Mister) is used when addressing a man by his last name. The first name is only used toward family and friends or toward children and teenagers. Don't use the first name toward someone your own age or older, unless specifically asked to do so.

B. MIRANDA WARNING

You are under arrest for ____.	*Está arrestado por ____.*	Ehs-TAH ah-rrhes-TAH-doh pohr ____.
You have the right to remain silent.	*Usted tiene el derecho de guardar silencio.*	Oos-TEHD TYEH-neh ehl deh-REH-choh deh gwahr-DAHR see-LEHN-syoh.
Anything you say can and will be used against you in a court of law.	*Todo lo que usted diga puede ser usado y va a ser usado contra usted ante un tribunal.*	TOH-doh loh keh oos-TEHD DEE-gah PWEH-deh sehr oo-SAH-doh ee vah ah sehr oo-SAH-doh KOHN-trah oos-TEHD AHN-teh oon tree-boo-NAHL.

You have the right to consult with a lawyer before questioning and to have a lawyer present during questioning.	*Tiene el derecho de hablar con un abogado antes del interrogatorio y a tenerlo presente durante el interrogatorio.*	TYEH-neh ehl deh-REH-choh deh ah-BLAHR kohn oon ah-boh-GAH-doh AHN-tehs dehl een-teh-roh-gah-TOH-ryoh ee ah teh-NEHR-loh preh-SEHN-teh doo-RAHN-teh ehl een-teh-roh-gah-TOH-ryoh.
If you are unable to afford an attorney one will be assigned to represent you without charge.	*Si no puede pagar a un abogado, se le asignará uno para que lo represente a usted sin cobrarle.*	See noh PWEH-deh pah-GAHR ah oon ah-boh-GAH-doh, seh leh ah-seeg-nah-RAH OO-noh PAH-rah keh loh reh-preh-SEHN-teh ah oos-TEHD seen koh-BRAHR-leh.
You can decide at any time to exercise these rights and not answer any questions or make any statements.	*En cualquier momento usted puede ejercer esos derechos y no contestar a las preguntas o decir nada.*	Ehn kwahl-KYEHR moh-MEHN-toh oos-TEHD pweh-deh eh-hehr-SEHR eh-sohs deh-REH-chos ee noh kohn-ehs-TAHR ah lahs preh-goon-tahs oh deh-seehr nah-dah.
Do you understand each of these rights I have read to you?	*¿Comprende usted cada uno de estos derechos que le acabo de leer?*	¿Kohm-PREHN-deh oos-TEHD KAH-dah OO-noh deh EHS-tohs deh-REH-chohs keh leh ah-KAH-boh deh leh-EHR?
Knowing your rights and knowing what you are doing, do you wish to speak or do you prefer to remain silent?	*Conociendo sus derechos y sabiendo lo que hace, ¿desea hablar o prefiere guardar silencio?*	Koh-noh-SYEHN-doh soos deh-REH-chohs ee sah-BYEHN-doh loh keh AH-seh, ¿deh-SEH-ah ah-BLAHR oh preh-FYEH-reh gwahr-DAHR see-LEHN-syoh?

GRAMMAR NOTE ••••

THE PRESENT TENSE In Spanish there are different verb endings for each of the subjects I, you, he, etc. performing an action. The present tense expresses actions that are occurring at the present moment. There are three sets of endings for the present tense of regular verbs in Spanish: one set of verb endings for infinitives ending in -ar, one set for those ending in -er, and another for -ir verbs.

TO WORK *TRABAJ-AR:*

SINGULAR
I	yo	trabaj- o
you (inf.)	tú	trabaj- as
he/she/you (form.)	él/ella/usted	trabaj- a

PLURAL
we	nosotros	trabaj- amos
you (inf.)	vosotros	trabaj- áis
they/you (form.)	ellos/ellas/ustedes	trabaj- an

TO UNDERSTAND *COMPREND-ER:*

SINGULAR
I	yo	comprend- o
you (inf.)	tú	comprend- es
he/she/you (form.)	él/ella/usted	comprend- e

PLURAL
we	nosotros	comprend- emos
you (inf.)	vosotros	comprend- éis
they/you (form.)	ellos/ellas/ustedes	comprend- en

TO LIVE *VIV-IR:*

SINGULAR
I	yo	viv- o
you (inf.)	tú	viv- es
he/she/you (form.)	él/ella/usted	viv- e

PLURAL
we	nosotros	viv- imos
you (inf.)	vosotros	viv- ís
they/you (form.)	ellos/ellas/ustedes	viv- en

C. ISSUING TICKETS

> # CULTURE NOTE ••••
>
> **GREETINGS**   Latinos usually are more formal than most non-Hispanic Americans, which is reflected not only in the two forms of address (*tú* and *usted*), but also in greetings. *Buenos días* (Good morning/Good day), *Buenas tardes* (Good afternoon), and *Buenas noches* (Good evening) can be used towards everybody, regardless of the person's age or social status, and no matter how well you know the person. *Hola* (Hello/Hi) is only used among family, friends and colleagues, or toward children and teenagers, and is best not used toward strangers. Just like in English, it is customary to inquire about a person's well-being: *¿Cómo está usted?* is used toward strangers, and *¿Cómo estás?* or *¿Qué tal?* toward family and friends.

OFFICER	*AGENTE*	
Good morning. I stopped you for ____.	*Buenos días. Lo paré a usted por ____.*	BWEH-nohs DEE-ahs. Loh pah-REH ah oos-tehd pohr ____.
What's your name?	*¿Cómo se llama?*	¿KOH-moh seh YAH-mah?
What's your date of birth?	*¿Cuál es su fecha de nacimiento?*	¿Kwahl ehs soo FEH-chah deh nah-see-MYEHN-toh?
Your address?	*¿Su dirección?*	¿Soo dee-rehk-SYOHN?
Your phone number?	*¿Su número de teléfono?*	¿Soo NOO-meh-roh deh teh-LEH-foh-noh?
May I see...	*¿Puedo ver...*	¿PWEH-doh vehr...

• your driver's license?	• *su licencia de manejar?*	• soo lee-sehn-SYAH deh mah-neh-HAHR?
• proof of insurance?	• *su prueba del seguro?*	• soo PRWEH-bah dehl seh-GOO-roh?
• your registration?	• *su registro del coche?*	• soo reh-HEES-troh dehl KOH-chech?
Do you work?	*¿Trabaja usted?*	¿Trah-BAH-hah oos-TEHD?
What type of work do you do?	*¿Qué tipo de trabajo hace usted?*	¿Keh TEE-poh deh trah-BAH-hoh AH-seh oos-TEHD?
What's your work address?	*¿La dirección de su trabajo?*	¿Lah dee-rehk-SYOHN deh soo trah-BAH-hoh?
Phone number at work?	*¿El número de teléfono en su trabajo?*	¿Ehl NOO-meh-roh deh teh-LEH-foh-noh ehn soo trah-BAH-hoh?
You have been charged because...	*Le he puesto una multa por...*	Leh eh PWEHS-toh OO-nah MOOL-tah pohr...
• your registration...	• *su registro del coche...*	• soo reh-HEES-troh dehl KOH-cheh...
• your license...	• *su licencia...*	• soo lee-SEHN-syah...
• your insurance...	• *su seguro...*	• soo seh-GOO-roh...
• ...is expired.	• *...está caducado/a.*	• ...ehs-TAH kah-doo-kah-doh/dah.
• ...is suspended.	• *...está suspendida.*	• ...ehs-TAH soos-pehn-DEE-dah.
Do you have another address?	*¿Tiene otra dirección?*	¿TYEH-neh OH-trah dee-rehk-syohn?
What name and address appear on your license?	*¿Qué nombre y dirección aparecen en su licencia?*	¿Keh NOHM-breh ee dee-rehk-SYOHN ah-pah-REH-sehn ehn soo lee-SEHN-syah?

You are required...	Usted tiene que...	Oos-TEHD TYEH-neh keh...
• to be in court by the date written here.	• ir a la corte el día escrito aquí.	• eer ah lah KOHR-teh EHL DEE-ah ehs-KREE-toh ah-KEE.
• to pay the fine within ____ days.	• pagar la multa dentro de ____ días.	• pah-GAHR lah MOOL-tah DEHN-troh deh ____ DEE-ahs.
• to follow the directions on the rear of this summons.	• seguir las instrucciones en la parte de atrás de esta citación.	• seh-GEER lahs eens-trook-SYOHN-ehs ehn lah PAHR-teh de ah-TRAHS deh EHS-tah see-tah-SYOHN.
Sign here, please.	Firme aquí, por favor.	FEER-meh ah-KEE, pohr fah-VOHR.
Just because you are signing this doesn't mean you are admitting guilt.	El hecho de firmar este papel no quiere decir que usted admite su culpabilidad.	Ehl EH-choh deh feer-MAHR EHS-teh pah-PEL noh KYEH-reh deh-seer keh oos-TEHD ahd-MEE-teh soo kool-pah-bee-lee-DAHD.
If you refuse to sign, I'll have to place you under arrest.	Si se niega a firmar, tendré que arrestarlo/la.	See seh NYEH-gah ah feer-MAHR, tehn-DREH keh ah-rehs-TAHR-loh/lah
Get out of the car.	Salga del carro.	SAHL-gah dehl KAH-rroh.
Come to the sidewalk.	Venga a la acera.	VEHN-gah ah lah ah-SEH-rah.

GRAMMAR NOTE ••••

ASKING FOR SOMEONE'S NAME   There are two ways to ask for somebody's name:

What's your name?
- ¿Cómo se llama? (form.)
- ¿Cómo te llamas? (inf.)
- ¿Cuál es su nombre? (form.)
- ¿Cuál es tu nombre? (inf.)

And there are two ways to answer:

My name is _____.
- Me llamo _____.
- Mi nombre es _____.

When you need somebody's name for a document, ask for:

Name and last names, please.
Nombre y apellidos, por favor.

Don't abbreviate any of the two last names when filling out forms, as they are both legal and identifying names.

D. CONSENT SEARCH

OFFICER	AGENTE	
Good afternoon. I'm Detective _____.	*Buenas tardes. Soy el detective _____.*	BWEH-nahs TAHR-dehs. Soy ehl deh-tehk-TEE-veh _____.
I need to look into your...	*Necesito registrar su...*	Neh-seh-SEE-toh reh-hees-TRAHR soo...
• house.	• *casa.*	• KAH-sah.
• car.	• *carro.*	• KAH-rroh.
• trunk.	• *cajuela.*	• ka-hoo-EH-lah
• coat.	• *abrigo.*	• ah-BREE-goh.
• yard.	• *jardín.*	• hahr-DEEN.
• garage.	• *garaje.*	• gah-RAH-heh.

You are not obligated to consent to the search.	*Usted no está obligado a consentir al registro.*	Oo-STEHD noh ehs-TAH oh-blee-GAH-doh ah kohn-sehn-TEER ahl reh-HEES-troh.
If you don't let me look, I will apply to the court for a search warrant.	*Si no consiente, voy a pedir al tribunal una orden de registro.*	See noh kohn-SYEHN-teh, voy ah peh-DEER ahl tree-boo-NAHL OO-nah OHR-dehn deh reh-HEES-troh.
I will be back once the warrant is granted.	*Volveré cuando tenga la orden.*	Vohl-veh-REH KWAHN-oh-TEHN-gah lah OHR-dehn.
I (don't) have a search warrant.	*(No) tengo una orden de registro.*	(Noh) TEHN-goh OO-nah OHR-dehn deh reh-HEES-troh.

E. SEARCH AND ARREST COMMANDS

Removal of High-Risk Suspects from Vehicles

Put your hands on the...	*Ponga las manos en el...*	POHN-gah lahs MAH-nohs ehn ehl...
• windshield.	• *parabrisas.*	• pah-rah-BREE-sahs.
• steering wheel.	• *volante.*	• voh-LAHN-teh.
Driver, slowly, with your left hand turn off the engine.	*Conductor, despacio, con la mano izquierda apague el motor.*	Kohn-dook-TOHR, dehs-PAH-syoh, kohn lah MAH-noh ees-KYEHR-dah ah-PAH-geh ehl moh-TOHR.
Hold/drop the keys out of the window.	*Tire las llaves por la ventana.*	TEE-reh lahs YAH-vehs pohr lah vehn-TAH-nah.
Driver, get out of the car and take two steps to the left.	*Conductor, salga del carro y camine dos pasos a la izquierda.*	Kohn-dook-TOHR, SAHL-gah dehl KAH-rroh ee kah-MEE-neh dohs PAH-sohs ah la ees-KYEHR-dah.

English	Spanish	Pronunciation
Put your hands high over your head.	*Levante las manos por encima de su cabeza.*	Leh-VAHN-teh lahs MAH-nohs pohr ehn-see-mah deh soo kah-BEH-sah.
Higher!	*¡Más ariba!*	¡MAHS ah-REE-bah!
Face away from me.	*No me mire.*	Noh meh MEE-reh.
Turn your back towards me.	*Voltéese de espaldas a mí.*	Vohl-TEH-eh-seh deh ehs-PAHL-dahs ah mee.
Slowly, walk backwards.	*Despacio, camine para atrás.*	Dehs-PAH-syoh, kah-MEE-neh PAH-rah ah-TRAHS.
Keep your hands up.	*No baje las manos.*	Noh BAH-heh lahs MAH-nohs.
Slowly, come down to your knees.	*Despacio, póngase de rodillas.*	Dehs-PAH-syoh, POHN-gah-seh deh roh-DEE-yahs.
Sit back on your feet.	*Siéntese en los talones.*	SYEHN-teh-seh ehn lohs tah-LOH-nehs.
Put your hands behind your head.	*Ponga las manos detrás de la cabeza.*	POHN-gah lahs MAH-nohs deh-TRAHS deh lah kah-BEH-sah.
Interlock your fingers.	*Cruce los dedos de las manos.*	KROO-seh lohs DEH-dohs deh lahs MAH-nohs.
Don't move.	*No se mueva.*	Noh seh MWEH-vah.
I will search you for...	*Lo voy a registrar para ver si acaso lleva...*	Loy voy ah reh-hees-TRAHR PAH-rah VEHR see ah-KAH-soh YEH-vah...
• weapons.	• *armas.*	• AHR-mahs.
• drugs.	• *drogas.*	• DROH-gahs.
• an ID.	• *identificación.*	• ee-dehn-tee-fee-kah-SYOHN.
Do you have any sharp objects in your pockets?	*¿Tiene objetos afilados en sus bolsillos?*	¿TYEH-neh ohb-HEH-tohs ah-fee-LAH-dohs ehn soos bohl-SEE-yohs?

VOCABULARY ••••

BODY PARTS

head	cabeza	kah-BEH-sah
hair	pelo, cabello	PEH-loh, kah-BEH-yoh
face	cara	KAH-rah
eyes	ojos	OH-hohs
nose	nariz	nah-REES
ears	orejas	oh-REH-hahs
mouth	boca	BOH-kah
teeth	dientes	DYEHN-tehs
tongue	lengua	LEHN-gwah
neck	cuello	KWEH-yoh
shoulders	hombros	OHM-brohs
arms	brazos	BRAH-sohs
hands	manos	MAH-nohs
fingers	dedos	DEH-dohs
wrist	muñeca	moo-NYEH-kah
elbow	codo	KOH-doh
chest	pecho	PEH-choh
back	espalda	ehs-PAHL-dah
waist	cintura	seen-TOO-rah
hip	cadera	kah-DEH-rah
stomach	estómago	ehs-TOH-mah-goh
legs	piernas	PYEHR-nahs
knees	rodillas	rroh-DEE-yahs
feet	pies	pyehs
toes	dedos del pie	DEH-dohs dehl pyeh
ankles	tobillos	toh-BEE-yohs

STANDING MODIFIED SEARCH AND FELONY PRONE COMMANDS

Stop!	¡Alto!/¡Párese!	¡AHL-toh!/¡PAH-reh-seh!
Hands up!	¡Manos arriba!	¡MAH-nohs ah-REE-bah!
Turn around slowly!	¡Voltéese despacio!	¡Vohl-TEH-eh-seh dehs-PAH-syoh!
Put your hands on your head!	¡Ponga las manos en la cabeza!	¡POHN-gah lahs MAH-nohs ehn lah KAH-beh-sah!
Kneel down!	¡Póngase de rodillas!	¡POHN-gah-seh deh roh-DEE-yahs!
Interlock your fingers!	¡Cruce los dedos de las manos!	¡KROO-seh lohs DEH-dohs deh lahs MAH-nohs!
Put your knees together!	¡Junte las rodillas!	¡Hoon-teh lahs roh-DEE-yahs!
Put your arms straight in front of you!	¡Extienda los brazos hacia adelante!	¡Ehk-STYEHN-dah lohs BRAH-sohs AH-syah ah-deh-LAHN-teh!
Down on your stomach!	¡Al suelo, boca abajo!	¡Ahl SWEH-loh, BOH-kah ah-BAH-hoh!
Cross your ankles!	¡Cruce los tobillos!	¡KROO-seh lohs toh-BEE-yohs!
Turn your head to the right/left!	¡Gire la cabeza a la derecha/izquierda!	¡HEE-reh lah kah-BEH-sah ah lah deh-REH-chah/ees-KYEHR-dah!
Don't move!	¡No se mueva!	¡Noh seh MWEH-vah!

GRAMMAR NOTE ••••

DIRECT COMMANDS   If you give an order to an adult you don't know, use the formal command form.

> (You) drop the gun!   *¡Suelte la pistola!*

You can also include yourself when giving an order:

> Let's drop the gun!   *¡Tiremos la pistola!*

The command forms of *-ar* verbs use the present tense endings of *-er* and *-ir* verbs.

> TO CALL *LLAM- AR:*
>
> | you (don't) call! | *(no) ¡llam- e!* |
> | you [pl.] (don't) call! | *(no) ¡llam- en!* |
> | let's (not) call! | *(no) ¡llam- emos!* |

-er and *-ir* verbs use *-ar* endings:

> TO RUN *CORR- ER:*
>
> | you (don't) run! | *(no) ¡corr- a!* |
> | you [pl.] (don't) run! | *(no) ¡corr- an!* |
> | let's (not) run! | *(no) ¡corr- amos!* |

> TO WRITE *ESCRIB- IR:*
>
> | you (don't) write! | *(no) ¡escrib- a!* |
> | you [pl.] (don't) write! | *(no) ¡escrib- an!* |
> | let's (not) write! | *(no) ¡escrib- amos!* |

F. BUILDING/AREA SEARCH WARNING

OFFICER	AGENTE	
Police Department!	*¡Departamento de Policía!*	¡Deh-pahr-tah-MEHN-toh deh poh-lee-SEE-ah!
If there's anyone inside the building, you must come out now.	*Si hay alguien dentro del edificio, debe salir ahora mismo.*	See ahy AHL-gyehn DEHN-troh dehl eh-dee-FEE-syoh, DEH-beh sah-LEER ah-OH-rah MEES-moh.

The building is surrounded by the police.	El edificio está rodeado por la policía.	Ehl eh-dee-FEE-syoh ehs-ehs-TAH roh-deh-AH-doh pohr lah poh-lee-SEE-ah.
We will release...	Soltaremos...	Sohl-tah-REH-mohs...
• a police dog.	• a un perro policía.	• ah oon PEH-rroh poh-lee-SEE-ah.
• tear gas.	• gas lacrimógeno.	• gahs lah-kree-MOH-heh-noh.
We are coming into the building.	Estamos entrando en el edificio.	Ehs-TA-mohs en-TRAN-doh ehn ehl eh-dee-FEE-syoh.
Give up now.	Ríndase.	REEN-dah-seh.
SUSPECT	**SOSPECHOSO**	
Don't send in the dog!	¡No suelte al perro!	¡Noh SWEHL-teh ahl PEH-rroh!
I'll come out now!	¡Salgo ahora mismo!	¡SAHL-goh ah-OH-rah MEES-moh!
Don't shoot!	¡No dispare!	¡Noh dees-PAH-reh!
I surrender!	¡Me entrego!	¡Meh ehn-TREH-goh!

GRAMMAR NOTE ••••

COMMANDS WITH PRONOUNS   When the verb indicates that the action is performed by oneself or directed to somebody else, a pronoun is attached to the command form in the affirmative. If the command is negative, the pronoun is placed before the verb.

to take sth. off	quitar	Take your jacket off!	¡Quítese la chaqueta!
		Don't take your jacket off!	¡No se quite la chaqueta!
to look at	mirar	Look at me!	¡Míreme!
		Don't look at me!	¡No me mire!

3. Field Tactics

CULTURE NOTE ••••

HEATED DISCUSSIONS Heated discussions among Latinos may be mistaken as fights. Latinos seem to talk all at the same time, interrupting each other loudly and gesturing profusely. This does not necessarily mean that violence is about to erupt. Latinos enjoy "blowing off steam" verbally. Latinos believe that *Perro que ladra no muerde* (A barking dog doesn't bite). When dealing with emotionally charged subjects, remain calm, try to calm down the subject, and call for the help of an interpreter immediately.

A. DEALING WITH UNCOOPERATIVE SUSPECTS AND WITNESSES

CULTURE NOTE ••••

TÚ OR USTED? In Spanish there are two forms of "you," the informal *tú*, used with family and friends, and the formal *usted*, used with everyone else. Please, be aware that using *tú* with Latinos you don't know personally may be considered disrespectful or condescending. Use the formal *usted* unless you are dealing with children or teenagers. However, when dealing with uncooperative witnesses or suspects, it may be appropriate to use *tú*.

SUBJECT	SOSPECHOSO	
Why am I here?	*¿Por qué me tienen aquí?*	¿Pohr KEH meh TYEH-nehn ah-KEE?
I didn't do anything.	*No he hecho nada.*	Noh eh EH-choh NAH-dah.
Let me go.	*Déjenme ir.*	DEH-hehn-meh eer.
Son of a bitch!	*¡Hijo de la chingada/puta!*	¡EE-hoh deh lah cheen-GAH-dah/POO-tah!
Fuck you!	*¡Qué se joda!*	¡Keh seh HOH-dah!
Shit!	*¡Mierda!*	¡MYEHR-dah!
You'll regret this.	*Va a lamentar esto.*	Vah ah lah-mehn-TAHR EHS-toh.
I will get you in trouble.	*Lo/la voy a joder.*	Loh/lah voy ah HOH-dehr.
Racist!	*¡Racista!*	¡Rah-SEES-tah!
OFFICER	**AGENTE**	
Take a seat.	*Siéntate.*	SYEHN-tah-teh.
Sit down!	*¡Siéntate!*	¡SYEHN-tah-teh!
Lie down!	*¡Acuéstate!*	¡Ah-KWEHS-tah-teh!
Turn around!	*¡Voltéate!*	¡Vohl-TEH-ah-teh!
Put the...down.	*Suelta...*	SWEHL-tah...
• knife	• *el cuchillo.*	• ehl koo-CHEE-yoh.
• gun	• *la pistola.*	• lah pees-TOH-lah.
Show me your hands.	*Enséñame las manos.*	Ehn-SEH-nyah-meh lahs MAH-nohs.
Stop!	*¡Para!*	¡PAH-rah!
Stop resisting!	*¡No resistas más!*	¡Noh reh-SEES-tahs mahs!
Put your hands...	*Pon las manos...*	POHN lahs MAH-nohs...
• behind your back.	• *detrás de la espalda.*	• deh-TRAHS deh lah ehs-PAHL-dah.

• above your head.	• *por encima de la cabeza.*	• pohr ehn-SEE-mah deh lah kah-BEH-sah.
• up.	• *arriba.*	• ah-REE-bah.
Calm down!	¡*Cálmate!*	¡KAHL-mah-teh!
Stay over there!	¡*Quédate ahí!*	¡KEH-dah-teh ah-EE!
Be quiet!	¡*No grites!*	¡Noh GREE-tehs!
Don't move!	¡*Estáte quieto!*	¡Ehs-TAH-teh KYEH-toh!
Shut up!	¡*Cállate!*	¡KAH-yah-teh!
Listen to me!	¡*Escúchame!*	¡Ehs-KOO-chah-meh!
No need…	*No necesitas*…	Noh neh-seh-SEE-tahs…
• to cry.	• *llorar.*	• yoh-RAHR.
• to curse.	• *maldecir.*	• mahl-deh-SEER.
• to scream.	• *gritar.*	• GREE-tahr.
• to swear.	• *jurar.*	• joo-RAHR.
• to yell.	• *gritar.*	• gree-TAHR.
Don't waste your time…	*No pierdas el tiempo*…	Noh PYEHR-dahs ehl TYEHM-POH…
• cursing.	• *maldiciendo.*	• mahl-dee-SYEHN-doh.
• crying.	• *llorando.*	• yoh-RAHN-doh.
• screaming.	• *gritando.*	• gree-TAHN-doh.
• swearing.	• *jurando.*	• joo-RAHN-doh.
Everything will be fine.	*Todo estará bien.*	TOH-doh ehs-tah-RAH byehn.
You'll be okay.	*No te pasará nada.*	Noh teh pah-sah-RAH NAH-dah.

VOCABULARY ••••

ADJECTIVES OF EMOTION

sad	*triste*	TREES-teh
happy	*contento/a*	kohn-TEHN-toh/tah
depressed	*deprimido/a*	deh-pree-MEE-doh/dah
tired	*cansado/a*	kahn-SAH-doh/dah
drunk	*borracho/a*	boh-RRAH-choh/chah
crazy	*loco/a*	LOH-koh/kah
nervous	*nervioso/a*	nehr-vee-OH-soh/sah
busy	*ocupado/a*	oh-koo-PAH-doh/dah
relaxed	*relajado/a*	reh-lah-HAH-doh/dah
tranquil	*tranquilo/a*	trahn-KEE-loh/lah
agitated	*agitado/a*	ah-hee-TAH-doh/dah
sick	*enfermo/a*	ehn-FEHR-moh/mah
angry	*enojado/a*	ehn-noh-HAH-doh/dah
dead	*muerto/a*	MWEHR-toh/tah
high (i.e., drugged)	*en onda*	ehn OHN-dah

GRAMMAR NOTE ••••

THE FAMILIAR COMMAND To give an order to a friend, family member, child, or anyone else you are on familiar terms with, use the informal command form.

The affirmative command uses the third person singular verb form. The negative command switches the endings: *-ar* verbs use *-er* or *-ir* endings; *-er* and *-ir* verbs use *-ar* endings.

TO CALL *LLAM- AR:*

| don't call! | ¡no llam- es! |
| call! | ¡llam- a! |

TO RUN *CORR- ER:*

| don't run! | ¡no corr- as! |
| run! | ¡corr- e! |

TO WRITE *ESCRIB- IR:*

| don't write! | ¡no escrib- as! |
| write! | ¡escrib- e! |

There are a few irregular informal commands:

put!	¡pon!
leave!	¡sal!
have!	¡ten!
come!	¡ven!
say!	¡di!
do!	¡haz!
go!	¡ve!
be!	¡sé!

B. REQUESTING AN INTERPRETER OR TRANSLATOR

CLERK/OFFICER   *OFICIAL*

I do not speak Spanish. *No hablo español.*   Noh AH-bloh ehs-pah-NYOHL.

I will have someone who speaks Spanish return your call.	*Voy a llamar a una persona que habla español para que le devuelva la llamada.*	Voy ah yah-MAHR ah OO-nah pehr-SOH-nah keh AH-blah ehs-pah-NYOHL PAH-rah keh leh deh-VWEHL-vah lah yah-MAH-dah.
Speak slowly.	*Hable más despacio.*	AH-bleh mahs dehs-PAH-syoh.
Repeat, please.	*Repita, por favor.*	Reh-PEE-tah, pohr fah-VOHR.
I don't understand.	*No comprendo.*	Noh kohm-PREHN-doh.
Wait. I'll bring in a translator.	*Espere. Llamaré a un traductor.*	Ehs-PER-reh. Yah-mah-REH ah oon trah-DOOK-tohr.
I'll call an interpreter.	*Llamaré a un intérprete.*	Yah-mah-REH ah oon een-TEHR-preh-teh.
Do you need…	*¿Necesita…*	¿Neh-seh-SEE-tah…
• a translator?	• *un traductor?*	• oon trah-dook-TOHR?
• an interpreter?	• *intérprete?*	• een-TEHR-preh-teh?
Do you…English?	*¿Usted…el inglés?*	¿Oos-TEHD…ehl een-GLEHS?
• speak	• *habla*	• AH-blah
• understand	• *comprende*	• kohm-PREHN-deh
Does anyone here speak English?	*¿Alguien aquí habla inglés?*	¿AHL-gyehn ah-KEE AH-blah een-GLEHS?
Can you help me translate?	*¿Puede ayudarme a traducir?*	¿PWEH-deh ah-yoo-DAHR-meh ah trah-doo-SEER?

GRAMMAR NOTE ••••

THE FUTURE TENSE The future tense describes events that will take place in the future. There is only one set of endings for all verbs. These endings are attached to the infinitive forms, as in the model below.

TO HELP *AYUDAR:*

I will help	*yo*	*ayudar- é*
you will help	*tú*	*ayudar- ás*
you/he/she will help	*usted/él/ella*	*ayudar- á*
we will help	*nosotros/as*	*ayudar- emos*
you all will help	*vosotros/as*	*ayudar- éis*
you all/they will help	*ustedes/ellos/ellas*	*ayudar- án*

We will help you. *Nosotros te ayudaremos.*

Another way to express the future is to use the verb *ir* + *a* + the infinitive of another verb. First, here's the verb *ir*.

I go	*yo*	*voy*
you go (inf.)	*tú*	*vas*
you go, he/she goes	*usted/él/ella*	*va*
we go	*nosotros/as*	*vamos*
you all go (inf.)	*vosotros/as*	*váis*
you all/they go	*ustedes/ellos/ellas*	*van*

Where are you going?	*¿Adónde van ustedes?*
We are going home.	*Vamos a casa.*

I'm going to arrest you.	*Voy a arrestarlo/la.*
You are not going to do this again.	*Tú no vas a hacer esto otra vez.*

IN CASE OF AN EMERGENCY

1. 911 Calls

A. ESTABLISHING THE EMERGENCY

DISPATCHER

_____ Police Department.

What's your emergency?

SUBJECT

There's...

* a medical emergency.

* a crime.

* an accident.

* a fight.

* a burglary.

* a bomb threat.

* an explosion.

OPERADORA DE EMERGENCIA

_Departamento de Policía de _____._

¿Cuál es su emergencia?

SUJETO

_Es..._

* _una emergencia médica._

* _un crimen._

* _un accidente._

* _una lucha._

* _un robo._

* _una amenaza de bomba._

* _una explosión._

Deh-pahr-tah-MEHN-toh deh poh-lee-SEE-ah deh _____.

¿Kwahl ehs soo eh-mehr-HEHN-syah?

Ehs...

* OO-nah eh-mehr HEHN-sayh MEH-dee-kah.

* oon KREE-mehn.

* oon ahk-see-DEHN-teh.

* oo-nah LOO-chah.

* oon ROH-boh.

* oon ah-mehn-NAH sah deh BOHM-bah.

* OO-nah eks-ploh-SYON.

• drug deal.	• *un negocio de drogas.*	• oon neh-goh-SYOH deh DRO-gahs.
• a fire.	• *un incendio.*	• oon een-SEHN-dyoh.

GRAMMAR NOTE ••••

THE VERBS *SER* AND *ESTAR* (TO BE)   The English "to be" has two different equivalents in Spanish: *ser* and *estar*. *Ser* describes constant quality. *Estar* describes a temporary state of being.

TO BE *SER:*

SINGULAR	PLURAL
yo soy	*nosotros/as somos*
tú eres	*vosotros/as sois*
él/ella/Ud. es	*ellos/ellas/Uds. son*

TO BE *ESTAR:*

SINGULAR	PLURAL
yo estoy	*nosotros/as estamos*
tú estás	*vosotros/as estáis*
él/ella/Ud. está	*ellos/ellas/Uds. están*

Use the verb *ser* for one's identity, physical description and traits, occupations, color, origin, and for telling time.

You are tall and generous.	*Usted es alto y generoso.*
I am a police officer.	*Yo soy policía.*
It's red.	*Es roja.*
Where are (all of) you from?	*¿De dónde son ustedes?*
Who is she?	*¿Quién es ella?*
What time is it?	*¿Qué hora es?*

The verb *estar*, on the other hand, is used for an emotional or physical state, physical location, or an action in progress:

How are you?	*¿Cómo está usted?*
Where are you?	*¿Dónde está usted?*
What are you doing?	*¿Qué está haciendo?*

B. ESTABLISHING THE IDENTITY OF THE CALLER

DISPATCHER	*OPERADORA DE EMERGENCIA*	
What's your name?	*¿Cómo se llama?*	¿KOH-moh seh YAH-mah?
What's your...	*¿Cuál es su...*	¿KWAHL ehs soo...
• address?	• *dirección?*	• dee-rehk-SYOHN?
• phone number?	• *número de teléfono?*	• NOO-meh-roh deh teh-LEH-foh-noh?

GRAMMAR NOTE ••••

ADDRESSES AND PHONE NUMBERS   When giving an address in Spanish, begin with the name of the street, followed by north, south, east, west, and the number.

What's your address?
My address is 99 East Pine Street.

¿Cuál es su dirección?
Mi dirección es Calle Pine Este, número noventa y nueve.

Phone numbers are grouped in pairs:

What's your phone number?

My number is 733-22-85.

¿Cuál es su número de teléfono?
Mi número de teléfono es el siete-treinta y tres-veintidós, ochenta y cinco.

Where are you calling from?	*¿De dónde llama?*	¿Deh DOHN-deh YAH-mah?
Where are you at this moment?	*¿Dónde está usted en este momento?*	¿DOHN-deh ehs-TAH oos-TEHD ehn EHS-teh moh-MEHN-toh?
• Is anybody...	• *¿Hay alguien...*	• ¿Ahy AHL-gyehn...

• Are you...	• ¿Está usted...	• ¿Ehs-TAH oos-TEHD...
• How many people are...	• ¿Cuántas personas están...	• ¿KWAHN-tahs pehr-SOH-nahs ehs-TAHN...
...hurt?	...herido/a/os?	...eh-REE-doh/dah/dohs?
Are they breathing?	¿Respiran?	¿Rehs-PEE-rahn?

SUBJECT | *SUJETO*

My name is ____.	Mi nombre es ____.	Mee NOHM-breh ehs ____.
My address is ____.	Mi dirección es ____.	Mee dee-rehk-SYOHN ehs ____.
I'm at ____.	Estoy en ____.	Ehs-TOY ehn ____.
The address here is ____, between ____ and ____ streets.	La dirección aquí es ____, entre las calles ____ y ____.	Lah dee-rehk-SYOHN ah-KEE ehs ehs ____, EHN-treh lahs KAH-yehs ____ ee ____.
I don't know the exact address.	No sé la dirección exacta.	Noh seh lah dee-rehk-SYOHN ek-SAHK-tah.
There's a...across the street.	Hay...al otro lado de la calle.	Ahy...ahl OH-troh LAH-doh deh lah KAH-yeh.
• gas station	• una gasolinera	• OO-nah gah-soh-lee-NEH-rah
• bank	• un banco	• oon BAHN-koh
• school	• una escuela	• OO-nah ehs-KWEH-lah
• park	• un parque	• oon PAHR-keh
• church	• una iglesia	• OO-nah ee-GLEH-syah
My phone number is ____.	Mi número de teléfono es ____.	Mee NOO-meh-roh deh teh-LEH-foh-noh ehs ____.
The phone number here is ____.	El teléfono aquí es ____.	Ehl teh-LEH-foh-noh ah-KEE ehs ____.
• Yes, I'm...	• Sí, estoy...	• See, ehs-TOY...

• No, I'm not…	• *No, no estoy…*	• Noh, noh ehs-TOY…
• Several people are…	• *Varias personas están…*	• VAH-ree-ahs pehr-SOH-nahs ehs-TAHN…
• One person is…	• *Una persona está…*	• OO-nah pehr-SOH-nah esh-TAH…
…hurt.	…*herido/a/as.*	…eh-REE-doh/dah/dahs.

C. MEDICAL EMERGENCIES

DISPATCHER	OPERADORA DE EMERGENCIA	
What is the nature of the injury?	*¿Qué tipo de herida es?*	¿Keh TEE-poh deh eh-REE-dah ehs?
How old is the injured person?	*¿Cuántos años tiene la persona herida?*	¿KWAHN-tohs AH-nyohs TYEH-neh lah per-SOH-nah eh-REE-dah?

SUBJECT	SUJETO	
My dad/mom/ someone…	*Mi padre/madre/ alguien…*	Mee PAH-dreh/MAH-dreh/AHL-gyehn…
• just had a heart attack.	• *acaba de tener un ataque al corazón.*	• ah-KAH-bah deh teh-NEHR oon ah-TAH-keh ahl koh-rah-SOHN.
• just had a stroke.	• *acaba de tener un ataque de apoplejía.*	• ah-KAH-bah deh teh-NEHR oon ah-TAH-keh deh ah-poh-pleh-HEE-ah.
• got burned.	• *se quemó.*	• seh keh-MOH.
• was drunk and passed out.	• *estaba borracho y perdió el conocimiento.*	• ehs-TAH-bah boh-RRAH-choh ee pehr-DYHO ehl koh-noh-see-MYEHN-toh.
• is bleeding.	• *está sangrando.*	• ehs-TAH sahn-GRAHN-doh.

• fell down the stairs.	• *se cayó por las escaleras.*	• seh kah-YOH pohr lahs ehs-kah-LEH-rahs.
• broke his/her...	• *se rompió...*	• seh rrohm-PYOH...
• leg.	• *la pierna.*	• lah PYEHR-nah.
• arm.	• *el brazo.*	• ehl BRAH-soh.
• hip.	• *la cadera.*	• lah kah-DEH-rah.
Someone...my father/mother.	*Alguien...a mi padre/madre.*	AHL-gyehn...ah mee PAH-dreh/MAH-dreh.
• stabbed	• *apuñaló*	• ah-poo-nya-LOH
• shot	• *disparó*	• dees-pah-ROH

D. CRIMINAL EMERGENCIES

GRAMMAR NOTE ••••

HAY (THERE IS, THERE ARE)

there is/there are	*hay*
There are drugs here.	*Hay drogas aquí.*
there was/there were	*había/hubo*
There was nobody in the building.	No *había nadie en el edificio.*

DISPATCHER	OPERADORA DE EMERGENCIA	
Are there any weapons involved?	*¿Hay armas implicadas?*	¿Ahy AHR-mahs eem-plee-KAH-dahs?
Where is the weapon?	*¿Dónde está el arma?*	¿DOHN-deh ehs-TAH ehl AHR-mah?
What happened?	*¿Qué pasó?*	¿Keh pah-SOH?

SUBJECT	SUJETO	
• My parents...	• Mis padres...	• Mees PAH-drehs...
• The neighbors...	• Los vecinos...	• Lohs veh-SEE-nohs...
• Some kids...	• Algunos niños...	• Ahl-GOO-nohs NEE-nyohs...
...are fighting.	...están peleando.	...ehs-TAHN peh-leh-AHN-doh.
There was an explosion.	Hubo una explosión.	OO-boh OO-nah eks-ploh-SYOHN.
A fire broke out in my...	Hay un incendio en mi...	Ahy oon een-SEHN-dyoh ehn mee...
• apartment.	• apartamento.	• ah-pahr-tah-MEHN-toh.
• house.	• casa.	• KAH-sah.
Somebody broke into the apartment/house...	Alguien entró en el apartamento/la casa...	AHL-gyehn ehn-TROH ehn ehl ah-pahr-tah MEHN-toh/lah KAH-sah...
• next door.	• de al lado.	• deh ahl LAH-doh.
• across the street.	• de enfrente.	• deh ehn-FREHN-teh.
I heard shots...	Oí disparos...	Oh-EE dees-PAH-rohs...
• in the park.	• en el parque.	• ehn ehl PAHR-keh.
• across the street.	• al otro lado de la calle.	• ahl OH-troh LAH-doh deh lah KAH-yeh.
• in my apartment building.	• en mi edificio de apartamentos.	• ehn mee eh dee-FEE-syoh deh ah-pahr-tah-MEHN-tohs.
• near here.	• cerca de aquí.	• SEHR-kah deh ah-KEE.
There was a car accident...	Hubo un accidente de carro...	OO-boh oon ahk-see-DEHN-teh deh KAH-rroh...
• nearby.	• cerca de aquí.	• SEHR-kah deh ah-KEE.
• between ____ and ____ streets.	• entre las calles ____ y ____.	• EHN-treh lahs KAH-yehs ____ ee ____.

There's something suspicious going on in...	*Algo sospechoso está ocurriendo en...*	AHL-goh sohs-peh-CHOH-soh ehs-TAH oh-koo-RYEHN-doh ehn...
• my yard.	• *mi jardín.*	• mee hahr-DEEN.
• the alley.	• *en el callejón.*	• ehn ehl kah-yeh-HOHN.
• behind my house.	• *detrás de mi casa.*	• deh-TRAHS deh mee KAH-sah.

E. DESCRIPTIONS OF POSSIBLE SUSPECTS

DISPATCHER	*OPERADORA DE EMERGENCIA*	
Can you describe the suspect?	*¿Puede describir al sospechoso?*	¿PWEH-deh dehs-kree-BEER ahl sohs-peh-CHOH-soh?
Is the suspect/are the suspects...	*¿Está el sospechoso/ están los sospechosos...*	¿Ehs-TAH ehl sohs-peh-CHOH-soh/ehs-TAHN lohs sohs-peh-CHOH-sohs...
• still in the house?	• *en la casa todavía?*	• ehn lah KAH-sah toh-dah-VEE-ah?
• at the scene?	• *en la escena?*	• eh la eh-SEH-nah?
• in the building?	• *en el edificio?*	• ehn ehl eh-dee-FEE-syoh?
• still there?	• *allá todavía?*	• ah-YAH-toh-dah-VEE-ah?
Which direction did he/she/they take?	*¿En qué dirección se fue/se fueron?*	¿Ehn keh dee-rehk-SYOHN seh FWEH/seh FWEH-rohn?
Can you describe the vehicle?	*¿Puede describir el vehículo?*	¿PWEH-deh dehs-kree-BEER ehl veh-EE-koo-loh?

SUBJECT	*SUJETO*	
He/she is/they are...	*Él/ella es/ellos son...*	Ehl/EH-yah ehs/EH-yohs sohn...
• tall.	• *alto/a/os/as.*	• AHL-toh/ah/ohs/ahs.

• young.	• *joven/jóvenes.*	• HOH-vehn/HOH-vehn-ehs.
• fat.	• *gordo/a/os/as.*	• GOHR-doh/dah/dohs/dahs.
• skinny.	• *delgado/a/os/as.*	• dehl-GAH-doh/dah/dohs/dahs.
He/she/they/left...	*Él/ella se fue/ellos se fueron...*	Ehl/EH-yah seh FWEH/EH-yohs seh FWEH-rohn...
• in a van.	• *en un camión.*	• ehn oon kah-MYOHN.
• in a car.	• *en un carro.*	• ehn oon KAH-rroh.
• on foot.	• *a pie.*	• ah pyeh.
• on a motorcycle.	• *en una moto.*	• ehn OO-nah MOH-toh.
He/they are still there.	*Todavía están allí.*	Toh-dah-VEE-ah ehs-tahn ah-YEE.
I don't know.	*No sé.*	Noh seh.
I couldn't see...	*No podía ver...*	Noh poh-DEE-ah vehr...
• the car.	• *el carro.*	• ehl KAH-rroh.
• the license plate.	• *la placa.*	• lah PLAH-kah.
• the suspect.	• *el/la sospechoso/a.*	• ehl/lah sohs-peh-CHOH-soh/sah.

F. CALMING DOWN THE CALLER

DISPATCHER	*OPERADORA DE EMERGENCIA*	
Is anyone else with you?	*¿Hay alguien más con usted?*	¿Ahy AHL-gyehn mahs kohn oos-TEHD?
Are you alone?	*¿Está solo/a?*	¿Ehs-TAH SOH-loh/ah?
Help is on the way.	*Le mandamos ayuda.*	Leh mahn-DAH-mohs ah-YOO-dah.
The police will be right there.	*La policía llegará pronto.*	Lah poh-lee-SEE-ah yeh-gahr-AH PROHN-toh.

Meet them outside.	*Encuéntrelos afuera.*	Ehn-KWEHN-treh-lohs ah-FWEH-rah.
We will send... immediately.	*Mandaremos... inmediatamente.*	Mahn dah-REH-mohs ...een-meh-dyah-tah-MEHN-teh.
• a patrol car	• *una patrulla*	• OO-nah pah-TROO-yah
• an ambulance	• *una ambulancia*	• OO-nah ahm-boo-LAHN-syah
Remain calm.	*Mantenga la calma.*	Mahn-TEHN-gah lah KAHL-mah.
Let the police in the door.	*Deje entrar a la policía.*	DEH-heh ehn-TRAHR ah la poh-lee-SYAH.

2. At the Scene of a Violent Crime or Accident

A. WITNESS INTERVIEW AT THE SCENE

CULTURE NOTE ••••

NONVERBAL COMMUNICATION   Latinos are highly expressive. Nonverbal communication is important, and it is often said that Latinos talk with their bodies. Shaking hands, kissing, embracing, and touching other people while talking is just as important as words. They usually stand closer to each other than most non-Hispanic Americans do during conversations.

OFFICER	AGENTE	
What happened?	¿Qué pasó?	¿Keh pah-SOH?
Did anybody see what happened?	¿Alguien vió lo que pasó?	¿Ahl-GYEHN VEE-OH loh keh pah-SOH?
WITNESS	TESTIGO	
I saw...	Yo vi...	Yoh vee...
• everything.	• todo.	• TOH-doh.
• what happened.	• lo que pasó.	• loh keh pah-SOH.
• the crash.	• el choque.	• ehl CHOH-keh.
A car crash.	Un accidente de carro.	Oon ahk-see-DEHN-teh deh KAH-rroh.
Two cars collided.	Dos carros chocaron.	Dohs KAH-rrohs choh-KAH-rohn.
• A man...	• Un hombre...	• Oon OHM-breh...
• A woman...	• Una mujer...	• OO-na MOO-HEHR
• A kid on a bicycle...	• Un niño en bicicleta...	• Oon NEEN-yoh ehn bee-see-KLEH-tah...
...was run over.	...fue atropellado/a.	...fwe ah-troh-peh-YAH-doh/dah.
They shot...	Le dispararon a...	Leh dees-pahr-RAHR-ohn ah...
• someone.	• alguien.	• AHL-gyehn.
• two men.	• dos hombres.	• dohs OHM-brehs.
Someone was stabbed.	Alguien fue apuñalado.	AHL-gyehn fweh ah-poo-nyeh-LAH-doh.
A hit and run.	Un carro chocó con otro y se escapó.	Oon KAH-rroh choh-KOH kohn OH-troh ee seh ehs-kah-POH.
OFFICER	AGENTE	
Do you live here?	¿Vive usted aquí?	¿VEE-veh oos-TEHD ah-KEE?
Do you know the victim?	¿Conoce a la víctima?	¿Koh-NOH-seh ah lah veek-TEE-mah?

WITNESS	TESTIGO	
I didn't know the victim.	No conocía a la víctima.	Noh kohn-noh-SEE-ah lah veek-TEEM-ah.
I knew the victim.	Conocía a la víctima.	Koh-noh-SEE-ah ah lah veek-TEEM-ah.
Yes, I live...	Sí, vivo...	See, VEE-voh...
• around the corner.	• alrededor de la esquina.	• ahl-rehd-deh-DOHR deh lah ehs-KEE-nah.
• in this building.	• en este edificio.	• ehn EHS-teh eh-dee-FEE-syoh.
No, I was just passing through.	No, sólo pasaba por aquí.	Noh, SOH-loh pah-SAH-bah pohr ah-KEEH.
No, I don't live around here.	No, no vivo por aquí.	Noh, noh VEE-voh pohr ah-KEEH.

OFFICER	AGENTE	
• When...	• ¿Cuándo...	• ¿DOHN-deh...
• Where...	• ¿Dónde...	• ¿KWAHN-doh...
...did the accident/ crime occur?	...ocurrió el accidente/crimen?	...oh-koo-RRYOH ehl ahk-see-DEHNTEH/ KREE-mehn?

WITNESS	TESTIGO	
Over there.	Allá.	Ah-YAH.
Right here.	Aquí.	Ah-KEE.
At the corner of _____ and _____ streets.	En la esquina de _____ y _____.	Ehn la ehs-KEE-nah deh _____ ee _____.
Inside the house.	Dentro de la casa.	DREHN-troh deh lah KAH-sah.
In the backyard.	En el patio de la casa.	Ehn ehl PAH-tyoh deh lah KAH-sah.
In this building.	En este edificio.	Ehn EHS-teh eh-dee-FEE-syoh.
Upstairs.	Arriba.	Ah-REE-bah.
Just a few minutes ago.	Hace unos minutos.	AH-seh OO-nohs mee-NOO-tohs.

| An hour ago. | *Hace una hora.* | AH-seh OO-nah OH-rah. |

OFFICER — *AGENTE*

Who did this?	*¿Quién lo hizo?*	¿Kyehn loh EE-soh?
Do you have a description...	*¿Tiene una descripción...*	¿TYEH-neh OO-nah dehs-kreep-SYOHN...
• of the subject?	• *del sujeto?*	• dehl soo-HEH-toh?
• of the vehicles involved in the accident/crime?	• *de los vehículos implicados en el accidente/crimen?*	• deh lohs veh-EE-koo-lohs eem-plee-KAH-dohs ehn ehl ahk-see-DEHN-teh/KREE-mehn?

OFFICER — *AGENTE*

Thank you for your cooperation.	*Gracias por su cooperación.*	GRAH-syahs pohr soo koh-oh-peh-rah-SYOHN.
Please give your name and address to the officer over there.	*Por favor, déle su nombre y dirección al agente allí.*	Pohr fah-VOHR, DEH-leh soo NOHM-breh ee dee-rehk-SYOHN ahl ah-HEHN-teh ah-YEE.
Please wait here until someone can take your statement.	*Por favor, quédese aquí hasta que alguien tome su informe.*	Pohr fah-VOHR, KEH-deh-seh ah-KEE AHS-tah keh AHL-gyehn TOH-meh soo een-FOHR-meh.

B. SECURING THE SCENE

OFFICER — *AGENTE*

We have to secure the scene.	*Tenemos que proteger la escena.*	Teh-NEH-mohs keh proh-teh-HEHR lah eh-SEH-nah.
Please...	*Por favor...*	Pohr fah-VOHR...
• go around.	• *vayan alrededor.*	• VAH-yahn ahl-reh-deh-DOHR.
• go to the other side of the street.	• *vayan al otro lado de la calle.*	• VAH-yahn ahl OH-troh LAH-doh deh lah KAH-yeh.

• use the sidewalk.	• *usen la acera.*	• OO-sehn lah ah-SEH-rah.
• move on.	• *circulen.*	• seer-KOO-lehn.
• stand back.	• *atrás.*	• ah-TRAHS.
• use the side street.	• *usen la calle de al lado.*	• OO-sehn lah KAH-yeh deh ahl LAH-doh.
• follow the detour signs.	• *sigan la señal de desvío.*	• SEE-gahn lah seh-NYAHL deh dehs-VEE-oh.
You can't...	*No pueden...*	Noh PWEH-dehn...
• go in there.	• *ir ahí.*	• eer ah-EE.
• go into the building.	• *entrar en el edificio.*	• ehn-TRAHR ehn ehl eh-dee-FEE-syoh.
• go into the apartment.	• *entrar en el apartamento.*	• ehn-TRAHR ehn ehl ah-pahr-tah-MEHN-toh.
Please be patient.	*Por favor, tengan paciencia.*	Pohr fah-VOHR, TEHN-gahn pah-SYEHN-syah.

GRAMMAR NOTE ••••

TENER (TO HAVE) AND TENER QUE (TO HAVE TO)

The verb *tener* indicates possession, while *tener que* + infinitive indicates obligation.

TO HAVE *TENER:*

SINGULAR	PLURAL
tengo	*tenemos*
tienes	*tenéis*
tiene	*tienen*

I have no weapons.	*Yo no tengo armas.*
You have to come to the station.	*Ustedes tienen que venir a la estación.*

ON THE ROAD

1. Roadside Assistance

OFFICER	AGENTE	
Good morning. I am officer ___.	*Buenos días. Soy el agente ___.*	BWEH-nohs DEE-ahs. Soy ehl ah-HEN-teh ___.
Is there a problem?	*¿Hay un problema?*	¿Ay oon proh-BLEH-mah?

DRIVER	CONDUCTOR	
Good morning, officer. I was driving along and suddenly my car broke down.	*Buenos días, agente. Estaba manejando y de repente mi carro dejó de funcionar.*	Bwen-NOHS DEE-ahs, ah-HEHN teh. Ehs-TAH-bah mah-neh-HAN-doh ee deh rrhe-PEHN-teh mee KAH-rroh deh-JOH deh foon-syoh-NAHR.

OFFICER	AGENTE	
Can you...?	*¿Puede usted ...?*	¿PWEH-deh oos-TEHD...?
• start the engine?	• *arrancar el motor?*	• ah-rrahn-KAHR ehl moh-TOHR?
• steer the vehicle?	• *girar el volante?*	• hee-RAHR ehl vohl-LAHN-teh?

GRAMMAR NOTE ••••

NEGATION In Spanish we express the negative with the word *no,* which precedes the conjugated verb:

Did you call the police?	*¿Llamó usted a la policía?*
I didn't (call them).	*No llamé a la policía.*

There are other words to express the negative.

never	*nunca*
nothing	*nada*
nobody	*nadie*
none	*ningún/o/a*
neither	*tampoco*
neither...nor	*ni...ni*

Except for *nada* (nothing) and *ningún* (nobody), these words can stand either before or after the verb. *Nada* and *ningún* always stand after the verb. Note the double negative if the negative stands after the verb.

I never drink tequila.	*Yo nunca bebo tequila.*
I never drink tequila.	*Yo no bebo tequila nunca.*

DRIVER	**CONDUCTOR**	
Yes, I can.	*Sí, puedo.*	See, PWEH-doh.
No, I can't.	*No, no puedo.*	Noh, no PWEH-doh.
OFFICER	**AGENTE**	
Do you have an AAA card?	*¿Tiene una tarjeta de Triple A?*	¿TYEHN-eh OO-nah tahr-HEH-tah deh TREE-pleh-ah?
Do you need...	*¿Necesita...*	¿Neh-seh-SEE-tah...
• to charge the battery?	• *cargar la batería?*	• kahr-GAHR lah bah-teh-REE-ah?

- a mechanic? • *un mecánico?* • oon meh-KAH-nee-koh?

- a push? • *un empujón?* • oon ehm-poo-HOHN?

- a new oil filter? • *un nuevo filtro para el aceite?* • oon NWEH-voh FEEL-troh PAH-rah ehl ah-SAY-teh?

- transmission fluid? • *aceite para la transmisión?* • ah-SAY-teh PAH-rah lah trahns-mee-SYOHN?

- a tow truck? • *una grúa?* • OO-nah GROO-ah?

- brake fluid? • *aceite para los frenos?* • ah-SAY-teh PAH-rah los FREH-nohs?

DRIVER | *CONDUCTOR*

Yes, I need ____. | *Sí, necesito ____.* | See, neh-seh-SEE-toh ____.

No, I don't need ____. | *No, no necesito ____.* | Noh, noh neh-seh-SEE-toh ____.

OFFICER | *AGENTE*

I think that... | *Pienso que...* | PYEHN-soh keh...

- the water tank is empty. • *el depósito del agua está vacío.* • ehl deh-POH-see-toh dehl AH-gwah ehs TAH vah-SEE-oh.

- the oil tank is empty. • *el tanque del aceite está vacío.* • ehl TAHN-keh dehl ah-SAY-teh ehs-TAH vah-SEE-oh.

- the gas tank is empty. • *el depósito de gasolina está vacío.* • ehl deh-POH-see-toh deh gahs-oh-LEE-nah ehs-TAH vah-SEE-oh.

- this tire is flat. • *esta llanta/goma está desinflada.* • EHS-tah YAHN-tah/GOH-mah ehs-TAH dehs-een-FLAH-dah.

- the battery is empty. • *la batería está descargada.* • lah bah-teh-REE-ah ehs-TAH dehs-kahr-GAH-dah.

Do you have... | *¿Tiene...* | ¿TYEH-neh...

• a wrench?	• *una llave inglesa?*	• OO-nah YAH-veh een-GLEH-sah?
• a hammer?	• *un martillo?*	• oon mahr-TEE-yoh?
• a screwdriver?	• *un desarmador?*	• oon dehs-ahr-mah-DOHR?
• a jack?	• *un gato?*	• oon GAH-toh?
• a wire?	• *un alambre?*	• oon ahl-AHM-breh?
• a flashlight?	• *una linterna?*	• OO-nah leen-TEHR-nah?
• the car manual?	• *el manual del carro?*	• ehl mah-NWAHL dehl KAH-rroh?
• a map?	• *un mapa?*	• oon MAH-pah?
• a spare tire?	• *una llanta/goma de repuesto?*	• OO-nah YAHN-tah/ GOH-mah deh rreh-PWEHS-toh?
• jumper cables?	• *los cables?*	• lohs KAH-blehs?
DRIVER	**CONDUCTOR**	
Yes, I have ____.	*Sí, tengo ____.*	See, TEHN-goh ____.
No, I don't have ____.	*No, no tengo ____.*	Noh, noh TEHN-goh ____.
OFFICER	**AGENTE**	
Let me see if I can help you…	*A ver si puedo ayudarle/a…*	Ah vehr see PWEH-doh ah-yoo-DAHR-leh/ lah…
• start the engine.	• *arrancar el motor.*	• ah-rrahn-KAHR ehl moh-TOHR.
• jump start the car with the cables.	• *arrancar el carro con los cables.*	• ah-rrahn-KAHR ehl KAHR-roh kohn lohs KAH-blehs.
• change the tire.	• *cambiar la llanta.*	• KAHM-byahr lah YAHN-tah.
I can…	*Puedo…*	PWEH-doh…
• call a tow truck.	• *llamar a la grúa.*	• yah-MAHR ah lah GROO-ah.

- take you to the nearest gas station.
- llevarlo a la gasolinera más cercana.
- yeh-VAHR loh ah lah gahs-oh-lee-NEH-rah mahs sehr-KAH-nah.

- call AAA for you.
- llamar a Triple A.
- yah-MAHR ah TREE-pleh Ah.

You are blocking traffic.

Está bloqueando el tráfico.

Ehs-TAH bloh-keh-AHN-doh ehl TRAH-fee-koh.

I must tow the vehicle.

Debo remolcar el vehículo.

DEH-boh reh-mohl-KAHR ehl veh-HEE-koo-loh.

DRIVER

CONDUCTOR

I've already called...

Ya llamé a...

Yah yah-MEH ah...

- the tow truck.
- la grúa.
- lah GROO-ah.

- AAA.
- Triple A.
- TREE-pleh A.

My friend/husband/ wife already went to get gas.

Mi amigo/a/marido/ esposa ya fue a una gasolinera.

Mee ah-MEE-goh/gah/ mah-REE-doh/ehs-POH-sah yah fweh ah OO-nah gah-soh-lee-NEH-rah.

That would be great!

¡Sería estupendo!

¡Seh-REE-ah ehs-too-PEHN-doh!

Thank you for your help!

¡Gracias por su ayuda!

¡GRAH-syahs pohr soo ah-YOO-dah!

OFFICER

AGENTE

You're welcome.

De nada.

Deh NAH-dah.

Have a good day!

¡Qué tenga un buen día!

¡Keh TEHN-gah oon bwehn DEE-ah!

Good-bye.

¡Adiós!

¡Ah-DYOHS!

VOCABULARY ••••

PARTS OF A VEHICLE

car	*carro, coche*	KAH-rroh, KOH-cheh
doors	*puertas*	PWEHR-tahs
seats	*asientos*	ah-SYEHN-tohs
bumper	*parachoques*	pah-rah-CHOH-kehs
clutch	*embrague*	ehm-BRAH-gueh
brakes	*frenos*	FREH-nohs
fender	*guardafangos*	gwahr-dah-FAHN-gohs
hood	*cofre/capó*	KOH-freh, kah-POH
glass	*vidrio*	VEE-dryoh
glove compartment	*cajuela*	kah-HWEH-lah
mirror	*espejo*	ehs-PEH-hoh
radio	*radio*	RRAH-dyoh
seat belt	*cinturón*	seen-too-ROHN
steering wheel	*volante*	voh-LAHN-teh
windshield	*parabrisas*	pah-rah-BREE-sahs
engine	*motor*	moh-TOHR
plate	*placa*	PLAH-kah
trunk	*maletero*	mah-leh-TEH-roh
tire	*llanta*	YAHN-tah
truck	*camión*	kah-MYOHN
window	*ventanilla*	vehn-tah-NEE-yah
trunk	*cajuela*	ka-hoo-EH-lah
hub cap	*tapón de cubo*	tah-POHN deh-KOO-boh
wheel	*volante*	voh-LAHN-teh
front end	*el frente*	ehl FREHN-teh
rear end	*parte posterior*	PAHR-teh pohs-teh-RYOHR

GRAMMAR NOTE ••••

POSSESSIVE There are short and long forms of possessive adjectives. The short forms precede the noun they accompany. The long forms are placed after the noun and the verb.

SHORT FORMS

my	*mi/s*
your (fam.)	*tu/s*
your/his/her/its/their	*su/s*
ours	*nuestro/a/os/as*
your (fam.)	*vuestro/a/os/as*

LONG FORMS

mine	*mío*
yours (fam.)	*tuyo*
yours/his/hers/its/theirs	*suyo/a/os/as*
our	*nuestro/a/os/as*
yours	*vuestro/a/os/as*

The knife is not mine.	*El cuchillo no es mío.*
It's John's. It's his knife.	*Es de Juan. Es su cuchillo.*
The pistol is not yours.	*La pistola no es tuya.*
It's ours. It's our pistol.	*Es de nosotros. Es nuestra pistola.*

In Spanish, the preposition *de* (of) is used to indicate possession.

This is John's knife.	*El cuchillo es de Juan.*

The possessive pronouns stand alone in the sentence because they substitute the noun they refer to. Their forms are the same as the long forms of the possessive adjective.

The knife? It's mine.	*¿El cuchillo? Es el mío.*
This house? It's ours.	*¿Esta casa? Es la nuestra.*

2. Basic Traffic Stop

CULTURE NOTE ••••

LA MORDIDA   In some Latin American countries, corruption within the police force has been a fact of life, although efforts have been made to correct the problem. Street police officers are reported to accept bribes (*las mordidas*) from motorists who want to avoid a ticket (*la multa*) for minor traffic violations. Accustomed to this practice, some Latinos may try to do the same here, unaware of the fact that this is unacceptable in the United States. In such situations it may be best to explain that bribery is considered a crime under United States law, and that you have to give them a ticket for their traffic violation.

OFFICER	AGENTE	
Good morning.	*Buenos días.*	BWEH-nohs DEE-ahs.
Do you know why I stopped you?	*¿Sabe por qué lo/la paré?*	¿SAH-be pohr keh loh/lah pah-REH?
DRIVER	CONDUCTOR	
No, officer.	*No, agente.*	Noh, ah-HEHN teh.
I don't think so.	*Creo que no.*	KREH-oh keh noh.

GRAMMAR NOTE ••••

STEM-CHANGING VERBS There are a few verbs in Spanish that don't follow the rules we established for the present tense. Some of them change the *-e* in their stem to an *-ie* in some forms.

> TO WANT *QUERER:*
>
> quiero   queremos
> quieres   queréis
> quiere   quieren

Other verbs following this pattern are: *pensar* (to think), *sentir* (to feel), *empezar* (to begin), *entender* (to understand), *preferir* (to prefer).

Other verbs change their *-o* to *-ue.*

> TO BE ABLE TO *PODER:*
>
> puedo   podemos
> puedes   podéis
> puede   pueden

Other verbs following this pattern are: *encontrar* (to find), *morir* (to die), *volver* (to return), *jugar* (to play), *dormir* (to sleep).

Pedir (to ask for) changes *e* to *i.*

> TO ASK FOR *PEDIR:*
>
> pido   pedimos
> pides   pedís
> pide   piden

OFFICER	AGENTE	
I stopped you for...	Lo/la paré por...	Loh/lah pah-REH pohr...

• speeding.	• *manejar con exceso del velocidad.*	• mah-neh-HAHR kohn ehk-SEH-soh deh veh-loh-see-DAHD.
• tailgating.	• *manejar muy cerca del otro carro.*	• mah-neh-HAHR mwee SEHR-kah dehl OH-troh KAH-rroh.
• driving from side to side.	• *ir zigzagueando.*	• eer see-sah-gweh-AHN-doh.
• running a red light.	• *pasarse un semáforo en rojo.*	• pah-SAHR-seh oon seh-MAH-foh-roh ehn RROH-hoh.
• making an illegal turn.	• *dar una vuelta ilegal.*	• dahr OO-nah VWEHL-tah ee-leh-GAHL.
• not having the right of way.	• *no tener derecho de vía.*	• noh teh-NEHR deh-REH-choh deh VEE-ah.
• driving too slowly.	• *manejar muy despacio.*	• mah-neh-HAHR mwee dehs-PAH-syoh.
• going the wrong way in a one-way street.	• *ir en dirección contraria.*	• eer een dee-rehk-SYOHN kohn-TRAH-ree-ah.
• cutting the corner.	• *recortar una esquina.*	• rreh-kohr-TAHR OO-nah ehs-KEE-nah.
• having too many passengers in your vehicle.	• *llevar demasiados pasajeros en su carro.*	• yeh-VAHR deh-mah-SYAH-dohs pah-sah-HEH-rohs ehn soo KAH-rroh.
• littering.	• *tirar basura en la carretera.*	• tee-RAHR bah-SOO-rah ehn lah kah-rreh-TEH-rah.
• driving in the car pool lane.	• *manejar por la vía reservada para grupos.*	• mah-neh-HAHR pohr lah VEE-ah reh-sehr-VAH-dah PAH-rah GROO-pohs.
• stopping suddenly without any apparent reason.	• *parar de repente sin razón aparente.*	• pah-RAHR deh reh-PEHN-teh seen rrah-SOHN ah-pahr-EHN-teh.

• crossing a double yellow line.	• *cruzar una doble raya amarilla.*	• kroo-SAHR OO-nah DOH-bleh RRAH-yah ah-mah-REE-yah.
• making an unsafe lane change.	• *hacer un cambio de carril peligroso.*	• ah-SEHR oon KAHM-byoh deh kah-RREEL peh-lee-GROH-soh.

I stopped you because...	*Lo/la paré porque...*	Loh/lah pah-REH pohr-KEH...
• you did not yield to traffic.	• *no cedió el paso.*	• noh seh-dee-OH ehl PAH-soh.
• you did not obey the street sign.	• *no obedeció la señal.*	• noh oh-beh-deh-see-OH lah seh-NYAHL.
• you did not use your turn signal.	• *no usó las direccionales.*	• noh oo-SOH lahs dee-rehk-syon-AH-lehs.
• your license plate has expired.	• *ya se venció la placa.*	• yah-seh vehn-SYOH lah PLAH-kah.
• your child is not in a child-safe seat.	• *su niño no está sujeto en un asiento infantil.*	• soo NEE-nyoh noh ehs-TAH soo-HEH-toh ehn oon ah-SYEHN-toh een-fahn-TEEL.
• you have no lights on.	• *las luces estan apagadas.*	• lahs LOO-sehs ehs-TAHN ah-pah-GAH-dahs.
• your tail lights are not working.	• *las luces traseras no funcionan.*	• lahs LOO-sehs trah-SEH-rahs noh foon-SYOH-nahn.
• your view is obstructed.	• *la vista está obstruida.*	• lah VEES-tah ehs-TAH ohbs-troo-EE-dah.
• your car looks like one I am looking for.	• *su coche se parece al que estoy buscando.*	• soo KOH-che seh pah-REH-seh ahl keh ehs-TOY boos-KAHN-doh.

DRIVER	**CONDUCTOR**	
I didn't know that...	*No sabía que...*	Noh sah-BEE-ah keh...
• I was speeding.	• *manejaba con exceso de velocidad.*	• mah-neh-HAH-bah kohn ehk-SEH-soh de veh-loh-see-DAHD.

• I ran a stop sign.	• me pasé una señal de stop.	• meh pah-SEH oon-ah sehn-YAHL deh "stop."
• my turn signal was not working.	• las direccionales no funcionaban.	• lahs DEE-rehk-see-yoh-NAH-lehs noh foon-syohn-NAH-bahn.
• I was driving too slowly.	• manejaba muy despacio.	• mah-neh-HAH-bah mwee dehs-PAH-see-oh.
• this turn was illegal.	• la vuelta era ilegal.	• lah voo-EHL-tah EH-rah ee-leh-GAHL.
• this is a one-way street.	• iba en dirección contraria.	• EEB-ah ehn dee-rehk-SYOHN kohn-TRAH-ree-ah.
I'm sorry, officer.	Lo siento, agente.	Loh SYEHN-toh, ah-HEN-teh.
I was speeding because...	Manejaba rápido porque...	Mah-neh-HAH-bah RRAH-pee-doh pohr-KEH...
• I am on my way to the hospital/ a wedding.	• voy al hospital/a una boda.	• voy ahl ohs-pee-TAHL/ah OO-nah BOH-dah.
• I have diarrhea.	• tengo diarrea.	• TEHN-goh dee-ah-RREH-ah.
• I have to go to the bathroom.	• tengo que ir al baño.	• TEHN-goh keh eer ahl BAH-nyoh.
My speedometer must not be working.	Mi velocímetro probablemente no funciona.	Mee veh-loh-SEE-meh-troh proh-bah-bleh-MEHN-teh noh-foon-SYOHN-nah.
I was on my way to renew my license plate.	Iba a renovar mi placa.	EE-bah ah reh-noh-VAHR mee PLAH-kah.
OFFICER	**AGENTE**	
May I see your...	¿Puedo ver su...	¿PWEH-doh vehr soo...
• driver's license?	• licencia de manejar?	• lee-SEHN-syah deh mah-neh-HAHR?
• vehicle's registration?	• registro del carro?	• rreh-HEE-stroh dehl kah-rroh?

English	Spanish	Pronunciation
• proof of insurance?	• *prueba del seguro?*	• PRWEH-bah dehl seh-GOO-roh?

DRIVER / *CONDUCTOR*

Yes, sir.	*Sí, señor.*	See, seh-NYOHR.
One second, please.	*Un momento, por favor.*	Ooon moh-MEHN-toh, pohr fah-VOHR.
I can't find my...	*No encuentro mi...*	Noh ehn-KWEN-troh mee...
• proof of insurance.	• *prueba del seguro.*	• PRWEH-bah dehl seh-GOO-roh.
• driver's license.	• *licencia de manejar.*	• lee-SEHN-syah deh mah-neh-HAHR.
I don't have...	*No tengo...*	Noh TEHN-goh...
• insurance.	• *el seguro.*	• ehl seh-GOO-roh.
• a driver's license.	• *una licencia de manejar.*	• OO-nah lee-SEYHN-syah deh mah-neh-HAHR.

OFFICER / *AGENTE*

| Who is the owner of the car? | *¿Quién es el dueño del carro?* | ¿Kyehn ehs ehl DWEH-nyoh dehl KAH-rroh? |

DRIVER / *CONDUCTOR*

It's...	*Es...*	Ehs...
• my car.	• *mi carro.*	• mee KAH-rroh.
• my Dad's car.	• *el carro de mi padre.*	• ehl KAH-rroh deh mee PAH-dreh.
• my friend's car.	• *el carro de mi amigo/a.*	• ehl KAH-rroh deh mee ah-MEE-goh/gah.
• a rental.	• *un carro alquilado.*	• oon KAH-rroh ahl-kee-LAH-doh.

OFFICER / *AGENTE*

| Is this your current address? | *¿Es éste su domicilio actual?* | ¿Ehs EHS-teh soo doh-mee-SEE-lyoh ahk-too-AHL? |

DRIVER / *CONDUCTOR*

| No, I moved recently. | *No, me mudé recientemente.* | Noh, meh moo-DEH reh-SYEHN-teh-MEHN-teh. |

| My new address is _____. | Mi nueva dirección es _____. | Mee NWEH-vah dee-rehk-SYOHN ehs _____. |
| Yes, sir. | Sí, señor. | See, seh-NYOHR. |

OFFICER — **AGENTE**

| I will have to issue you a ticket. | Tengo que darle una multa. | TEHN-goh keh DAHR-leh OO-nah MOOL-tah. |

DRIVER — **CONDUCTOR**

Please don't give me a ticket.	Por favor, no me dé una multa.	Pohr fah-VOHR, noh meh DEH OO-nah MOOL-tah.
I have no...	No tengo...	Noh TEHN-goh...
• money.	• dinero.	• dee-NEH-roh.
• time.	• tiempo.	• TYEHM-poh.
I am in poor health.	No estoy bien de salud.	Noh ehs-TOY byehn deh sah-LOOD.
Can't you let me go this time?	¿No puede dejarme ir esta vez?	¿Noh PWEH-deh deh-HAHR-meh eer EHS-tah vehs?
I wasn't driving that fast.	No manejaba tan rápido.	Noh mahn-eh-HA-bah tahn RAH-pee-doh.
I didn't endanger anyone.	No puse en peligro a nadie.	Noh POO-seh ehn peh-LEE-groh ah NAH-dyeh.
You can't see the stop sign behind the trees.	El "stop" no se puede ver detrás de los árboles.	Ehl "stop" noh seh POO-eh-de VEHR deh-TRAHS deh lohs AHR-boh-lehs.

OFFICER — **AGENTE**

| This time I'll issue you a warning. | Esta vez lo dejo ir. | EHS-tah vehs loh DEH-hoh eer. |
| I'm sorry. It's the law. | Lo siento. Es la ley. | Loh SYEHN-toh. Ehs lah leh. |

You can fight it in court.	Puede protestarlo en el tribunal.	PWEH-deh proh-tehs-TAHR-loh ehn ehl tree-boo-NAHL.
Please stay in the car.	Por favor, quédese en el carro.	Pohr fah-VOHR, keh-deh-seh ehn ehl KAH-rroh.
Sign your name here.	Firme aquí.	FEER-meh ah-KEE.
By signing this ticket, you are not necessarily admitting your guilt.	Al firmar esta multa, usted no necesariamente admite su culpabilidad.	Ahl feer-MAHR EHS-tah MOOL-tah, OOS-tehd noh neh-seh-SAH-ree-ah-MEHN-teh ahd-MEE-teh soo kool-pah-beel-lee-DAHD.
You may go now.	Puede irse ahora.	PWEH-deh EER-seh ah-OH-rah.
Carefully, enter into the first lane.	Con cuidado, entre en el primer carril.	Khon kwee-DAH-doh, EHN-treh ehn ehl pree-MEHR kah-RREEHL.

GRAMMAR NOTE ••••

VERBS WITH IRREGULAR *YO* FORMS   The following verbs are irregular in the *yo* form only: *poner* (to put), *salir* (to leave), *traer* (to bring), *caer* (to fall), *hacer* (to do), *venir* (to come), *oir* (to hear), *decir* (to say). Please note that the other forms of the verb are regular.

I put	pongo	we put	ponemos
I leave	salgo	we leave	salimos
I bring	traigo	we bring	traemos
I fall	caigo	we fall	caemos
I do	hago	we do	hacemos
I come	vengo	we come	venimos
I hear	oigo	we hear	oimos
I say	digo	we say	decimos

3. Towing a Vehicle

OFFICER	AGENTE	
I'm towing your vehicle because...	*La grúa se ha llevado el vehículo porque...*	Lah GROO-ah seh ah yeh-VAH-doh ehl veh-EE-koo-loh pohr-KEH...
• your car is parked in a "no parking" zone.	• *su carro está estacionado en un lugar prohibido.*	• soo KAH-rroh ehs-TAH ehsTAH-syoh-NAH-doh ehn oon loo-GAHR proh-ee-BEE-doh.
• your car is parked on a private parking lot.	• *su carro está estacionado en un estacionamento privado.*	• soo KAH-rroh ehs-TAH ehs-tah-syoh-NAH-doh ehn oon ehs-tah-syohn-ah-MYEHN-toh pree-VAH-doh.
• your car has been parked on this road for three days.	• *su carro ha estado estacionado en esta carretera por tres días.*	• soo KAH-rroh ah ehs-TAH-doh ehs-tah-syoh-NAH-doh ehn EHS-tah kah-rreh-TEH-rah pohr trehs DEE-ahs.

SUBJECT	SUJETO	
I'm sorry, officer.	*Lo siento, agente.*	Loh SYEHN-toh, ah-HEHN-teh.
I parked here because...	*Lo estacioné ahí porque...*	Loh ehs-tah-syoh-NEH ah-EE pohr-KEH...
• there was no parking available for many blocks.	• *no había espacio libre por muchas cuadras.*	• noh ah-BEE-ah ehs-PAH-syoh LEE-breh pohr MOO-chahs KWAH-drahs.
• I just needed to go in and out of this building.	• *sólo necesitaba entrar y salir en este edificio rápidamente.*	• SOH-loh neh-seh-see-TAH-bah ehn-TRAHR ee sah-LEER ehn EHS-teh eh-dee-FEE-syoh RAH-pee-dah-mehn-teh.

- the car broke down and won't start.

- *el carro se descompuso y no puedo arrancarlo.*

- ehl KAH-rroh seh des-kohm-POO-soh ee noh PWEH-doh ah-rrahn-KAHR-loh.

Where has my car been towed to?

¿Adónde se llevaron mi carro?

¿Ah-DOHN-deh seh yeh-VAH-rohn mee kah-rroh?

OFFICER

AGENTE

It has been towed to _____.

Se lo llevaron a _____.

Seh loh yeh-VAH-rohn ah _____.

Can anyone come to pick you up?

¿Puede venir alguien a recogerlo/la?

¿PWEH-deh veh-NEER AHL-gyehn ah rreh-koh-HEHR-loh/lah?

SUBJECT

SUJETO

I need to call someone.

Necesito llamar a alguien.

Neh-seh-SEE-toh yah-MAHR ah AHL-gyehn.

Yes. Thank you.

Sí. Gracias.

See. GRAH-syahs.

How much does it cost to get my car released?

¿Cuánto cuesta recobrar mi carro?

¿KWAHN-toh KWEHS-tah rreh-koh-BRAHR mee KAH-rroh?

OFFICER

AGENTE

I don't know.

No sé.

Noh seh.

You need to pay a fee for the citation and a fee for towing.

Usted tiene que pagar la multa y otra suma para recobrar su carro.

Oos-TEHD TYEH-neh keh pah-GAHR lah MOOL-tah ee OH-trah SOO-mah PAH-rah reh-koh-BRAHR soo KAH-rroh.

SUBJECT

SUJETO

When can I get my car back?

¿Cuándo puedo recobrar mi carro?

¿KWAHN-doh PWEH-doh rreh-koh-BRAHR mee KAH-rroh?

OFFICER	AGENTE	
This...	Esta...	EHS-tah...
• afternoon.	• tarde.	• TAHR-deh.
• evening.	• noche.	• NOH-cheh.
Tomorrow morning.	Mañana por la mañana.	Mah-NYAH-nah pohr lah mah-NYAH-nah.
Here is the address where you can go to pick it up.	Aquí está la dirección para ir a recogerlo.	Ah-KEE ehs-TAH lah dee-rehk-SYOHN PAH-rah eer ah reh-koh-HEHR-loh.

4. DUI Investigations

A. PRELIMINARY QUESTIONS DURING A GENERAL DUI STOP

OFFICER	AGENTE	
Have you been drinking?	¿Ha estado bebiendo?	¿Ah ehs-TAH-doh beh-BYEHN-doh?
How many drinks have you had?	¿Cuántas bebidas ha tomado?	¿KWAHN-tahs beh-BEE-dahs ah toh-MAH-doh?
When?	¿Cuándo?	¿KWAHN-doh?

SUBJECT	SUJETO	
Yes, I have been drinking.	Sí, he estado bebiendo.	See, eh ehs-TAH-doh beh-BYEHN-doh.
Yes, but only a couple of beers/drinks.	Sí, pero sólo un par de cervezas/bebidas.	See, PEH-roh SOH-loh oon pahr deh sehr-VEH-sahs/beh-BEE-dahs.
No, I haven't been drinking.	No, no he estado bebiendo.	Noh, noh eh ehs-TAH-doh beh-BYEHN-doh.

OFFICER	AGENTE	
Have you taken any drugs?	¿Ha tomado drogas?	¿Ah toh-MAH-doh DROH-gahs?

SUBJECT	SUJETO	
No, I haven't taken any drugs.	No, no he tomado drogas.	Noh, noh eh toh-MAH-doh DROH-gahs.
I smoked a joint.	Fumé un leño.	Foo-MEH oon LEH-nyoh.
Just my medication.	Sólo medicamentos.	SOH-loh meh-dee-kah-MEHN-tohs.

OFFICER	AGENTE	
I'm going to have you do some physical tests.	Voy a hacerle tomar unas pruebas físicas.	Voy ah ah-SEHR-leh toh-MAHR OO-nahs PRWEH-bahs FEE-see-kahs.
Do you understand that this test is voluntary?	¿Entiende que estas pruebas son voluntarias?	¿Ehn-TYEHN-deh keh EHS-tahs proo-EH-bahs sohn voh-loon-TAH-ree-ahs?
Do you have any physical problems that may prevent you from performing this test?	¿Tiene algún problema físico que le impide hacer estos ejercicios?	¿TYEH-neh ahl-GOON proh-BLEH-mah FEE-see-koh keh leh eem-PEE-deh ah-SEHR ehs-tohs eh-hehr-SEE-syohs?
Follow my instructions.	Siga mis instrucciones.	SEE-gah mees eens-trook-SYOH-nehs.

SUBJECT	SUJETO	
Yes, I understand.	Sí, entiendo.	See, ehn-TYEHN-doh.
I don't want to take the test.	No quiero hacer la prueba.	Noh KYEH-roh ah-SEHR lah PRWEH-bah.
Go ahead.	Como guste.	KOH-moh GOOS-teh.
I don't have any physical problems.	No tengo problemas físicos.	Noh TEHN-goh proh-BLEH-mahs FEE-see-kohs.
I'm legally blind in one eye.	Estoy legalmente ciego de un ojo.	Ehs-TOY leh-gahl-MEHN-teh SYEH-goh deh oon OH-hoh.
I limp.	Estoy cojo.	Ehs-TOY KOH-hoh.
I have a sprained ankle.	Me he torcido el tobillo.	Meh eh tohr-SEE-doh ehl toh-BEE-yoh.

GRAMMAR NOTE ••••

THE AUXILIARY VERB *HABER* (TO HAVE)

PRESENT	IMPERFECT
he	había
has	habías
ha	había
hemos	habíamos
habéis	habíais
han	habían

I have smoked a little bit.   *He fumado muy poco.*

B. CONDUCTING THE GENERAL DUI TEST

OFFICER	AGENTE	
Stand with your feet together.	*Párese con los pies juntos.*	PAH-reh-seh kohn lohs pyehs HOON-tohs.
Hands to your sides.	*Manos a los lados.*	MAH-nohs ah lohs LAH-dohs.
Tilt your head back.	*Mueva la cabeza para atrás.*	Moo-EH-vah lah kah-BEH-sah PAH-rah ah-TRAHS.
Close your eyes.	*Cierre los ojos.*	SYEH-rreh lohs OH-hohs.
Stay that way until I say stop.	*Siga así hasta que le diga alto.*	SEE-gah ah-SEE AHS-tah keh leh DEE-gah AHL-toh.
Please begin.	*Por favor, empiece.*	Pohr fah-VOHR, ehm-PYEH-seh.
Thank you.	*Gracias.*	GRAH-syahs.
Put your hands to your side.	*Ponga los brazos a los lados.*	POHN-gah lohs BRAH-sohs ah lohs LAH-dohs.

Put your left foot in front of your right foot.	*Ponga el pie izquierdo enfrente del pie derecho.*	POHN-gah ehl pyeh ees-KYEHR-doh ehn-FREHN-teh dehl pyeh deh-REH-choh.
Walk nine steps forward, heel-to-toe.	*Camine nueve pasos talón-dedo-talón hacia adelante.*	Kah-MEE-neh NWEH-veh PAH-sohs tah-LOHN—DEH-doh—TAHL-lohn AH-syah ah-deh-LAHN-teh.
Turn around, slowly.	*Voltéese, despacio.*	Vohl-TEH-eh-seh, dehs-PAH-syoh.
Walk five steps, heel-to-toe, back to where you started.	*Camine cinco pies, talón-dedo-talón, para atrás.*	Kah-MEE-neh SEEN-koh pyehs, tah-LOHN —DEH-doh—tah-LOHN, PAH-rah ah-TRAHS.
Thank you.	*Gracias.*	GRAH-syahs.
Stand facing me.	*Párese enfrente de mí.*	PAH-reh-seh ehn-FREHN-teh deh mee.
Put your hands to your side and your feet together.	*Ponga las manos a los lados y los pies juntos.*	POHN-gah lahs MAH-nohs ah lohs LAH-dohs ee lohs pyehs HOON-tohs.
Put your arms straight out to the sides.	*Extienda los brazos a lo largo del cuerpo.*	Ehks-TYEHN-dah lohs BRAH-sohs ah loh LAHR-goh dehl KWEHR-poh.
Touch the tip of your nose with your...	*Tóquese la punta de la nariz con...*	Toh-KEH-seh lah POON-tah deh lah nah-REES kohn...
• right finger.	• *el dedo derecho.*	• ehl DEH-doh deh-REH-choh.
• left finger.	• *el dedo izquierdo.*	• ehl DEH-doh ees-KYEHR-doh.
Return your hand to your side.	*Vuelva la mano a su posición normal.*	VWEHL-vah lah MAH-noh ah soo poh-see-SYOHN nohr-MAHL.

Touch the tip of your right index finger to your right ear lobe.	*Tóquese el lóbulo derecho de la oreja con el dedo índice de la mano derecha.*	Toh-KEH-seh ehl LOH-boo-loh deh-REH-choh deh lah oh-REH-hah kohn ehl DEH-doh EEN-dee-seh deh lah MAH-noh deh-REH-chah.
Now, left finger to the right ear lobe.	*Ahora, el lóbulo derecho con el dedo índice izquierdo.*	Ah-OH-rah, ehl LOH-boo-loh deh REH-choh kohn ehl DEH-doh EEN-dee-seh ees-KYEHR-doh.
Open your eyes.	*Abra los ojos.*	AH-brah lohs OH-hohs.
Turn and face away from me.	*Voltéese y míre para allá.*	Vohl-TEH-eh-seh ee MEE-reh PAH-rah ah-YAH.

Grammar Note ••••

THE PERFECT TENSES The perfect tenses are formed with a conjugated form of the auxiliary verb *haber* (to have) and the past participle of the main verb. Participle endings are:

-ado for verbs in *-ar:* robbed *rob-ado*
-ido for verbs in *-er* and *-ir:* drank *beb-ido*

I have robbed. *Yo he robado.*
We have robbed. *Nosotros hemos robado.*

Irregular past participles are:

broken	*roto*
said	*dicho*
made, done	*hecho*
put	*puesto*
seen	*visto*
returned	*vuelto*
written	*escrito*

C. MAKING THE ARREST

OFFICER	AGENTE	
You are under arrest for driving under the influence of alcohol or drugs.	Está arrestado por manejar bajo la influencia del alcohol o de drogas.	Ehs-TAH ah-rrehs-TAH-doh POHR mah-neh-HAHR BAH-hoh lah een-floo-EHN-syah deh AHL-kohl oh deh DROH-gahs.
You have to take a chemical test of your blood or breath.	Tiene que hacer una prueba química de la sangre o del aliento.	TYEH-neh keh ah-SEHR OO-nah proo-EH-bah KEE-mee-kah deh lah SAHN-greh oh dehl ah-LYEHN-toh.
Which chemical test do you wish to take?	¿Cuál prefiere hacer?	¿Kwahl preh-FYEHR-eh ah-SEHR?
SUSPECT	SOSPECHOSO	
The breath test.	La prueba del aliento.	Lah proo-EH-bah dehl ahl-LYEHN-toh.

D. CONDUCTING THE BREATH TEST

OFFICER	AGENTE	
Do you have dentures?	¿Tiene dientes postizos?	¿TYEH-neh DYEHN-tehs pohs-TEE-sohs?
If you have dentures, please remove them.	Si tiene dientes postizos, por favor, sáqueselos.	See-TYEH-neh DYEHN-tehs pohs-TEE-sohs, pohr fah-VOHR, SAH-keh-seh-lohs.
Have you belched in the last twenty minutes?	¿Ha eructado en los últimos veinte minutos?	¿Ah eh-rook-TAH-doh ehn lohs OOL-tee-mohs VAYN-teh mee-NOO-tohs?
Do you have anything in your mouth?	¿Tiene algo en la boca?	¿TYEH-neh AHL-goh ehn lah BOH-kah?

Hold this tube and blow into the mouthpiece until I tell you to stop.	*Agarre este tubo y sople dentro del aparato por la boca hasta que le diga "alto."*	Ah-GAH-rreh EHS-teh TOO-boh ee SOH-pleh DEHN-troh dehl ah-pahr-AH-toh por lah BOH-kah AHS-tah keh leh DEE-gah "AHL-toh."
Take a deep breath and blow.	*Respire profundamente y sople.*	Reh-SPEE-reh proh-foon-dah-MEHN-teh ee SOH-pleh.
Don't suck on the mouthpiece.	*No chupe la dentadura.*	Noh CHOO-peh lah dehn-tah-DOO-rah.
Blow...Keep blowing...harder...	*Sople...Siga soplando...más fuerte...*	SOH-pleh...SEE-gah soh-PLAHN-doh... mahs FWEHR-teh...
Okay. You can stop.	*Bien. Puede parar.*	BYEHN. PWEH-deh pah-RAHR.
Thank you.	*Gracias.*	GRAH-syahs.
You have to take the test again.	*Tiene que hacer la prueba otra vez.*	TYEH-neh keh ah-SEHR lah proo-EH-bah OH-trah vehs.
If you don't blow I will charge you with refusal.	*Si no lo hace lo multaré por negarse.*	See noh loh ah-seh loh mool-tah-REH pohr neh-GAHR-seh.

E. CONDUCTING OTHER FIELD SOBRIETY TESTS

Horizontal Gaze Nystagmus

OFFICER	AGENTE	
Listen!	*¡Escuche!*	¡Ehs-KOO-cheh!
Keep your head still and follow the tip of my fingers with your eyes only.	*Mantenga la cabeza fija y siga mi dedo con los ojos sólamente.*	Mahn-TEHN-gah lah kah-BEH-sah fee-hah ee SEE-gah mee DEH-doh khon lohs OH-hohs soh-lah-MEHN-teh.
Do not move your head!	*¡No mueva la cabeza!*	¡Noh MWEH-vah lah kah-BEH-sah!

| Eyes only! | ¡Los ojos sólamente! | ¡Lohs OH-hohs soh-lah-MEHN-teh! |
| Thank you. | Gracias. | GRAH-syahs. |

FINGER TO NOSE

Listen!	¡Escuche!	¡Ehs-KOO-cheh!
Put your feet together, heels and toes!	¡Junte los pies, talones y dedos!	¡HOOHN-teh lohs pyehs, tah-LOH-nehs ee DEH-dohs!
Raise your arms like this!	¡Levante los brazos así!	¡Leh-VAHN-teh lohs BRAH-sohs ah-SEE!
When I tell you, close your eyes.	Cuando se lo diga, cierre los ojos.	KWAHN-doh seh loh DEE-gah, SYEH-rreh lohs OH-hohs.
When I tell you, touch the tip of your nose with the tip of your right or left index finger.	Cuando se lo diga, toque la punta de la nariz con la punta de su dedo índice derecho o izquierdo.	KWAHN-doh seh loh DEE-gah, TOH-keh lah POON-tah deh lah nah-REES kohn lah POON-tah deh soo DEH-doh EEN-dee-seh deh-REH-choh oh ees-KYEHR-doh.
I will say right or left.	Le diré si el derecho o el izquierdo.	Leh dee-REH see ehl deh-REH-choh oh ehl ees-KYEHR-doh.
Do you understand?	¿Comprende?	¿Kohm-PREHN-deh?
Close your eyes.	Cierre los ojos.	SYEH-rreh lohs OH-hohs.
Touch your nose with your left/right index finger.	Toque la nariz con su dedo índice izquierdo/derecho.	TOH-keh lah nariz kohn soo DEH-doh ENN-dee-seh ees-KYEHR-doh/deh-REH-choh.
Thank you.	Gracias.	GRAH-syahs.

Modified Position of Attention

Listen!	*¡Escuche!*	¡Ehs-KOO-cheh!
Put your feet together, heels and toes!	*¡Junte los pies, talones y dedos!*	¡HOON-teh lohs pyehs, tah-LOH-nehs ee DEH-dohs!
Put your hands on your side!	*¡Ponga las manos al lado del cuerpo!*	¡POHN-gah lahs MAH-nohs ahl LAH-doh dehl KWEHR-poh!
With your eyes open, tilt your head back.	*Con los ojos abiertos, mueva la cabeza para atrás.*	Kohn lohs OH-hohs ah-BYEHR-tohs, moo-EH-vah lah kah-BEH-sah PAH-rah ah-TRAHS.
Further back.	*Más atrás.*	MAHS ah-TRAHS.
Do not move.	*No se mueva.*	Noh seh MWE-vah.
Close your eyes.	*Cierre los ojos.*	SYEH-rreh lohs OH-hohs.
Do not open them until I tell you.	*No los abra hasta que se lo diga.*	Noh lohs AH-brah AHS-tah keh seh loh dee-gah.
Stop. Open your eyes.	*Alto. Abra los ojos.*	AHL-toh. AH-brah lohs OH-hohs.
Lower your head. Stop.	*Baje la cabeza. Alto.*	BAH-heh lah kah-beh-sah. AHL-toh.
Thank you!	*¡Gracias!*	¡GRAH-syahs!

Standing on One Foot

Listen!	*¡Escuche!*	¡Ehs-KOO-cheh!
Put your feet together, heels and toes!	*¡Junte los pies, talones y dedos!*	¡HOON-teh lohs pyehs, tah-LOH-nehs ee DEH-dohs!
Put your hands on your side!	*¡Ponga las manos al lado del cuerpo!*	¡POHN-gah lahs MAH-nohs ahl LAH-doh dehl KWEHR-poh!
Watch me. Do not do anything yet.	*Míreme. No haga nada todavía.*	MÉ-reh-meh. Noh AH-gah NAH-dah toh-dah-VEE-ah.

When I tell you, raise one foot six inches off the ground and do not move.	Cuando se lo diga, levante un pie seis pulgadas del suelo y no se mueva.	KWAN-doh seh loh DEE-gah, leh-VAHN-teh oon pyeh dehl SWEH-loh ee noh seh MWE-vah.
Now, go ahead.	Ahora, hágalo.	Ah-OH-rah, AH-gah-loh.
Count from one to thirty.	Cuente de uno a treinta.	KWEHN-teh deh OO-noh ah TREH-een-tah.
Thank you.	Gracias.	GRAH-syahs.

STANDING AND WALKING HEEL TO TOE

Listen!	¡Escuche!	¡Ehs-KOO-cheh!
Place your right foot in front of your left foot, like this.	Ponga el pie derecho enfrente del pie izquierdo, así.	POHN-gah ehl pyeh deh-REH-choh ehn-FREHN-teh dehl pyeh ees-KYEHR-do, ah-SEE.
Put your hands to your side.	Ponga los brazos al lado del cuerpo.	POHN-gah lohs BRAH-sohs ahl LAH-doh dehl KWEHR-poh.
Do not move.	No se mueva.	Noh seh MWE-vah.
Do you understand?	¿Comprende?	¿Kohm-PREHN-deh?
When I tell you to begin, take nine heel-to-toe steps in a straight line.	Cuando se lo diga, dé nueve pasos de talón a dedo en línea recta.	KWAHN-doh seh loh DEE-gah, DEH NWEH-veh PAH-sohs deh tah-LOHN ah DEH-doh ehn LEE-neh ah REHK-tah.
Then turn around and take nine steps back, heel-to-toe.	Después voltéese y dé nueve pasos para atrás de talón a dedo.	Dehs-PWEHS vohl-TEH-eh-see ee DEH NWEH-veh PAH-sohs PAH-rah ah-TRAHS deh tah-LOHN ah DEH-doh.
Make the turn keeping one foot on the line and use the other foot to turn.	Voltéese y mantenga un pie en la línea y use el otro pie para dar la vuelta.	Vohl-TEH-eh-seh ee mahn-TEHN-gah oon pyeh ehn lah LEE-neh ah ee OO-seh ehl OH-troh pyeh PAH-rah dahr la VWEHL-tah.

Watch how I do it.	*Mire como lo hago.*	MEE-reh KOH-moh loh AH-goh.
Keep your hands at your side and watch your feet.	*Baje los manos al lado del cuerpo y mire los pies.*	BAH-heh lahs MAH-nohs ahl LAH-doh dehl KWEHR-poh ee MEE-reh lohs pyehs.
Count your steps aloud.	*Cuente sus pasos en voz alta.*	KWEHN-teh soosPAH-sohs ehn vohsAHL-tah.
Do it!	*¡Hágalo!*	¡AH-gah-lo!
Thank you!	*¡Gracias!*	¡GRAH-syahs!

THUMB TO FINGER COUNT

Listen!	*¡Escuche!*	¡Ehs-KOO-cheh!
Watch me. Do not do anything yet.	*Míreme. No haga nada todavía.*	MEE-reh-meh. Noh AH-gah NAH-dah toh-dah-VY-ah.
With either hand, touch the tip of each finger to the tip of your thumb and count like this.	*Con cualquier mano, tóquese la punta de cada dedo con la punta del pulgar y cuente así.*	Kohn kwahl-KYEHR MAH-noh, toh-KEH-seh lah POOHN-tah deh KAH-dah DEH-doh kohn lah POOHN-tah dehl POOL-gahr ee KWEHN-teh ah-SEE.
One, two, three, four, and then four, three, two, one.	*Uno, dos, tres, cuatro, y luego cuatro, tres, dos, uno.*	OO-noh, dohs, trehs, KWAH-troh, ee LWE-goh KWA-troh, trehs, dohs, OO-noh.
Do this three times.	*Hágalo tres veces.*	AH-gah loh trehs VEH-cehs.
Count aloud.	*Cuente en voz alta.*	KWEHN-teh ehn vohs AHL-tah.
Thank you!	*¡Gracias!*	¡GRAH-syahs!

ADMINISTRATIVE SERVICES

CULTURE NOTE ••••

DEALING WITH AUTHORITY The Latinos you as a police officer may come in contact with will not only be from a variety of cultural and national backgrounds, but also from a variety of educational and socio-economic backgrounds. Most Latinos from the middle and upper classes are rather well educated, speak English quite well and have assimilated to the culture in the United States. Among Latinos from a less privileged background, you may find many that have not completed high school, don't speak English well, and have not yet adjusted to the U.S. American way of life. Not quite familiar with the laws and rules of their new country, they will avoid any conflict with the law, and may not even turn to the police for help for fear that they will be mistreated, arrested, or even deported. While these fears may be unreasonable, they are very real and may have an effect on an individual's behavior. Therefore, a reluctance to be forthcoming with information may not be due to a guilty conscience, but rather due to a general distrust of authority in a strange land.

1. Theft Report

A. OBTAINING GENERAL INFORMATION

VICTIM / **VÍCTIMA**

I need to file a theft report.	Vengo a denunciar un robo.	VEHN-goh ah deh-noon-SYAHR oon RROH-boh.
I want to report a...	Quiero poner una denuncia...	KYEH-roh poh-NEHR OO-nah deh-NOON-SYAH...
• theft.	• por robo.	• pohr RROH-boh.
• burglary.	• por robo.	• pohr RROH-boh.

OFFICER / **AGENTE**

| Your name, address, and phone number, please? | ¿Su nombre, dirección, y número de teléfono, por favor? | ¿Soo NOHM-breh, dee-rehk-SYOHN, ee NOO-meh-roh deh teh-LEH-foh-noh, pohr fah-VOHR? |
| You have to fill out this report. | Tiene que llenar este formulario. | TYEH-ne keh yeh-NAHR EHS-teh fohr-moo-LAH-ryoh. |

VICTIM / **VÍCTIMA**

Pardon, what did you say?	Perdone, ¿qué me dijo?	Pehr-DOH-neh, ¿keh meh DEE-hoh?
I don't speak English very well.	No hablo inglés muy bien.	Noh AH-bloh een-GLEHS mwee byehn.
Repeat slowly, please.	Repita más despacio, por favor.	Reh-PEE-tah mahs dehs-PAH-syoh, pohr fah-VOHR.
Where do I write the answers?	¿Dónde escribo las respuestas?	¿DOHN-deh ehs-KREE-boh lahs rrehs-PWEHS-tahs?

OFFICER / **AGENTE**

What's your name?	¿Cómo se llama?	¿KOH-moh seh YAH-mah?
Where do you live?	¿Dónde vive?	¿DOHN-deh VEE-veh?
What's your phone number?	¿Cuál es su número de teléfono?	¿Kwahl ehs soo NOO-meh-roh deh teh-LEH-foh-noh?

What's your date of birth?	¿Cuál es su fecha de nacimiento?	¿Kwahl ehs soo FEH-chah deh nah-see-MYEHN-toh?
Please, write the answers here.	Por favor, escriba las respuestas aquí.	Pohr fah-VOHR, ehs-KREE-bah lahs rrehs-PWEHS-tahs ah-KEE.
You need to write your...	Necesita poner...	Neh-seh-SEE-tah poh-NEHR...
• name and last name/s.	• su nombre y apellido/s.	• soo NOHM-breh ee ah-peh-YEE-doh/dohs.
• address.	• su dirección.	• soo dee-rehk-SYOHN.
• phone number.	• su número de teléfono.	• soo NOO-meh-roh deh teh-LEH-foh-noh.
• birthdate.	• su fecha de nacimiento.	• soo FEH-chah deh nah-see-MYEHN-toh.
Thank you.	Gracias.	GRAH-syahs.

GRAMMAR NOTE ••••

DATES AND BIRTH DATES   In Spanish the day is always mentioned first:

What is the date today?
Today is February 25, 1997.

¿Qué día es hoy?
Hoy es el 25 de febrero de 1997.

What's your date of birth?

¿Cuál es su fecha de nacimiento?

2/25/97
When were you born?
My date of birth is February 15, 1968.

25/2/97
¿Cuándo nació usted?
Mi fecha de nacimiento es el quince de febrero de mil novecientos sesenta y ocho.

I was born on February 15, 1968.
2/15/68

Nací el 15 de febrero de 1968.
15/2/68

B. OBTAINING DETAILS ABOUT THE CIRCUMSTANCES OF THE THEFT OR ROBBERY

OFFICER	AGENTE	
What...	¿Qué...	¿Keh...
• are you missing?	• le falta?	• lah FAHL-tah?
• did they take?	• le robaron?	• leh rroh-BAH-rohn?

VICTIM	VICTIMA	
They took my...	Me robaron...	Meh-rroh-BAH-rohn...
• car.	• el carro.	• ehl KAH-rroh.
• stereo/car stereo.	• el estéreo/...de mi carro.	• ehl ehs-TEH-reh-oh/ ...deh mee KAH-rroh.
• car phone.	• teléfono celular.	• teh-LEH-foh-noh seh-loo-LAHR.
• TV.	• la tele.	• lah teh-LEH.
• purse.	• mi bolsa.	• mee BOHL-sah.
• jewelry.	• mis joyas.	• mees HOH-yahs.
• money.	• el dinero.	• ehl dee-NEH-roh.
• suitcase.	• la maleta.	• lah mah-LEH-tah.
• computer.	• la computadora.	• lah kohm-poo-tah-DOH-rah.
• bicycle.	• la bicicleta.	• lah bee-see-KLEH-tah.

OFFICER	AGENTE	
What is the value of the items taken?	¿Cuál es el valor de lo robado?	¿KWAHL ehs ehl vah-LOHR deh loh roh-BAH-doh?
Where was it/were they taken from?	¿De dónde se lo/la/los/ las robaron?	¿Deh DOHN-deh seh loh/lah/lohs/lahs rroh-BAH-rohn?

VICTIM	VICTIMA	
It was/they were stolen from...	Me lo/la/los/las robaron...	Meh loh/lah/lohs/lahs rroh-BAH-rohn...
• the house.	• de la casa.	• deh lah KAH-sah.
• the car.	• del carro.	• dehl KAH-rroh.
• the garage.	• del garaje.	• dehl gah-RAH-heh.

• my purse.	• *de mi bolsa.*	• deh mee BOHL-sah.
• my backyard.	• *del jardín.*	• del har-DEEN.
OFFICER	*AGENTE*	
When did this happen?	*¿Cuándo ocurrió esto?*	¿KWAHN-doh oh-koo-RYOH EHS-toh?
VICTIM	*VICTIMA*	
This...	*Esta...*	EHS-tah...
• morning.	• *mañana.*	• mah-NYAH-nah.
• afternoon.	• *tarde.*	• TAHR-deh.
Last night.	*Anoche.*	Ah-NOH-cheh.
Within the last five hours.	*En las últimas cinco horas.*	Ehn lahs OOL-tee-mahs SEEN-koh OH-rahs.
Overnight.	*Durante la noche.*	Doo-RAHN-teh lah NOH-cheh.
Yesterday.	*Ayer.*	Ah-YEHR.
A few hours/minutes ago.	*Hace unas horas/ minutos.*	AH-seh OO-nahs OH-rahs/mee-NOO-tohs.
The day before yesterday.	*Anteayer.*	Ahn-teh-ah-YEHR.
Between 4:00 P.M. and 6:00 P.M.	*Entre las 4:00 y las 6:00 de la tarde.*	EHN-treh lahs KWAH-troh ee lahs says deh lah TAHR-deh.
Around 1:00 A.M.	*Alrededor de la 1:00 de la mañana.*	Ahl-reh-deh-DOHR deh lah OO-nah deh lah mahn-NYAH-nah.
At midnight.	*A medianoche.*	Ah meh-dyah-NOH-cheh.
At around noon.	*Alrededor del mediodía.*	Ahl-reh-deh-DOHR dehl meh-dyoh-DEE-ah.
While I was...	*Cuando estaba...*	KWAHN-doh ehs-TAH-bah...
• at work.	• *en mi trabajo.*	• ehn mee trah-BAH-hoh.
• sleeping.	• *durmiendo.*	• door-MYEHN-doh.
• shopping.	• *de compras.*	• deh KOHM-prahs.

• working.	• *trabajando.*	• trah-bah-HAHN-doh.
OFFICER	*AGENTE*	
Did you see/hear anything?	*¿Oyó/vio algo?*	¿Oh-YOH/VEE-oh AHL-goh?
VICTIM	*VICTIMA*	
I didn't hear/see anything.	*No oí/vi nada.*	Noh oh-EE/vee NAH-dah.
I heard a noise in the backyard.	*Oí un ruido en el jardín.*	Oh-EE oon RROOH-ee-doh ehn el har-DEEHN.
I wasn't...	*No estaba...*	Noh ehs-TAH-bah...
• in the house.	• *en casa.*	• ehn KAH-sah.
• there.	• *allí.*	• ah-YEE.
OFFICER	*AGENTE*	
What is the value of your property?	*¿Cuál es el valor de lo robado?*	¿KWAHL ehs ehl vah-LOHR deh loh rroh-BAH-doh?
VICTIM	*VICTIMA*	
$____.	____ dólares.	____ DOH-lahr-ehs.
I don't know exactly.	*No sé exactamente.*	Noh seh ek-sahk-tah-MEHN-teh.
About ____ dollars.	*Alrededor de ____ dólares.*	Ahl-reh-dah-DOHR deh ____ DOH-lahr-ehs.

C. DESCRIPTION OF THE STOLEN PROPERTY

OFFICER	*AGENTE*	
Can you describe your...	*¿Puede describir su...*	¿PWEH-deh dehs-kree-BEER soo...
• property?	• *propiedad?*	• proh-pyeh-DAHD?
• car?	• *carro?*	• KAH-rroh?
• bicycle?	• *bicicleta?*	• bee-see-KLEH-tah?
Do you know...	*¿Sabe usted...*	¿SAH-beh oos-TEHD...
• the serial number?	• *el número de la serie?*	• ehl NOO-meh-roh deh lah SEH-ryeh?

• the brand name?	• *la marca?*	• lah MAHR-kah?
• the make and year of the car?	• *la marca y el año del carro?*	• lah MAHR-kah ee ehl AN-nyoh dehl KAH-rroh?
• the license plate number?	• *el número de la placa?*	• ehl NOO-meh-roh deh la PLAH-kah?
• the color?	• *el color?*	• ehl coh-LOHR?
How much money was stolen?	*¿Cuánto dinero le robaron?*	¿KWAHN-toh dee-NEH-roh leh rroh-BAH-rohn?

VICTIM	**VICTIMA**	
I don't know.	*No sé el número.*	Noh seh ehl NOO-meh-roh.
I don't have...	*No tengo...*	Noh tehn-goh...
• the serial number.	• *el número de la serie.*	• ehl NOO-meh-roh deh lah SEH-ryeh.
• the brand name.	• *la marca.*	• lah MAHR-kah.
Here is the serial number.	*Aquí está el número de la serie.*	Ah-KEE ehs-TAH ehl NOO-meh-roh deh lah SEH-ryeh.
It was...	*Era...*	EH-rah...
• a 29" Sony color TV.	• *una tele Sony de veintinueve pulgadas.*	• lah teh-lee-vee-SOHR Sony deh VAYN-eh ee noo-EH-veh pool-GAH-dahs.
• a Pioneer car stereo with a...	• *el estéreo del carro que tenía...de la marca Pioneer.*	• ehl ehs-TEH-reh-oh dehl KAH-rroh keh teh-NEE-ah... deh lah MAHR-kah Pioneer.
• a radio.	• *una radio*	• OO-nah RAH-dyoh
• a cassette player.	• *una casetera*	• OO-nah kah-seh-TEH-rah
• a CD player.	• *un CD*	• oon seh-DEH
• a mountain bike.	• *una bicicleta de montaña.*	• OO-nah bee-see-KLEH-tah deh mohn-TAH-nyah.

• a ten-speed road bike.	• *una bicicleta de diez velocidades.*	• OO-nah bee-see-KLEH-tah deh dyehs veh-loh-see-DAHD-dehs.
• an eighteen-karat gold necklace.	• *un collar de oro de dieciocho quilates.*	• oon koh-YAHR deh OH-roh deh dee-eh-see-OH-choh kee-LAH-tehs.
• a gold diamond ring.	• *un anillo de oro con un diamante.*	• un ah-NEE-YOH deh OH-roh kohn oon dee-ah-MAHN-teh.
• a '96 blue, four-door Subaru.	• *un Subaru azul de cuatro puertas del noventa y seis.*	• oon Soo-BAH-roo ah-SOOL deh KWAH-troh PWEHR-tahs dehl noh-VEHN-tah ee says.
• a Toyota four-wheel drive.	• *un Toyota de doble tracción.*	• oon Toyota deh DOH-bleh trahk-SYOHN.
• a PC computer.	• *una computadora PC.*	• OO-nah kohm-poo-tah-DOH-rah peh-SEH.
• a laptop.	• *una computadora portátil.*	• OO-nah kohm-poo-tah-DOH-rah pohr-TAH-teel.

OFFICER	AGENTE	
Sign...	*Firme...*	FEER-meh...
• here.	• *aquí.*	• ah-KEE.
• down below.	• *aquí abajo.*	• ah-KEE ah-BAH-hoh.
• on the dotted line with an "X."	• *en la línea marcada con una "equis."*	• ehn lah LEE-nee-ah mahr-KAH-dah kohn OO-nah "EH-kees."
We will...	*Trataremos de...*	Trah-tahr-EH-mohs deh...
• track it down for you.	• *encontrarlo/la.*	• ehn kohn-TRAHR-loh/lah.
• give you a call if we find out anything.	• *llamarle si tenemos alguna pista.*	• yah-MAHR-leh see teh-NEH-mohs ahl-GOON-ah PEES-tah.

- see what we can do for you.
- *ver cómo podemos ayudarlo/la.*
- vehr KOH-moh poh-DEH-mohs ah-yoo-DAHR-loh/lah.

A detective will call you to follow-up.

Un agente llamará enseguida.

Oon ah-HEHN-teh yah-mah-RAH ehn-seh-GEE-dah.

2. Retrieving Property and Evidence

VICTIM

VÍCTIMA

Do you have my property?

¿Tienen mis cosas aquí?

¿TYEH-nehn mees KOH-sahs ah-KEE?

POLICE

POLICÍA

Do you have your case report number?

¿Tiene el número de su informe?

¿TYEH-neh ehl NOO-meh roh deh soo een-FOHR-meh?

VICTIM

VÍCTIMA

What's that?

¿Qué es eso?

Keh ehs EH-soh?

POLICE

POLICÍA

The number the officer gave you for your case.

El número que la policía le dio para su caso.

Ehl NOO-meh-roh keh lah poh-lee-SEE-ah leh DEE-oh PAH-rah soo KAH-soh.

VICTIM

VÍCTIMA

Yes, I have it.

Sí, lo tengo.

See, loh TEHN-goh.

No, I don't have it.

No, no lo tengo.

Noh, noh loh TEHN-goh.

I've lost it.

Lo he perdido.

Loh eh pehr-DEE-doh.

I don't know where it is.

No sé donde está.

Noh seh DOHN-deh ehs-TAH.

I left it at home.

Lo dejé en casa.

Loh deh-HEH ehn KAH-sah.

POLICE

POLICÍA

What's your name?

¿Cómo se llama?

¿KOH-moh seh YAH-mah?

| Do you have a picture ID? | ¿Tiene identificación con foto? | ¿TYEH-neh ee-dehn-tee-fee-kah-SYOHN kohn FOH-toh? |

VICTIM — **VÍCTIMA**

| Here is my ID. | Aquí está. | Ah-KEE ehs-TAH. |
| You have my ID. | Ustedes la tienen. | Oos-TEH-dehs lah TYEH-nehn. |

POLICE — **POLICÍA**

| What's your date of birth? | ¿Cual es su fecha de nacimiento? | ¿Kwahl ehs soo FEH-chah deh nah-see-MYEHN-toh? |

VICTIM — **VÍCTIMA**

| I was born on the 4th of July 1976. | Nací el cuatro de julio de mil novecientos setenta y seis. | Nah-SEE ehl KWAH-troh deh HOO-lyoh deh meel noh-veh-SYEHN-tohs seh-TEHN-tah ee says. |
| My date of birth is 7/4/76. | Mi fecha de nacimiento es el 4/7/76. | Mee FEH-chah deh nah-see-MEHN-toh ehs ehl 4/7/76. |

POLICE — **POLICÍA**

| What is it that we have of yours? | ¿Qué cosas suyas tenemos aquí? | ¿Keh KOH-sahs SOO-yahs tehn-EH-mohs ah-KEE? |

VICTIM — **VÍCTIMA**

My...	Mi/mis...	Mee/mees...
• keys.	• llaves.	• YAH-vehs.
• ID.	• identificación.	• ee-dehn-tee-fee-kah-SYOHN.
• wallet.	• cartera.	• kahr-TEH-rah.
• coat.	• abrigo.	• ah-BREE-goh.
• jewelry.	• joyas.	• HOH-yahs.
• bag.	• bolsa.	• BOHL-sah.

POLICE — **POLICÍA**

| We can't release them/it yet. | No podemos darle su/s cosa/s todavía. | Noh poh-DEH-mohs DAHR-leh soo/s KOH-sah/s toh-dah-VEE-ah. |

You have to talk to the detective in charge of your case.	Usted tiene que hablar con el detective encargado de su caso.	Oos-STEHD TYEH-neh keh ah-BLAHR kohn ehl deh-tehk-TEE-veh ehn kahr-GAH-doh deh soo KAH-soh.
Here is the name of the agent and the case number.	Aquí está el nombre del agente y el número de su caso.	Ah-KEE ehs-TAH ehl NOHM-breh dehl ah-HEHN-teh ee ehl NOO-meh-roh deh soo KAH-soh.
You need to call this number.	Usted necesita llamar a este número.	Oos-STEHD neh-seh-SEE-tah yah-MAHR ah EHS-teh NOO-meh-roh.
May I see your ID?	¿Puedo ver su identificación?	¿PWEH-doh vehr soo ee-dehn-tee-fee-kah-SYOHN?
Sign your name here.	Firme aquí.	FEER-meh ah-KEE.
Write your address.	Escriba su dirección.	Ehs-KREE-bah soo dee-rehk-SYOHN.
I have to take your fingerprints.	Tengo que tomar sus huellas digitales.	TEHN-goh keh toh-mahr soos WEH-yahs dee-hee-TAH-lehs.
Give me your right index finger.	Déme su dedo índice derecho.	DEH-meh soo DEH-doh EEN-dee-seh deh-REH-choh.
Do not press.	No presione.	Noh preh-SYOH-neh.
I will do the pressing.	Yo haré la presión.	Yoh ah-REH lah preh-SYOHN.
Thank you.	Gracias.	GRAH-syahs.

3. Retrieving a Vehicle from Impounds and Records

SUBJECT	SUJETO	
Good afternoon.	Buenas tardes.	BWEH-nahs TAHR-dehs.
I'm looking for my car.	Busco mi carro.	BOOS-koh mee KAH-rroh.

I don't know...	No sé...	Noh seh...
• where my car is.	• donde está mi carro.	• DOHN-deh ehs-TAH mee KAH-rroh.
• if the police towed my car.	• si la grúa se llevó mi carro.	• see lah GROOH-ah seh yeh-VOH mee KAH-rroh.
• if my car was stolen.	• si robaron mi carro.	• see roh-BAH-rohn mee KAH-rroh.

RECORDS OFFICER	**OFICIAL DE ARCHIVOS**	
What kind of car do you have?	¿Qué tipo de carro tiene usted?	¿Keh TEE-poh deh KAH-rroh TYEH-neh oo-STEHD?

SUBJECT	**SUJETO**	
A '97 Chevy.	Un Chevy del noventa y siete.	Oon Chevy dehl noh-VEHN-tah ee SYEH-teh.
A '90 Honda Civic.	Un Honda Civic del noventa.	Oon Honda Civic dehl noh-VEHN-tah.
A pick-up truck.	Una camioneta.	OO-nah kah-myoh-NEH-tah.
A blue van.	Un camión azul.	Oon kah-MYOHN ah-SOOL.
A station wagon.	Una camioneta.	Oo-nah kah-myoh-NEH-tah.
I'm not sure.	No estoy seguro/a.	Noh ehs-TOY seh-GOO-roh/rah.

RECORDS OFFICER	**OFICIAL DE ARCHIVOS**	
When and where did you see your car last?	¿Cuándo y dónde vio su carro la última vez?	¿KWAHN-doh ee DOHN-deh VEE-oh soo-KAH-rroh lah OOL-tee-mah vehs?

SUBJECT	**SUJETO**	
This morning at 1:00 A.M.	Esta madrugada a la 1:00.	EHS-tah mah-droo-GAH-dah ah lah OO-nah.
Last night at 10:00 P.M.	Anoche a las 10:00.	Ah-NOH-cheh ah lahs DEE-ehs.

At midnight.	*A medianoche.*	Ah meh-dee-ah-NOH-cheh.
Today at noon.	*Hoy al mediodía.*	OH-ee ahl meh-dee-oh-DEE-ah.
At the corner of ____.	*En la esquina de ____.*	Ehn lah ehs-KEE-nah deh ____.
Between ____ and ____ streets.	*Entre las calles ____ y ____.*	EHN-treh lahs KAH-yehs ____ ee ____.
In the parking lot of the library.	*En el estacionamiento de la biblioteca.*	Ehn ehl ehs-tah-syohn-ah-MYEHN-toh deh la bee-blyoh-TEH-kah.

RECORDS OFFICER — *OFICIAL DE ARCHIVOS*

What's your license plate number?	*¿Cuál es el número de su placa?*	¿Kwahl ehs ehl NOO-meh-roh deh soo PLAH-kah?

SUBJECT — *SUJETO*

I don't know.	*No sé*	Noh seh.
Colorado BEY 482.	*Colorado BEY cuatro, ocho, dos.*	Koh-loh-RAH-doh Beh Eh ee-gree-EH-gah KWAH-troh, OH-choh, dohs.

RECORDS OFFICER — *OFICIAL DE ARCHIVOS*

Let me check the computer.	*Déjeme ver en la computadora.*	DEH-heh-meh vehr ehn lah kohm-poo-tah-DOH-rah.
Yes, we have your car.	*Sí, tenemos su carro.*	See, teh-NEH-mohs soo KAH-rroh.
No, we don't have your car.	*No, no tenemos su carro.*	No, noh teh-NEH-mohs soo KAH-rroh
You should report your car as stolen.	*Debe denunciar su carro como robado.*	DEH-beh deh-NOON-syahr soo KAH-rroh KOH-moh roh-BAH-doh.
Are you the owner of the car?	*¿Es usted el dueño del carro?*	¿Ehs oos-TEHD ehl DWEH-nyoh dehl KAH-rroh?

SUBJECT — *SUJETO*

Yes.	*Sí.*	See.

Why was my car towed?	¿Por qué se llevó mi carro la grúa?	¿Pohr keh seh yeh-VOH mee KAH-rroh lah groo-ah?

RECORDS OFFICER **OFICIAL DE ARCHIVOS**

Because it was parked...	Porque estaba estacionado...	Pohr-keh ehs-TAH-bah ehs-tah-syoh-NAH-doh...
• in a "no parking" zone.	• en un lugar prohibido.	• ehn oon loo-GAHR proh-ee-BEE-doh.
• in a private parking lot.	• en una zona privada.	• ehn OO-nah SOH-nah pree-VAH-dah.
• on that road for days.	• en la carretera por días.	• ehn lah kah-rreh-TEH-rah por DEE-ahs.

SUBJECT **SUJETO**

Yes, I'm the owner of the car.	Sí, soy el dueño del carro.	See, SOH-ee ehl DWEH-nyoh dehl KAH-rroh.

RECORDS OFFICER **OFICIAL DE ARCHIVOS**

Can I see your...	¿Puedo ver...	¿PWEH-doh vehr...
• registration?	• su registro del carro?	• soo rreh-HEES-troh dehl KAH-rroh?
• title?	• el título de propiedad?	• ehl tee-too-loh de proh-pyeh-dad.
• driver's license?	• su licencia de manejar?	• soo lee-SEHN-syah deh mah-neh-HAHR?
• some other identification?	• otra identificación?	• OH-trah ee-dehn-tee-fee-kah-SYOHN?

SUBJECT **SUJETO**

Yes, here is my driver's license.	Sí, aquí está mi licencia de manejar.	See, ah-KEE ehs TAH mee lee-SEHN-syah deh mah-neh-HAHR.

RECORDS OFFICER **OFICIAL DE ARCHIVOS**

Go to this address and show this document.	Vaya a esta dirección y muestre este documento.	VAH-yah ah EHS-tah dee-rehk-SYOHN ee MWEHS-treh EHS-teh doh-koo-MEHN-toh.

There they will give you your car.	Allí le darán su carro.	Ah-YEE-leh dah-RAHN soo KAH-rroh.
The car can only be towed out.	El carro sólo puede ser remolcado.	Ehl KAH-rroh SOH-loh PWEH-deh sehr reh-mohl-KAH-doh.
You cannot drive the car.	No puede manejar el coche.	Noh PWEH-de mah-neh-HAHR ehl KOH-che.

SUBJECT / *SUJECTO*

No, I'm not the owner of the car.	No, no soy el dueño del carro.	Noh, noh soy ehl DWEH-nyoh dehl KAH-rroh.
It's...	Es...	Ehs...
• my husband's car.	• el carro de mi marido.	• ehl KAH-rroh deh mee mah-REE-doh.
• a rental.	• un carro de alquiler.	• oon KAH-rroh deh ahl-kee-LEHR.
• a borrowed car.	• un carro prestado.	• oon KAH-rroh prehs-TAH-doh.

RECORDS OFFICER / *OFICIAL DE ARCHIVOS*

I'm sorry.	Lo siento.	Loh see-EHN-toh.
I can't give you the car.	No puedo darle el carro.	Noh PWEH-doh DAHR-leh ehl KAH-rroh.
The owner of the car needs to come in person with a form of identification or driver's license.	El dueño del carro tiene que venir en persona con su identificación o licencia de manejar.	Ehl DWEH-nyoh dehl KAH-rroh TYEH-neh keh veh-NEER ehn pehr-SOH-nah kohn soo ee-dehn-tee-fee-kah-SYOHN oh soo lee-SEHN-syah deh mah-neh-HAHR.
The owner of the car can give you permission in writing with his signature and the signature of a notary public.	El dueño del carro puede darle permiso por escrito con su firma y la firma de un notario público.	Ehl DWEH-nyoh dehl KAH-rroh PWEH-deh DAHR-leh pehr-MEE-soh phor ehs-KREE-toh kohn soo FEER-mah ee lah deh oon noh-TAH-ree-oh POO-blee-koh.

Please sign here and write your address and phone number for our records.	*Por favor, firme aquí y escriba su dirección y número de teléfono para nuestros archivos.*	Pohr fah-VOHR, FEER-meh ah-KEE ee ehs-KREE-bah soo dee-rehk-SYOHN ee NOO-meh-roh deh teh-LEH-foh-noh PAH-rah NWEHS-trohs ahr-CHEE-vohs.

4. Report Release

SUBJECT	**SUJETO**	
I'd like to have a copy of my case report.	*Quiero una copia del reporte de mi caso.*	KYEH-roh OO-nah KOH-pyah deh mee KAH-soh.
CLERK	**EMPLEADO**	
Do you have the case report number?	*¿Tiene usted el número de su caso?*	¿TYEH-neh oos-tehd ehl NOO-meh-roh deh soo KAH-soh?
Is it a criminal report or accident report?	*¿Es el informe de un crimen o accidente?*	¿Ehs ehl een-fohr-meh deh oon KREE-mehn oh akh-see-DEHN-teh?
SUBJECT	**SUJETO**	
It's an accident report.	*Es el informe de un accidente.*	Ehs ehl een-FOHR-meh deh oon akh-see-DEHN-teh.
CLERK	**EMPLEADO**	
The report cannot be released.	*No podemos entregarle el informe.*	Noh poh-DEH-mohs ehn-treh-GAHR-leh ehl een-FOHR-meh.
Your insurance company has to make the request.	*Su compañía de seguro tiène que hacer la petición.*	Soo kohm-pah-NEE-ah deh seh-GOO-roh TYEH-neh keh ah-SEHR lah peh-tee-SYON.
Your lawyer must make the request.	*Su abogado debe hacer la petición.*	Soo ah-boh-GAH-doh deh-beh ah-SEHR lah peh-tee-SYON.

English	Spanish	Pronunciation
Come with me to fill out a request.	*Venga y llene una solicitud.*	VEHN-gah eeh yeh-neh OO-nah soh-lee-see-TOOD.
There will be a $____ charge.	*Le costará ____ dólares.*	Leh kohs-tah-RAH ____ DOH-lah-rehs.
Bring the case report number.	*Traiga el número de su caso.*	TRAY-gah ehl NOO-meh-roh deh soo KAH-soh.

SUBJECT — *SUJETO*

It's a criminal report.	*Es el informe de un crimen.*	Ehs ehl een-FOHR-meh deh oon KREE-mehn.

CLERK — *EMPLEADO*

Fill out the request.	*Llene la solicitud.*	YEH-neh lah soh-lee-see-TOOD.
Pay the $____ charge.	*Pague los ____ dólares.*	PAH-geh lohs ____ DOH-lah-rehs.
We will mail it to you.	*Se lo enviaremos por correo.*	Seh loh ehn-vyah-REH-mohs pohr koh-rreh-oh.
We must send it to Investigations for approval.	*Tenemos que mandarlo a Investigaciones para que lo aprueben.*	Teh-NEH-mohs keh mahn-DAHR-loh ah een-vehs-tee-gah-SYOH-nehs pah-rah keh loh ah PRWEH-behn.
It takes three working days.	*Tarda tres días laborables.*	TAHR-dah trehs DEE-ahs lah-boh-RAH-blehs.
Allow five to seven days for processing.	*Déle de cinco a siete días para que lo aprueben.*	DEH-leh deh SEEN-koh ah SYEH-teh DEE-ahs PAH-rah keh loh ah-PRWEH-behn.
To mail in for a copy, send a letter requesting a copy.	*Para pedir una copia, envíe una carta solicitando una copia.*	PAH-rah peh-DEER OO-nah KOH-pyah, ehn-VEE-eh OO-nah KAHR-tah soh-lee-see-TAHN-doh OO-nah KOH-pyah.
Include the case report number, name, birthdate, location,	*Incluya el número del caso, su nombre, fecha de nacimiento, lugar,*	Eehn-CLOO-yah ehl NOO-meh-roh dehl KAH-soh, soo NOHM-

and date of occurrence.	*y fecha de lo ocurrido.*	breh, FEH-chah deh nah-see-MYEHN-toh, loo-GAHR, ee feh-chah deh loh oh-koo-RREE-doh.
Send a check for _____ dollars and a self-addressed, stamped envelope.	*Envíe un cheque por _____ dólares y un sobre con estampilla.*	Ehn-VEE-eh oon CHEH-keh pohr _____ DOH-lah-rehs ee oon SOH-breh kohn ehs-tahm-PEE-yah.

5. Booking a Suspect

C ULTURE NOTE ••••

EYE CONTACT   When being disciplined, children rarely make eye contact with their parents, as this would be considered insolent and defiant. This behavior often extends into adulthood: eye contact with an authority figure such as a teacher, a police officer, a doctor, a priest, an elder, or anyone in a position of authority is avoided. While this may be interpreted as proof of a guilty conscience in non-Hispanic cultures, it is considered a sign of respect in Latino culture.

A. TAKING DOWN PERSONAL INFORMATION

OFFICER	AGENTE	
What's...	*¿Cuál es...*	¿Kwahl ehs...
• your name and last name/s?	• *su nombre y apellido/s?*	• soo NOHM-breh ee ah peh-YEE-doh/dohs?
• your mother's last name?	• *el apellido de su madre?*	• ehl ah peh-YEE-doh deh soo MAH-dreh?

Do you have an alias or nickname?	¿Tiene un alias o apodo?	¿TYEH-neh oon AH-lyahs oh ah-POH-doh?
SUSPECT	*SOSPECHOSO*	
They call me "Chico."	Me llaman "Chico."	Meh YAH-mahn "Chico."
No, I don't have an alias.	No, no tengo apodo.	Noh, noh TEHN-goh ah-POH doh.
OFFICER	*AGENTE*	
What's…	¿Cuál es…	¿Kwahl ehs…
• your phone number?	• su número de teléfono?	• soo NOO-meh-roh deh teh-LEH-foh-noh?
• your address?	• su dirección?	• soo dee-rehk-SYOHN?
Where do you live?	¿Dónde vive?	¿DOHN-deh VEE-veh?
SUSPECT	*SOSPECHOSO*	
My address is ___.	Mi dirección es ___.	Mee dee-rehk-SYOHN ehs ___.
I live at ___.	Vivo en ___.	VEE-voh ehn ___.
I'm staying…	Me estoy quedando…	Meh ehs-TOY keh-DAN-doh…
• at ___.	• en ___.	• ehn ___.
• in a motel.	• en un motel.	• ehn oon moh-TEHL.
• with friends.	• en casa de unos amigos.	• ehn KAH-sah deh OO-nohs ah-MEE-gohs.
I don't have an address.	No tengo dirección.	Noh TEHN-goh dee-rehk-SYOHN.
OFFICER	*AGENTE*	
Whom should we…	¿A quién debemos…	¿Ah kyehn deh-BEH-mohs…
• notify?	• avisar?	• ah-vee-SAHR?
• call?	• llamar?	• yah-MAHR?
Whom should we tell about your arrest?	¿A quién le debemos contar de su arresto?	¿Ah kyehn leh deh-BEH-mohs kon-TAHR deh soo ah-RREHS-toh?

SUSPECT	SOSPECHOSO	
You can notify my...	*Puede avisarle a mi...*	PWEH-deh ah-vee-SAHR-leh ah mee...
• mother/father.	• *madre/padre.*	• MAH-dreh/PAH-dreh.
• friend.	• *amigo/a*	• ah-MEE-goh/gah.
• lawyer.	• *abogado/a.*	• ah-boh-GAH-doh/dah.
• boss.	• *jefe.*	• HEH-feh.
• wife/husband.	• *esposo/a.*	• ehs-POH-soh/sah.
• brother/sister.	• *hermano/a.*	• ehr-MAH-noh/nah.
• neighbor.	• *vecino/a.*	• veh-SEE-noh/nah.

OFFICER	AGENTE	
Where can we find him/her/them?	*¿Dónde podemos encontrarlo/la/los?*	¿DOHN-deh poh-DEH-mohs ehn-kohn-TRAHR-loh/lah/lohs?

SUSPECT	SOSPECHOSO	
Call them at _____.	*Llámeles al _____.*	YAH-meh-lehs al _____.
Why have I been arrested?	*¿Por qué me arrestan?*	¿Pohr-KEH meh ahr-REHS-tahn?

OFFICER	AGENTE	
For...	*Por...*	Pohr...
• drug possession.	• *posesión de drogas.*	• poh-seh-SYOHN deh DROH-gahs.
• drug dealing.	• *venta de drogas.*	• VEHN-tah deh DROH-gahs.
• car theft.	• *robo de coches.*	• RROH-boh deh KOH-chehs.
• homicide.	• *homicidio.*	• oh-mee-SEE-dyoh.
• assault.	• *asalto.*	• ah-SAHL-toh.
• drunk driving.	• *manejar borracho.*	• mah-neh-HAHR boh-RRAH-choh.
• spousal abuse.	• *abusar a la esposa.*	• ah-boo-SAHR ah lah ehs-POH-sah.
• petty theft.	• *robar.*	• rroh-BAHR.

• child abuse.	• *abuso a los niños.*	• ah-BOO-soh ah lohs NEE-nyohs.
• solicitation.	• *solicitación.*	• soh-lee-see-tah-SYOHN.
• loitering.	• *tirar basura.*	• tee-RAHR bah-SOO-rah.
• public drunkenness.	• *emborracharse en público.*	• ehm-boh-rra-CHAHR-seh ehn POO-blee-koh.

SUSPECT / *SOSPECHOSO*

You are arresting the wrong person.	*Está arrestando a la persona equivocada.*	Ehs-TAH ah-rrehs-TAHN-doh ah lah pehr-SOH-nah eh-kee-voh-KAH-dah.
I don't...	*No...*	Noh...
• sell drugs.	• *vendo drogas.*	• VEHN-doh DROH-gahs.
• have any drugs.	• *tengo drogas.*	• TEHN-goh DROH-gahs.
I didn't...	*No he...*	Noh eh...
• steal anything.	• *robado nada.*	• rroh-BAH-doh NAH-dah.
• assault anybody.	• *asaltado a nadie.*	• ah-sahl-TAH-doh ah NAH-dyeh.
• kill anybody.	• *matado a nadie.*	• mah-TAH-do ah NAH-dyeh.
Where are you taking me?	*¿Adónde me llevan?*	¿Ah-DOHN-deh meh YEH-vahn?

OFFICER / *AGENTE*

You are going to jail.	*Usted va a la cárcel.*	Oo-STEHD vah ah lah KAHR-sehl.

SUSPECT / *SOSPECHOSO*

How can I get out?	*¿Cómo salgo de la cárcel?*	¿KOH-moh SAHL-goh deh lah KAHR-sehl?

OFFICER / *AGENTE*

You need to post a bond.	*Necesita una fianza.*	Neh-seh-SEE-tah OO-nah FYAHN-sah.

SUSPECT	SOSPECHOSO	
How do I do that?	¿Cómo?	¿KOH-moh?
Where do they need to take the money?	¿Adónde necesitan llevar el dinero?	¿Ah-DOHN-deh neh-seh-SEE-tahn yeh-VAHR ehl dee-NEH-roh?
How much does it cost?	¿Cuánto cuesta?	¿KWAHN-toh KWEHS-tah?
Do I need a bondsman?	¿Necesito un fiador?	¿Neh-seh-SEE-toh oon fee-ah-DOHR?

OFFICER	AGENTE	
Talk to your lawyer.	Hable con su abogado.	HA-bleh kohn soo ah-boh-GAH-doh.
He'll give you the right information.	Él le dará la informacion correcta.	Ehl leh dah-RAH lah een-fohr-mah-SYOHN koh-RREHK-tah.

B. TAKING A MUG SHOT

POLICE	POLICÍA	
Please stand on the arrows on the floor facing the camera.	Por favor, párese en las flechas en el piso y mire hacia la cámara.	Pohr fah-VOHR, PAH-reh-seh ehn lahs FLEH-chahs ehn ehl PEE-soh ee MEE-reh AH-syah lah KAH-mah-rah.
Keep your eyes open.	Mantenga los ojos abiertos.	Mahn-TEHN-gah lohs OH-hohs ah-bee-EHR-tohs.
Hold this board up next to your chest with both hands.	Ponga esta tabla contra su pecho con las dos manos.	POHN-gah EHS-tah TAH-blah KOHN-trah soo PEH-choh kohn lahs dohs MAH-nohs.
Please face that direction and tuck your hair behind your ear so that I may see your ear.	Por favor, mire en aquella dirección y ponga el pelo detrás de la oreja para que pueda verla.	Pohr fah-VOHR, MEE-reh ehn ah-KEH-yah dee-rehk-SYOHN ee POHN-gah ehl PEH-loh deh-TRAHS deh lah oh-REH-hah PAH-rah keh PWEH-dah VEHR-lah.

Do not make any faces.	*No haga gestos.*	Noh AH-gah HEHS-tohs.
Please take off your glasses and we will do this again.	*Por favor, sáquese los lentes para hacer esto otra vez.*	Pohr fah-VOHR, SAH-keh-seh lohs LEHN-tehs PAH-rah ah-SEHR EHS-toh OH-trah vehs.
Thank you.	*Gracias.*	GRAH-syahs.

GRAMMAR NOTE ••••

OBJECT PRONOUNS   The direct object pronoun refers to objects or people directly relating to the action of the verb. It usually precedes the verb, but is attached to the affirmative command.

me	*me*
you (inf.)	*te*
him/her/it/you (form.)	*lo/la*
us	*nos*
you (inf.)	*os*
them/you (form.)	*los/las*

Do you know Jim?	*¿Conoces a Jim?*
Yes, I know him.	*Sí, lo conozco.*
The money? He has it.	*¿El dinero? Lo tiene él.*
Bring it.	*Tráigalo.*
Call us.	*Llámenos.*

The indirect object pronoun refers to the person or thing receiving the action. It precedes the verb and the direct object pronoun, and is attached to the affirmative command.

to me	*me*
to you (inf.)	*te*
to you (form.)/him/her	*le*
to us	*nos*
to you all (inf.)	*os*
to them/you all (form.)	*les*

He gave the car keys to us.	*Él nos dio las llaves del carro.*

C. FINGERPRINTING

POLICE	POLICÍA	
Please step over here next to me.	*Por favor, acérquese, aquí a mi lado.*	Pohr fah-VOHR, ah-SEHR-keh-seh, ah-KEE ah mee LAH-doh.
These are your fingerprint cards.	*Estas son las tarjetas para sus huellas digitales.*	EHS-tahs sohn lahs tahr-HEH-tahs PAH-rah soos WEH-yahs dee-hee-TAH-lehs.
Please sign the cards where the x's are.	*Por favor, firme las tarjetas donde están las equis.*	Pohr fah-VOHR, FEER-meh lahs tahr-HEH-tahs DOHN-deh ehs-TAHN lahs EH-kees.
I will take your fingerprints now.	*Tomaré sus huellas digitales ahora.*	Toh-mah-REH soos WEH-yahs dee-hee-TAH-lehs ah-OH-rah.
Take off your coat.	*Quítese el abrigo.*	KEE-teh-seh ehl ah-BREE-goh.
Roll up your sleeves.	*Súbase las mangas.*	SOO-bah-seh las MAHN-gahs.
I will start with your right hand.	*Empiezo con su mano derecha.*	Ehm-PYEH-soh kohn soo-MAH-noh deh-REH-chah.
Please relax your fingers.	*Por favor, relaje los dedos.*	Pohr fah-VOHR, reh-LAH-heh lohs DEH-dohs.
Left hand, please.	*La mano izquierda, por favor.*	Lah MAH-noh ees-KYEHR-dah, pohr fah-VOHR.
Now I need your fingers together.	*Ahora necesito sus dedos juntos.*	Ah-OH-rah neh-seh-SEE-toh soos DEH-dohs HOON-tohs.
Now I need your...	*Ahora necesito el...*	Ah-OH-rah neh-seh-SEE-toh ehl...
• thumb.	• *pulgar.*	• POOL-gahr.
• index finger.	• *índice.*	• EEN-dee-seh.
• middle finger.	• *cordial.*	• kor-dee-AHL.

• ring finger.	• *anular.*	• ah-noo-LAHR.
• pinky.	• *pequeño.*	• peh-KEH-nyoh.
Please step over here and face the table.	*Por favor, venga aquí y mire hacia la mesa.*	Pohr fah-VOHR, VEHN-gah ah-KEE ee MEE-reh AH-syah lah MEH-sah.
May I see your right hand?	*¿Puedo ver su mano derecha?*	¿PWEH-doh vehr soo MAH-noh deh-REH-chah?
Please keep your fingers together and your thumb separate.	*Por favor, siga con los dedos juntos y el pulgar separado.*	Pohr fah-VOHR, SEE-gah kohn loh DEH-dohs HOON-tohs ee ehl pool-GAHR seh-pah-RAH-doh.
Relax your fingers.	*Relaje los dedos.*	Reh-LAH-heh lohs DEH-dohs.
Do not press.	*No presione.*	Noh preh-SYOH-neh.
I will do all the work.	*Yo haré el trabajo.*	Yoh ah-REH ehl trah-BAH-hoh.
Hold your hand like this.	*Sostenga la mano así.*	Sohs-TEHN-gah lah MAH-noh ah-SEE.
I'll guide your hand.	*Yo dirijo su mano.*	Yoh dee-REE-hoh soo MAH-noh.
Please try not to grab the roller.	*Por favor, no agarre el rodillo.*	Pohr fah-VOHR, noh ah-GAH-rreh ehl roh-DEE-yoh.
Please keep your hand flat.	*Por favor, mantenga la mano estirada.*	Pohr fah-VOHR, mahn-TEHN-gah lah MAH-noh ehs-tee-RAH-dah.
Next, I'll do the side of your hand.	*Luego, voy a hacer el lado de la mano.*	LWEH-goh, voy ah ah-SEHR ehl LAH-doh deh lah MAH-noh.
I'll do the same thing with your left hand.	*Ahora, voy a hacer lo mismo con la mano izquierda.*	Ah-OH-rah, voy ah ah-SEHR loh MEES-moh kohn lah MAH-noh ees-KYEHR-dah.

Please stand over here to clean your hands.	Por favor, párese aquí para limpiar las manos.	Pohr fah-VOHR, PAH-reh-seh ah-KEE PAH-rah leem-PYAHR lahs MAH-nohs.
Wipe your hands with the paper towel.	Séquese las manos con la toalla de papel.	SEH-keh-seh lahs MAH-nohs kohn lah toh-AH-yah deh pah-PEHL.
Thank you.	Gracias.	GRAH-syahs.

D. STRIP SEARCH

Take your clothes off.	Quítese la ropa.	KEE-teh-seh lah ROH-pah.
Hand them to me.	Démela a mí.	DEH-meh-lah ah mee.
Face us.	Mírenos.	MEE-reh-nohs.
Run your hand through your hair.	Pase los dedos de la mano por su cabello.	PAH-seh lohs DEH-dohs deh lah MAH-noh pohr soo kah-BEH-yoh.
Expose the back side of your ears.	Enseñe la parte de atrás de las orejas.	Ehn-SEH-nyeh lah PAHR-teh deh ah-TRAHS deh lahs oh-REH-hahs.
Open your mouth.	Abra la boca.	AH-brah lah BOH-kah.
Roll back your tongue.	Levante la lengua.	Leh-VAHN-teh lah LEHN-gwah.
Pull the bottom and top of your lip.	Estire el labio inferior y el labio superior.	Ehs-TEE-reh ehl lah-byoh eehn-feh-RYOHR ee ehl LAH-byoh soo-peh-RYOHR.
Raise your arms.	Levante los brazos.	Leh-VAHN-teh lohs BRAH-sohs.
Open your fingers.	Abra los dedos.	AH-brah lohs DEH-dohs.

Raise your...	Levante...	Leh-VAHN-teh...
• testicles.	• los testículos.	• lohs tehs-TEE-koo-lohs.
• breasts.	• los pechos.	• lohs PEH-chohs.
Show the bottom of your feet.	Enseñe las plantas de los pies.	Ehn-SEH-nyeh lahs PLAHN-tahs deh lohs pyehs.
Bend forward and spread your cheeks.	Dóblese hacia adelante y separe las nalgas.	DOH-bleh-seh AH-syah ah-deh-LAHN-teh ee seh-PAH-reh lahs NAHL-gahs.
Did you put something in there?	¿Puso algo ahí?	¿POO-soh AHL-goh ah-EE?
Squat down and cough.	Agáchese y tosa.	Ah-GAH-cheh-seh ee TOH-sah.
Hold one foot up and spread your toes.	Levante un pie y extienda los dedos.	Leh-VAHN-teh oon pyeh ee ehks-TYEHN-dah lohs DEH-dohs.
Now the other foot.	Ahora el otro pie.	Ah-OH-rah ehl OH-troh pyeh.
The medical staff is going to look under your bandage.	El personal médico va a mirar debajo de su venda.	Ehl pehr-soh-NAHL MEH-dee-koh vah ah mee-RAHR deh-BAH-hoh deh soo VEHN-dah.

6. Handling Prisoners' Concerns

INMATE	PRISIONERO	
When do I go to court?	¿Cuándo voy a la corte?	¿KWAHN-doh voy ah lah KOHR-teh?
What's my court date?	¿Qué día voy a la corte?	¿Keh DEE-ah voy ah lah KOHR-teh?
At what time do I need to be in court?	¿A qué hora voy a la corte?	¿Ah keh OH-rah voy ah lah KOR-teh?

GUARD	GUARDA	
We'll look it up in the computer.	*Lo miraremos en la computadora.*	Loh mee-rah-REH-mohs ehn lah kohm-poo-tah-DOH-rah.
I'll let you know on _____ at _____.	*Se lo diré el día _____ a las _____.*	Seh loh dee-REH ehl DEE-ah _____ ah lahs _____.

INMATE	PRISIONERO	
What about...	*¿Y acerca del/de...*	¿Ee ah-SEHR-kah dehl/deh...
• my mail?	• *correo?*	• koh-REEH-oh?
• personal visits?	• *las visitas?*	• lahs vee-SEE-tahs?
• phone calls?	• *llamadas de teléfono?*	• yah-MAH-dahs deh teh-LEH-foh-noh?
• Where can I send mail?	• *¿Adónde puedo mandar el correo?*	• ¿Ah-DOHN-deh PWEH-doh mahn-DAHR ehl koh-RREH-oh?
• When will I receive mail?	• *¿Cuándo puedo recibir el correo?*	• ¿KWAHN-doh PWEH-doh reh-see-BEER ehl koh-RREH-oh?

GUARD	GUARDA	
If you send mail out, you must write... in the envelope.	*Si usted envía una carta, debe poner... en el sobre.*	See oos-TEHD ehn-VEE-ah OO-nah KAHR-tah, DEH-beh poh-NEHR...ehn ehl SOH-breh.
• your full name	• *su nombre y apellidos*	• soo NOHM-breh ee ah-peh-YEE-dohs
• your return address	• *su remite*	• soo reh-MEE-teh
If you are receiving mail, the envelope must contain... of the sender.	*Si recibe el correo, el sobre debe contener...de la persona que le escribe.*	See reh-SEE-beh ehl koh-RREH-oh, ehl SOH-breh DEH beh kohn-teh-NEHR... deh lah pehr-SOH-nah keh leh ehs-KREE-beh.
• the name	• *el nombre*	• ehl NOHM-breh

• the return address	• *el remite*	• ehl reh-MEE-teh
You may have visits from…at any time.	*Puede tener visitas… en cualquier momento.*	PWEH-deh teh-NEHR vee-SEE-tahs… ehn kwah-KEYHR moh-MEHN-toh.
• clergy	• *de un clérigo*	• deh oon KLEH-ree-goh
• attorneys	• *de los abogados*	• deh lohs ah-boh-GAH-dohs
• authorized personnel	• *personal autorizado*	• pehr-soh-NAHL ah-oo-toh-ree-SAH-doh
You are allowed _____ visits per week, starting on Sunday and ending on Saturday.	*Usted puede tener _____ visitas personales por semana, empezando el domingo y terminando el sábado.*	Oos-TEHD PWEH-deh teh-NEHR _____ vee-SEE-tahs pehr-soh-NAH-lehs pohr seh-MAH-nah, ehm-peh-SAHN-doh ehl doh-MEEN-goh ee rehr-mee-NAHN doh ehl SAH-bah-doh.
Visits are allowed daily between…	*Las visitas pueden ser diarias, entre…*	Lahs vee-SEE-tahs PWEH-dehn sehr dee-AH-ree-ahs, EHN-treh…
• 9:00 and 10:30 A.M.	• *las nueve y las diez y media de la mañana.*	• lahs NWEH-veh ee lahs dyehs ee MEH-dy-ah deh lah mah-NYAH-nah.
• 1:00 and 4:00 P.M.	• *la una y las cuatro de la tarde.*	• lah OO-nah ee lahs KWAH-troh deh lah TAHR-deh.
• 7:00 and 8:30 P.M.	• *las siete y las ocho y media de la tarde.*	• lahs SYEH-teh ee lahs OH-choh ee MEH-dyah deh lah TAHR-deh.
No more than three visitors at a time are allowed in the visiting area.	*No se permiten más de tres visitantes a la vez en la zona para las visitas.*	Noh seh pehr-MEE-tehn mahs deh trehs vee-see-TAHN-tehs ah lah vehs ehn lah SOH-nah PAH-rah lahs vee-SEE-tahs.

If you have a visitor, you must go to the visiting booth number assigned to you.	Si tiene una visita, debe ir al lugar para las visitas asignado para usted con un número.	See TYEH-neh OO-nah vee-SEE-tah, DEH-beh eer ahl loo-GAHR PAH-rah lahs vee-SEE tahs ah-seeg-NAH-doh PAH-rah oos-TEHD kohn oon NOO-meh-roh.
You can call collect to contact...	Usted puede llamar a cobro revertido...	Oos-TEHD PWEH-deh yah-MAHR a KOH-broh reh-vehr-TEE-doh...
• attorneys.	• a los abogados.	• ah lohs ah-boh-GAH-dohs.
• relatives.	• a sus parientes.	• ah soos pah-RYEHN-tehs.
• the staff here.	• al personal aquí.	• ahl pehr-soh-NAHL ah-KEE.
• your employer.	• a su jefe en el trabajo.	• ah soo HEH-feh ehn ehl trah-BAH-hoh.
We will not take messages for you unless...	No le daremos los mensajes a menos que...	Noh leh dah-REH-mohs lohs mehn-SAH-hehs ah MEH-nohs keh...
• there's a death in your family.	• haya una muerte en su familia.	• AH-yah OO-nah MWEHR-teh ehn soo fah-MEE-lee-ah.
• your attorney needs to speak to you.	• su abogado necesite hablarle.	• soo ah-boh-GAH-doh neh-seh-SEE-teh ah-BLAHR-leh.
INMATE	*PRISIONERO*	
What about...	¿Y acerca de...	¿Ee ah-SEHR-kah deh...
• my money?	• mi dinero?	• mee dee-NEH-roh?
• recreation?	• recreo?	• reh-KREH-oh?

GUARD	GUARDA	
Family or friends can deposit money into your account, during normal business hours.	*Su familia o sus amigos pueden depositar dinero en su cuenta durante las horas normales de trabajo.*	Soo fah-MEE-lee-ah oh soos ah-MEE-gohs PWEH-dehn deh-poh-see-TAHR dee-NEH-roh ehn soo KWEHN-tah doo-rahn-TEH lahs OH-rahs nohr-MAH-lehs deh trah-BAH-hoh.
They will accept...	*Se aceptan...*	Seh ahk-SEHP-tahn...
• U.S. currency.	• *dinero al contado.*	• dee-NEH-roh ahl kohn-TAH-doh.
• money orders.	• *giro postal.*	• HEE-roh pohs-tahl.
• traveler's checks.	• *cheques de viajero.*	• CHEH-kehs deh vee-ah-HEH-roh.
• cashier checks.	• *cheques al cajero.*	• CHEH-kehs ahl kah-HEH-roh.
• certified funds.	• *certificados de depósito.*	• sehr-tee-fee-KAH-dohs deh deh-POH-see-toh.
• government checks.	• *cheques del gobierno.*	• CHEH-kehs dehl goh-BYEHR-noh.
For recreation, you can go to...	*Para su recreo, puede ir a...*	PAH-rah soo reh-CREH-oh PWEH-deh eer ah...
• Bible studies.	• *los estudios de la Biblia.*	• lohs ehs-TOO-dyohs deh lah BEE-bly-ah.
• the recreational facilities.	• *las zonas de recreo.*	• lahs ZOH-nahs deh reh-KREH-oh.
• the library.	• *la biblioteca.*	• lah bee-blyoh-TEH-kah.
GUARD	GUARDA	
Are there any other questions?	*¿Tiene otras preguntas?*	¿TYEH-neh OH-trahs preh-GOON-tahs?
Do you get along with your inmates?	*¿Se lleva bien con sus compañeros de celda?*	¿Seh YEH-vah byehn kohn soos kohm-pah-NYEH-rohs deh SEHL-dah?

134

INMATE	PRISIONERO	
I don't get along with ____.	*No me llevo bien con ____.*	Noh meh YEH-voh byehn kohn ____.
Somebody is...	*Alguien me...*	AHL-gyehn meh...
• picking on me.	• *está molestando.*	• ehs-TAH moh-lehs-TAHN-doh.
• making obscene gestures at me.	• *haciendo gestos obscenos cuando me mira.*	• ah-SYEHN-doh HEHS-tohs ohb-SEH-nohs. KWAHN-doh meh MEE-rah.
• threatening me.	• *me amenaza.*	• meh ah-meh-NAH-sah.
• being rude to me.	• *me trata mal.*	• meh TRAH-tah mahl.
• too loud at night.	• *hace ruido por la noche.*	• Ah-seh RWEE-doo pohr lah NOH-cheh.

GUARD	GUARDA	
Always close your cell door.	*Siempre cierre la puerta de su celda.*	SYEHM-preh SYEH-rreh lah PWEHR-tah deh soo SEHL-dah.
It's a violation of rules if you leave your cell door open.	*Es una violación del reglamento si deja la puerta de su celda abierta.*	Ehs OO-nah vyoh-lah SYOHN dehl reh-glah-MEHN-toh see DEH-hah lah PWEHR-tah deh soo SEHL-dah ah-BYEHR-tah.
Next time you have a complaint...	*La próxima vez que tenga una queja...*	Lah PROHK-see-mah vehz keh TEHN-gah OO-nah KEH-hah...
• identify the person.	• *identifique a la persona.*	• ee-dehn-tee-FEE-keh ah lah pehr-SOH-nah.
• give the information to a deputy.	• *déle la información a un diputado.*	• DEH-leh lah een-fohr-mah-SYOHN ah oon dee-poo-TAH-doh.

The staff will take disciplinary action.	*El personal corregirá el problema con la acción adecuada.*	Ehl pehr-soh-NAHL koh-rreh-hee-RAH ehl proh-BLEH-mah kohn lah ahk-SYOHN ah-deh-KWAH-dah.
If you have any more questions, let us know.	*Si tiene más preguntas, díganoslo.*	See TYEH-neh mahs preh-GOON-tahs, DEE-gah-nohs-loh.
We will help you.	*Lo/la ayudaremos.*	Loh/lah ah-yoo-dah-REH-mohs.
When you get out of jail, you will be screened by...	*Cuando salga de la cárcel, será examinado por...*	KWAHH-doh SAHL-gah deh lah KAHR-sehl, seh-RAH ehk-sah-mee-NAH-doh pohr...
• medical personnel.	• *el personal médico.*	• ehl pehr-soh-nahl MEH-dee-koh.
• a counselor.	• *un/una consejero/a.*	• oon/OO-nah kohn-seh-HEH-roh/rah.
INMATE	*PRISIONERO*	
Thank you.	*Gracias.*	GRAH-syahs.

7. Prisoner Release

CLERK	*EMPLEADO*	
A bond has been posted for your release.	*Se depositó una fianza para su libertad.*	Seh deh-poh-see-TOH OO-nah FYAHN-sah PAH-rah soo lee-behr-TAHD.
Do you understand what that means?	*¿Entiende usted lo que quiere decir esto?*	¿Ehn-TYEHN-deh oos-TEHD loh keh KYEH-rah deh-SEER EHS-toh?
INMATE	*PRISIONERO*	
No, I don't understand.	*No, no entiendo.*	Noh, noh ehn-TYEHN-doh.
CLERK	*EMPLEADO*	
Someone has paid your bond.	*Alguien pagó su fianza.*	AHL-gyehn pah-GOH soo FYAHN-sah.

You can go home now.	Ya puede irse a su casa.	Yah PWEH-deh EER-seh ah soo KAH-sah.
You have to be in court on _____.	Tiene que estar en la corte el día _____.	TYEH-neh keh ehs-TAHR ehn lah KOHR-tah ehl DEE-ah _____.
If you don't go to court, a warrant will be issued for your arrest.	Si usted no va, se pedirá una orden de arresto contra usted.	See oos-TEHD noh vah, seh peh-dee-RAH OO-nah OHR-dehn deh ah-RREHS-toh KOHN-trah oos-TEHD.
Do you understand?	¿Comprende?	¿Kohm-PREHN-deh?

INMATE — *PRISIONERO*

| I understand. | Comprendo. | Kohn-PREHN-doh. |

CLERK — *EMPLEADO*

| Has all of your property been returned to you? | ¿Ya le han devuelto sus cosas? | ¿Yah leh ahn deh-VWEHL-toh soos KOH-sahs? |
| Pick up your property at the desk. | Recoja sus pertenencias en el mostrador. | Reh-KOH-hah soos pehr-teh-NEHN-syahs ehn ehl mohs-trah-DOHR. |

INMATE — *PRISIONERO*

| Where is my car? | ¿Dónde está mi carro? | ¿DOHN-deh ehs-TAH mee KAH-rroh? |
| Was my car impounded? | ¿Han embargado mi carro? | ¿Ahn ehm-bahr-GAH-doh mee KAH-rroh? |

CLERK — *EMPLEADO*

Your car has been impounded at _____.	Su carro se lo llevaron a _____.	Soo KAH-rroh seh loh yeh-VAH-rohn ah _____.
You need to fill out these forms, here.	Necesita llenar estos formularios.	Ne-seh-SEE-tah ye-NAHR EHS-tohs for-moo LAH-ree-ohs.
Then Sgt. _____ will release you.	Después, el Sargento _____ lo dejará libre.	Dehs-PWEHS ehl sahr-HEHN-toh _____ loh deh-hah-RAH LEE-breh.

Take the elevator... to get out.	*Tome el ascensor... para salir.*	TOH-meh ehl ahs-sehn-SOHR...PAH-rah sah-LEER.
• to the right	• *a la derecha*	• ah lah deh-REH-chah
• to the left	• *a la izquierda*	• ah lah ees-KYEHR-dah
Good luck!	*¡Buena suerte!*	¡BWEH-nah SWEHR-teh!

CRIMES AND MISDEMEANORS

Vocabulary ••••

CRIMES

homicide	*homicidio*	oh-mee-SEE-dyoh
rape	*violación*	vyoh-lah-SYOHN
assault	*asalto*	ah-SAHL-toh
threat	*amenaza*	ah-meh-NAH-sah
obscene call	*llamada obscena*	yah-MAH-dah ohbs-SEH-nah
murder	*asesinato*	ah-seh-see-NAH-toh
suicide	*suicidio*	swee-SEE-dyoh
accident	*accidente*	ahk-see-DEHN-teh
manslaughter	*homicidio involuntario*	oh-mee-SEE-dyoh een-voh-loon-TAH-ryoh.

(cont'd.)

Crimes *(cont'd.)*

drive-by shooting	*disparo desde un carro*	dees-PAH-roh DEHS-deh oon KAH-rroh
crime of passion	*crimen pasional*	KREE-mehn pah-syoh-NAHL
first degree	*primer grado*	pree-MEHR GRAH-doh
second degree	*segundo grado*	seh-GOON-doh GRAH-doh
armed robbery	*robo a mano armada*	ROH-boh ah MAH-noh ahr-MAH-dah
theft	*robo*	ROH-boh
smuggling	*contrabando*	kohn-trah-BAHN-doh
arson	*incendio premeditado*	een-SEHN-dyoh preh-meh-dee-TAH-doh
counterfeiting	*falsificación*	fahl-see-fee-kah-SYOHN
embezzling	*desfalco*	dehs-FAHL-koh
extortion	*extorsión*	ehks-tohr-SYOHN
fraud	*fraude*	FROW-deh
gambling	*juego de apuestas*	HWEH-goh deh ah-PWEHS-tahs
kidnapping	*secuestro*	seh-KWEHS-troh
trespassing	*intrusión*	een-troo-SYOHN
vandalism	*vandalismo*	vahn-dah-LEES-moh
sexual harassment	*acosamiento sexual*	ah-koh-sah-MYEHN-toh sehk-SWAHL
strangulation	*estrangulación*	ehs-trahn-goo-lah-SYOHN
massacre	*matanza*	mah-TAHN-sah
solicitation	*incitación*	een-see-tah-SYOHN
domestic violence	*violencia doméstica*	vyoh-LEHN-syah doh-MEHS-tee-kah

CULTURE NOTE ••••

COOPERATION Regardless of their specific cultural or national background, Latinos will most likely side with each other rather than an outsider. Thus, an individual will assist family members and friends regardless of the consequences, and expect the same in return. A sense of honor is so important in Latino culture that it may keep an individual from cooperating with the police against a friend or a family member, even though he or she may not condone any of the actions.

1. Homicide

A. TALKING TO THE REPORTING PARTY

DISPATCHER	OPERADORA DE EMERGENCIA	
What's your emergency?	¿Cuál es su emergencia?	¿Kwahl ehs soo eh-mehr-HEHN-syah?

WITNESS	TESTIGO	
Somebody is hurt.	Alguien está herido.	AHL-gyehn ehs-TAH eh-REE-doh.
Two men were stabbed.	Apuñalaron a dos hombres.	Ah-poo-nyah-LAH-rohn ah dohs OHM-brehs.
A woman was beaten up.	Le pegaron a una mujer.	Leh peh-GAHR-ohn ah OO-nah moo-HEHR.
• My brother...	• a mi hermano.	• ah mee ehr-MAH-noh.
• My uncle...	• a mi tío.	• ah mee TEE-oh.
• My grandfather...	• a mi abuelo.	• ah mee ah-BWEHL-loh.

• My friend...	• *a mi amigo.*	• ah mee ah-MEE-goh.
• My neighbor...	• *a mi vecino.*	• ah mee veh-SEE-noh.
...was shot.	*Dispararon...*	Dees-pah-RAH-rohn...
...stabbed.	*Apuñalaron...*	Ah-poo-nyah-LAH-rohn...
...was hit by a car.	*Atropellaron...*	Ah-troh-peh-YAH-rohn...
...was beaten up.	*Le pegaron...*	Leh peh-GAH-rohn...
He's/she's...	*Él/ella está...*	Ehl/EH-yah ehs-TAH...
• lying there.	• *ahí en el suelo.*	• ah-EE ehn ehl SWEH-loh.
• bleeding.	• *sangrando.*	• sahn-GRAHN-doh.
• not moving.	• *inmóvil.*	• een-MOH-veel.
• hurt.	• *herido/a.*	• eh-REE-doh/dah.
• dead.	• *muerto/a.*	• MWEHR-toh/tah.

DISPATCHER	*OPERADORA DE EMERGENCIA*	
Where are you calling from?	*¿Desde dónde llama?*	¿DEHS-deh DOHN-deh YAH-mah?
Confirm your...	*Confirme su...*	Kohn-FEER-meh soo...
• address.	• *dirección.*	• dee-rehk-SYOHN.
• name.	• *nombre.*	• NOHM-breh.
• phone number.	• *número de teléfono.*	• NOO-meh-roh deh teh-LEH-foh-noh.

WITNESS	*TESTIGO*	
I'm calling from...	*Llamo desde...*	Yah-MOH DEHS-deh...
• a phone booth.	• *una cabina telefónica.*	• OO-nah kah-BEE-nah teh-leh-FOH-nee-kah.
• my house.	• *mi casa.*	• mee KAH-sah.
• my neighbor's house.	• *la casa de mi vecino.*	• lah KAH-sah deh mee veh-SEE-noh.
• my car phone.	• *el teléfono en mi carro.*	• ehl teh-LEH-foh-noh ehn mee KAH-rroh.
My name is ____.	*Me llamo ____.*	Meh YAH-moh ____.

142

| I live at ___. | Vivo en ___. | VEE-voh ehn ___. |
| My phone number is ___. | Mi número de teléfono es ___. | Mee NOO-meh-roh deh teh-LEH-foh-noh ehs ___. |

DISPATCHER

OPERADORA DE EMERGENCIA

Where did this happen?	¿Dónde ocurrió esto?	¿DOHN-deh oh-koo-RYOH EHS-toh?
Are there any weapons involved?	¿Hay armas implicadas?	¿Ahy AHR-mahs eem-plee-KAH-dahs?
Is anyone else hurt?	¿Hay alguien más herido?	¿Ay AHL-gyehn mahs eh-REE-doh?

WITNESS

TESTIGO

It happened...	Ocurrió...	Oh-koo-RYOH...
• across the street.	• al otro lado de la calle.	• ahl oh-troh LAH doh lah KAH-yeh.
• in the park.	• en el parque.	• ehn ehl PAHR-keh.
• next door.	• en la casa de al lado.	• ehn lah KAH-sah deh ahl LAH-doh.
• in the alley.	• en el callejón.	• ehn ehl kah-yeh-HOHN.
Nobody else is hurt.	No hay más heridos.	Noh ahy mahs eh-REE-dohs.
Two people are hurt.	Hay dos personas heridas.	Ahy dohs per-SOH-nahs eh-REE-dahs.
There was/were... involved.	Había... involucrado/a/os/as.	Ah-BEE-ah...een-voh-loo-KRAH-doh/dah/dohs/dahs.
• guns	• pistolas	• pees-TOH-lahs
• a broken bottle	• una botella rota	• OO-nah boh-TEH-yah ROH-tah
• a baseball bat	• un palo de béisbol	• oon PAH-loh deh BEHS-bohl
• a knife	• un cuchillo	• oon koo-CHEE-yoh
I didn't see any weapons.	No vi armas.	Noh vee AHR-mahs.

DISPATCHER	OPERADORA DE EMERGENCIA	
An ambulance is on the way.	*Ya viene una ambulancia.*	Yah VYEH-neh OO-nah ahm-boo-LAHN-syah.
The police are on their way.	*Ya viene la policía.*	Yah vee-EH-neh lah poh-lee-SEE-ah.

GRAMMAR NOTE ••••

THE PRETERITE The preterite is one of the three different past tenses in Spanish (the others are the perfect tense and the imperfect tense). It indicates that an action began and ended at a specific time in the past.

TO TAKE, TO WEAR *LLEVAR:*

I took	*llev- é*
you took (inf.)	*llev- aste*
you (form.)/he/she took	*llev- ó*
we took	*llev- amos*
you all took (inf.)	*llev- ásteis*
you all (form.)/they took	*llev- aron*

-er and *-ir* verbs have the same endings.

TO LIVE *VIVIR:*

I lived	*viv- í*
you lived (inf.)	*viv- iste*
you (form.)/he/she lived	*viv- ió*
we lived	*viv- imos*
you all lived (inf.)	*viv- isteis*
you all (form.)/they lived	*viv- ieron*

TO SEE *VER:*

I saw	*v- i*
you saw (inf.)	*v- iste*
you (form.)/he/she saw	*v- io*
we saw	*v- imos*
you all saw (inf.)	*v- isteis*
you all (form.)/they saw	*v- ieron*

B. AT THE SCENE: ESTABLISHING THE VICTIM'S IDENTITY

OFFICER	AGENTE	
I'm officer_____.	Soy el agente _____.	Soy ehl ah-HEHN-teh _____.
Do you know who...	¿Sabe quién/quiénes...	¿SAH-beh kyehn/KYEH-nehs...
• this person is?	• es esta persona?	• ehs EHS-tah pehr-SOH-nah?
• these people are?	• son estas personas?	• sohn EHS-tahs pehr-SOH-nahs?

WITNESS	TESTIGO	
Yes, I know him/her/them.	Sí, lo/la/los/las conozco.	See, loh/lah/lohs/lahs koh-NOHS-koh.
No, I don't know him/her/them.	No, no lo/la/los/las conozco.	Noh, noh loh/lah/lohs/koh-NOHS-koh.
That's...	Es...	Ehs...
• my neighbor.	• mi vecino.	• mee veh-SEE-noh.
• my brother.	• mi hermano.	• mee ehr-MAH-noh.
• a friend.	• un amigo.	• oon ah-MEE-goh.
She was the murderer's wife/girlfriend.	Era la mujer/amiga del asesino.	EH-rah lah moo-HEHR/ah-MEE-gah dehl ah-seh-SEE-noh.

OFFICER	AGENTE	
Do you know...	¿Sabe...	¿SAH-beh...
• his/her name?	• su nombre?	• soo NOHM-breh?
• how old he/she was?	• cuántos años tenía?	• KWAHN-tohs AH-nyohs teh-NEE-ah?
• what he/she was doing here?	• qué hacía aquí?	• keh ah-SEE-yah ah-KEE?
• who he/she was with?	• con quién estaba?	• kohn kyehn ehs-TAH-bah?
• where he/she lived?	• dónde vivía?	• DOHN-deh vee-VEE-ah?
• whether he/she worked?	• si trabajaba?	• see trah-bah-HAH-bah?

WITNESS	TESTIGO	
I don't know...	No sé...	Noh seh...
• his/her name.	• su nombre.	• soo NOHM-breh.
• whether he/she had a job.	• si tenía un trabajo.	• see teh-NEE-ah trah-BAH-hoh.
• where he/she worked.	• dónde trabajaba.	• DOHN-deh trah-bah-HAH-bah.
He/she was visiting...	Visitaba...	Vee-see-TAH-bah...
• his/her relatives.	• a sus parientes.	• ah soos pah-RYEHN-tehs.
• my neighbor.	• a mi vecino.	• ah mee veh-SEE-noh.
He/she lived _____.	Él/Ella vivía en _____.	Ehl/Eh-yah vee-VEE-ah ehn.
He/she worked at _____.	Él/Ella trabajaba en _____.	Ehl/EH-yah trah-bah-HAH-bah ehn _____.

OFFICER	AGENTE	
Do you know the victim's family?	¿Conoce a la familia de la víctima?	¿Koh-NOH-seh ah lah fah-MEE-lyah deh lah VEEK-tee-mah?
Where is the victim's family?	¿Dónde está la familia de la víctima?	¿DOHN-deh ehs-TAH lah fah-MEE-lyah deh lah VEEK-tee-mah?

WITNESS	TESTIGO	
I don't know his/her family.	No conozco a su familia.	Noh kohn-NOHS-koh ah soo fah-MEE-lyah.
I don't know...	No sé...	Noh seh...
• where his/her family lives.	• donde vive su familia.	• DOHN-deh VEE-veh soo fah-MEE-lyah.
• how to reach his/her/family.	• como contactar a su familia.	• KOH-moh kohn-tahk-TAHR ah soo fah-MEE-lyah.
He/she...	Él/ella...	Ehl/EH-yah...
• lived alone.	• vivía solo/a.	• vee-VEE-yah SOH-loh/lah.

• didn't have a family.	• *no tenía familia.*	• noh teh-NEE-ah fah-MEE-lyah.
His/her family lives...	*Su familia vive...*	Soo fah-MEE-lyah VEE-veh...
• on the other side of town.	• *al otro lado de la ciudad.*	• ahl OH-troh LAH-doh deh lah syoo-DAHD.
• out of town.	• *fuera de la ciudad.*	• FWEH-rah deh lah syoo-DAHD.
• in another state.	• *en otro estado.*	• ehn OH-troh ehs-TAH-doh.

C. ESTABLISHING THE CIRCUMSTANCES OF THE CRIME

OFFICER	AGENTE	
• When...	• *¿Cuándo...*	• ¿KWAHN-doh...
• Where...	• *¿Dónde...*	• ¿DOHN-deh...
...was the last time you saw him/her?	...*la última vez que lo/la vio?*	...lah OOL-tee-mah vehs keh loh/lah VEE-oh?
Do you know... he/she got killed?	*¿Sabe...fue asesinado/a?*	¿SAH-beh... fweh ah-sah-see-NAH-doh/dah?
• how	• *cómo*	• KOH-moh
• where	• *dónde*	• DOHN-deh
• when	• *cuándo*	• KWAHN-doh
• why	• *por qué*	• pohr KEH
WITNESS	TESTIGO	
The last time I saw him/her was...	*La última vez que lo/la vi fue...*	Lah OOL-tee-mah vehs keh loh/lah vee fweh...
• last night.	• *anoche.*	• ah-NOH-cheh.
• this morning.	• *esta mañana.*	• EHS-tah mah-NYAH-nah.
• a week ago.	• *la semana pasada.*	• lah seh-MAH-nah pah-SAH-dah.

He/she was...	Le...	Leh...
• punched in the head.	• pegaron en la cabeza.	• peh-GAH-roh ehn lah kah-BEH-sah.
• kicked.	• dieron patadas.	• DYEH-rohn pah-TAH-dahs.
• clubbed to death.	• apalearon.	• ah pah-leh-AH-rohn.
• shot.	• dispararon.	• dees-pah-rah-ROHN.
He/she was stabbed.	Lo/la apuñalaron.	Loh/lah ah-poo-nyahl-AH-rohn.
I don't know...he/she was killed.	No sé...lo/la asesinaron.	Noh seh...loh/lah ah-seh-see-NAH-rohn.
• how	• cómo	• KOH-moh
• when	• cuándo	• KWAHN-doh
• why	• por qué	• pohr KEH
OFFICER	**AGENTE**	
Where there any weapons involved?	¿Había armas implicadas?	¿Ah-BEE-ah AHR-mahs eem-plee-KAH-dahs?
Do you know where the weapon is?	¿Sabe dónde está el arma?	¿SAH-beh DOHN-deh ehs-TAH ehl AHR-mah?
Did he/she leave anything behind?	¿Él/ella dejó algo?	¿Ehl/EH-yah deh-HOH AHL-goh?
WITNESS	**TESTIGO**	
There was no weapon.	No había armas.	Noh ah-BEE-ah AHR-mahs.
I didn't see a weapon.	No vi un arma.	Noh vee oon AHR-mah.
He/she had a gun/knife.	Tenía una pistola/un cuchillo.	Teh-NEE-ah OO-nah pees-TOH-lah/un koo-CHEE-yoh.
They had baseball bats.	Ellos tenían palos de béisbol.	EH-yohs teh-NEE-ahn PAH-los deh BEHS-bohl.
They used their fists.	Usaron los puños.	Oo-SAH-rohn lohs POO-nyohs.

I think he/she/they dropped...	Creo que se le cayó/cayeron...	KREH-oh keh se leh kah-yoh/kah-YEH-rohn...
• a hat.	• un sombrero.	• oon sohm-BREH-roh.
• keys.	• las llaves.	• lahs YAH-vehs.
• a wallet.	• la cartera.	• lah kahr-TEH-rah.
• the gun.	• la pistola.	• lah pees-TOH-lah.
• the knife.	• el cuchillo.	• ehl koo-CHEE-yoh.

OFFICER	AGENTE	
How do you know what happened?	¿Cómo sabe lo que pasó?	¿KOH-moh SAH-beh loh keh pah-SOH?
What did you see?	¿Qué vio?	¿Keh vee-OH?
Where were you?	¿Dónde estaba?	¿DOHN-deh ehs-TAH-bah?

WITNESS	TESTIGO	
I was...	Estaba...	Ehs-TAH-bah...
• walking down the street.	• caminando por la calle.	• kah-mee-NAHN-doh pohr lah-KAH-yeh.
• watching TV.	• mirando la tele.	• mee-RAHN-doh lah TEH-leh.
• looking out of the window.	• mirando por la ventana.	• mee-RAHN-doh pohr lah vehn-TAH-nah.
• visiting my neighbor.	• visitando a mi vecino.	• vee-see-TAHN-doh ah mee veh-SEE-noh.
I heard shots.	Oí disparos.	Oh-EE dees-PAH-rohs.
I saw...	Vi...	Vee...
• a fight.	• una pelea.	• OO-nah peh-LEH-ah.
• a man with a gun/knife.	• un hombre con una pistola/un cuchillo.	• oon OHM-breh kohn OO-nah pees-TOH-lah/oohn koo-CHEE-yoh.
• a car speeding away.	• un carro acelerando.	• oon KAH-rroh ah-seh-leh-RAHN-doh.
• a few teenagers with sticks.	• unos adolescentes con palos.	• OO-nohs ah-doh-lehs-SEHN-tehs kohn PAH-lohs.

A man/woman was...	*Un hombre/una mujer estaba...*	Oon OHM-breh/unah muh-HER ehs-TAH-bah...
• kicking him/her.	• *dándole patadas.*	• DAHN-doh-leh pah-TAH-dahs.
• beating him/her up.	• *pegándole.*	• peh-GAHN-doh-leh.
• stabbing him/her.	• *apuñalándolo/la.*	• ah-poo-nyah-LAHN-doh-loh/lah.
• fighting with him/her.	• *peleando con él/ella.*	• peh-leh-AHN-doh kohn ehl/EH-yah.

GRAMMAR NOTE ••••

THE IMPERFECT OF *SER* (TO BE)

I was	era
you (inf.) were	eras
you (form.) were, he/she was	era
we were	éramos
you (inf.) all were	érais
you all (form.)/ they were	eran

D. ESTABLISHING SUSPECTS

OFFICER	AGENTE	
Do you know who did it?	*¿Sabe quién lo hizo?*	¿SAH-beh kyehn loh EE-soh?
Could you describe this person?	*¿Puede describir a esa persona?*	¿PWEH-deh dehs-kree-BEER ah EH-sah pehr-SOH-nah?
Can you describe them?	*¿Puede describirlos a ellos?*	¿PWEH-deh dehs-kree-BEER-lohs ah EH-yohs?
WITNESS	TESTIGO	
I don't know who did it.	*No sé quién lo hizo.*	Noh seh kyehn loh EE-soh.

I've never seen him/her/them before.	No lo/la/los/las he visto nunca.	Noh loh/lah/lohs/lahs eh VEES-toh NOON-kah.
He/she was...	Era...	EH-rah...
• an acquaintance.	• un conocido.	• oon koh-noh-SEE-doh.
• an associate.	• un compadre.	• oon kohm-PAH-dreh.
• an old friend.	• un viejo amigo.	• oon VYEH-hoh ah-MEE-goh.
• her husband/boyfriend.	• su marido/novio.	• soo mah-REE-doh/NOH-vyoh.
• his wife/girlfriend.	• su mujer/novia.	• soo moo-HEHR/NOH-vyah.
It happened so fast.	Ocurrió tan rápido.	Oh-koo-rree-OH tahn RAH-pee-doh.
It was dark.	Estaba oscuro.	Ehs-TAH-bah oh-SKOO-roh.
I couldn't see him/her/them clearly.	No podía verlo/la/los/las claramente.	Noh poh-DEE-ah VEHR-loh/lah/lohs/lahs klah-rah-MEHN-teh.
I can't describe him/her/them.	No puedo describirlo/la/los/las.	Noh PWEH-doh dehs-kree-BEER-loh/lah/lohs/lahs.
They were...	Eran...	EH-rahn...
• teenagers	• jóvenes.	• HOH-vehn-ehs.
• gang members.	• pandilleros.	• pahn-dee-YEH-rohs.
OFFICER	**AGENTE**	
How did he/she/they get away?	¿Cómo se fue él/ella/fueron ellos/as?	¿KOH-moh seh fweh ehl/EH-yah/FWEH-rohn EH-yohs/ahs?
WITNESS	**TESTIGO**	
He/she/they left...	Se fueron...	Seh FWEH-rohn...
• on foot.	• a pie.	• ah pyeh.
• by car.	• en carro.	• ehn KAH-rroh.
• running.	• corriendo.	• koh-RRYEHN-doh.
A car picked him/her/them up.	Un carro se lo/la/los/las llevó.	Oon KAH-rroh seh loh/lah/lohs/lahs yeh-VOH.

He/she/they drove away.	*Él/ella se fue/ellos/ellas se fueron manejando.*	Ehl/EH-yah seh fweh/ EH-yohs/EH-yahs seh FWEH-rohn mah-neh-HAHN-doh.
He/she is/they are still in the house.	*Él/ella está/ellos están en la casa todavía.*	Ehl/EH-yah ehs-TAH/ EH-yohs ehs-TAHN ehn lah KAH-sah toh-dah-VEE-ah.

OFFICER — **AGENTE**

Did you see what he/she was/they were driving?	*¿Vio que carro manejaba/manejaban?*	¿VEE-oh key KAH-rroh mah-neh-HAH-bah/ mah-neh-HAH-bahn?
Can you describe the vehicle?	*¿Puede describir el vehículo?*	¿PWEH-deh dehs-kree-BEER ehl veh-EE-koo-loh?

WITNESS — **TESTIGO**

I couldn't see anything.	*No podía ver nada.*	Noh poh-DEE-ah vehr NAH-dah.
He/she was/they were driving...	*Manejaba/ manejaban...*	Mah-neh-HAH-bah/ mah-neh-HAH-bahn...
• a pick-up truck.	• *una camioneta.*	• OO-nah kah-myoh-NEH-tah.
• a black Chevy.	• *un Chevy negro.*	• oon Chevy NEH-groh.
• a blue van.	• *una camioneta azul.*	• OO-nah kah-myoh-NEH-tah ah-SOOL.

OFFICER — **AGENTE**

Thank you very much for your help/ cooperation.	*Muchas gracias por su ayuda/ cooperación.*	MOO-chas GRAH-syahs pohr soo ah-YOO-dah/koh-oh-peh-rah-SYOHN.
Please call us if you...	*Por favor, llámenos si...*	Pohr fah-VOHR, YAH-meh-nohs see...
• can think of anything else.	• *piensa que hay algo más.*	• PYEHN-sah keh AH-ee AHL-goh mahs.
• remember anything else.	• *recuerda algo más.*	• reh-KWEHR-dah AHL-goh mahs.
• hear or see anything.	• *oye o ve algo.*	• OH-yeh oh veh AHL-go.

| Here is my business card. | *Aquí está mi tarjeta.* | Ah-KEE ehs-TAH mee tahr-HEH-tah. |
| Here is the number where you can call. | *Aquí está el número donde puede llamar.* | Ah-KEE ehs-TAH ehl NOO-meh-roh DOHN-deh PWEH-deh yah-MAHR. |

VOCABULARY ••••

WEAPONS

club	*macana, garrote*	mah-KAH-nah, gah-RROH-teh
billy club	*porra*	POH-rrah
black jack	*cachiporra*	kah-chee-POH-rrah
blade	*hoja, fila*	OH-hah, FEE-lah
dagger	*puñal*	poo-NYAHL
knife	*cuchillo, fila*	koo-CHEE-oh, FEE-lah
hunting knife	*cuchillo de caza*	koo-CHEE-oh deh KAH-sah
butcher knife	*cuchillo de carnicero*	koo-CHEE-yoh deh kahr-nee-SEH-roh
pocket knife	*navaja*	nah-VAH-hah
stick	*palo*	PAH-loh
night stick	*porra*	POH-rrah
gun	*pistola, cuete*	pees-TOH-lah, KWEH-teh
hammer	*martillo*	mahr-TEE-yoh
shotgun	*escopeta*	ehs-koh-PEH-tah
rifle	*rifle*	REE-fleh
mase	*gas lacrimógeno*	gahs lah-kree-MOH-heh-noh

2. Child Abuse Investigations

GRAMMAR NOTE ••••

THE IMPERFECT TENSE This is one of the three past tenses in Spanish (the others are the preterite and the perfect tenses). It emphasizes the duration or repetition of an event in the past, rather than its completion, beginning, or ending. It's also used to describe the background or scenario of an action that took place at a specific time in the past. There are two sets of endings for the imperfect tense. One for -*ar* verbs, and another for -*er* and -*ir* verbs.

TO WORK *TRABAJAR:*

trabaj- aba
trabaj- abas
trabaj- aba
trabaj- ábamos
trabaj- abais
trabaj- aban

TO HAVE *TENER:*

ten- ía
ten- ías
ten- ía
ten- íamos
ten- íais
ten- ían

TO LIVE *VIVIR:*

viv- ía
viv- ías
viv- ía
viv- íamos
viv- íais
viv- ían

A. TALKING TO THE REPORTING PARTY

REPORTING PARTY	INFORMANTE	
I suspect this child has been...	*Sospecho que este niño ha sido...*	Sohs-PEH-cho keh EHS-teh NEE-nyoh ah SEE-doh...
• molested.	• *abusado.*	• ah-boo-SAH-doh.
• physically abused.	• *físicamente maltratado.*	• FEE-see-kah-mehn-teh mahl-trah-TAH-doh.
• beaten.	• *azotado.*	• ah-soh-TAH-doh.

OFFICER	AGENTE	
What's your name?	*¿Cómo se llama?*	¿KOH-moh seh YAH-mah?
What's...	*¿Cuál es...*	¿KWAL ehs...
• the name of the child?	• *el nombre del niño?*	• ehl NOHM-breh dehl NEE-nyoh?
• your address and phone number?	• *su dirección y número de teléfono?*	• soo dee-REHK-SYOHN ee NOO-meh-roh deh teh-LEH-foh-noh?
• your relationship to the child?	• *su relación con el niño?*	• soo reh-lah-SYOHN kohn ehl NEE-nyoh?
How old is the child?	*¿Cuantos años tiene el niño?*	¿KWAHN-tohs AH-nyohs TYEHN-eh ehl NEE-nyoh?
How old is the suspect?	*¿Cuantos años tiene el sospechoso?*	¿KWAHN-tohs AH-nyohs TYEHN-eh ehl sohs-peh-CHOH-soh?

REPORTING PARTY	INFORMANTE	
I'm...	*Soy...*	Soy...
• his/her therapist.	• *su psicólogo/a.*	• soo see-KOH-loh-goh/gah.
• his/her teacher.	• *su maestro/a.*	• soo mah-EHS-troh/trah,
• a friend of the family.	• *un amigo/a de la familia.*	• oon ah-MEE-goh/gah deh lah fah-MEE-lyah.

• his/her mother/father.	• *su madre/padre.*	• soo MAH-dreh/PAH-dreh.
• a relative.	• *un pariente.*	• oon pah-RYEHN-teh.
• a neighbor.	• *un/una vecino/a.*	• oon/OO-nah veh-SEE-noh/ah.

OFFICER

AGENTE

How did you find out about this?	¿*Cómo se enteró de esto?*	¿KOH-moh seh ehn-teh-ROH deh EHS-toh?
What makes you suspect...	¿*Qué le hace sospechar...*	¿Keh leh AH-seh soh-speh-CHAR...
• physical abuse?	• *abuso físico?*	• ah-BOO-soh FEE-see-koh?
• molestation?	• *abuso sexual?*	• ah-BOO-soh sehk-SWAHL?

REPORTING PARTY

INFORMANTE

I have observed the abuse/injury.	*He observado el abuso.*	Eh ohb-sehr-VAH-doh ehl ah-BOO-soh.
• A friend of the child...	• *Un amigo/a del niño/de la niña...*	• Oon ah-MIHGOH/ah dehl NEE-nyoh/deh lah NEE-nyah...
• The child...	• *El niño...*	• Ehl NEE-nyoh...
...told me about it.	...*me lo dijo.*	...meh loh DEE-hoh.
I saw bruises on the child's...	*He visto moretones en...del niño.*	Eh VEES-toh moh-reh-TOH-nehs ehn...dehl NEE-nyoh.
• arm.	• *el brazo*	• ehl BRAH-soh
• leg.	• *la pierna*	• lah PYEHR-nal
• neck.	• *el cuello*	• ehl KWEH-yoh
• head.	• *la cabeza*	• lah kah-BEH-sah
• face.	• *la cara*	• lah KAH-rah

OFFICER

AGENTE

How often did you see bruises?	¿*Cuántas veces vio usted moretones?*	¿KWAHN-tahs VEH-sehs VEE-oh oo-STEHD moh-reh-TOH-nehs?

Did you notice any particular behavior or demeanor on the child?	¿Ha notado usted algún comportamiento o actitud diferente en el niño?	¿Ah noh-TAH-doh oo-STEHD ahl-GOON kohm-pohr-tah-MYEHN-toh oh ahk-tee-TOOD dee-feh-REHN-teh ehn ehl NEE-nyoh?

REPORTING PARTY — *INFORMANTE*

I saw bruises...	Vi moretones...	Vee moh-reh-TOH-nehs...
• every day.	• todos los días.	• TOH-dohs lohs DEE-ahs.
• once.	• una vez.	• OO-nah vehs.
• once a week.	• una vez por semana.	• OO-nah vehs pohr seh-MAH-nah.
The child was...	El niño/la niña estaba...	Ehl NEE-nyoh/lah NEE-nyah ehs-TAH-bah...
• crying.	• llorando/a.	• yoh-RAHN-doh/ah.
• hysterical.	• histérico/a.	• ees-TEH-ree-koh/ah.
• excited.	• nervioso/a.	• nehr-vee-OH-soh/ah.
• quiet.	• callado/a.	• kah-YAH-doh/ah.
• scared.	• asustado/a.	• ah-soos-TAH-doh/ah.
The child seemed shy.	El niño/la niña parecía tímido/a.	Ehl NEE-nyoh/lah NEE-nyah pah-reh-SEE-ah TEE-mee-doh/ah.

OFFICER — *AGENTE*

What did the child tell you?	¿Qué le dijo el niño?	¿Keh leh DEE-hoh ehl NEE-nyoh?
Is there a relationship between the child and the suspect?	¿Hay alguna relación entre el niño y el sospechoso?	¿Aye ahl-GOO-nah reh-lah-SYOHN EHN-treh ehl NEE-nyoh ee ehl sohs-peh-CHOH-soh?

REPORTING PARTY — *INFORMANTE*

The child told me that...	El niño me dijo que...	Ehl NEE-nyoh meh DEE-hoh keh...

- somebody physically/ sexually assaulted him/her.
- *alguien le asaltó físicamente/ sexualmente.*
- AHL-gyehn leh ah ah-sahl-TOH FEE-see-kah-MEHN-teh/sehk-swahl-MEHN-teh.

- somebody touched him/her where they shouldn't have.
- *alguien le tocó donde no debía.*
- ahl-GYEHN leh toh-KOH DOHN-deh noh deh-BEE-ah.

- he/she fell down.
- *se cayó.*
- seh kah-YOH.

- nothing happened.
- *nada ocurrió.*
- NAH-dah oh-koo-RRYOH.

The suspect is the child's...

El sospechoso es... del niño.

Ehl sohs-peh-CHOH-soh...dehl NEE-nyoh.

- father.
- *el padre*
- ehl PAH-dreh

- brother.
- *el hermano*
- ehl hehr-MAH-noh

- teacher.
- *el maestro*
- ehl mah-EHS-troh

- priest.
- *el sacerdote*
- ehl sah-sehr-DOH-teh

OFFICER

AGENTE

Has this happened before?

¿Ha ocurrido antes?

¿Ah oh-koo-RREE-doh AHN-tehs?

Have you suspected something before?

¿Ha sospechado algo antes?

¿Ah sohs-peh-CHAH-doh AHL-goh AHN-tehs?

Has anyone mentioned this to you before?

¿Le han mencionado esto a usted antes?

¿Leh ahn mehn-syoh-NAH-doh EHS-toh ah oo-STEHD AHN-tehs?

REPORTING PARTY

INFORMANTE

Yes, it has happened before.

Sí, ha ocurrido antes.

See, ah oh-koo-RREE-doh AHN-tehs.

No. It has never happened before.

No, no ha ocurrido antes.

Noh, noh ah oh-koo-RREE-doh AHN-tehs.

B. TALKING TO THE CHILD

C**ULTURE NOTE** ••••

THE FAMILIAR *TÚ* When talking to a child or a younger teenager, be sure to use the familiar form of address *tú* and the second person singular verb form.

OFFICER	AGENTE	
Do you know why I'm talking to you?	¿Sabes por qué estoy hablando contigo?	¿SAH-behs pohr KEH ehs-TOY ah-BLAHN-doh kohn-TEE-goh?
Don't be afraid.	No tengas miedo.	Noh TEHN-gahs MYEH-doh.
I want to help you.	Quiero ayudarte.	KYEH-roh ah-yoo-DAHR-teh.

CHILD	NIÑO	
Yes, I do.	Sí. Lo sé.	See. Loh seh.
It's because my... touched me.	Es porque mi...me tocó dónde no debía.	Ehs pohr-KEH mee... meh toh-KOH DOHN-deh noh deh-BEE-ah.
• mom	• mamá	• mah-MAH
• dad	• papá	• pah-PAH
• sister	• hermana	• ehr-MAH-nah
• brother	• hermano	• ehr-MAH-noh
• friend	• amigo	• ah-MEE-goh
• uncle	• tío	• TEE-oh
• aunt	• tía	• TEE-ah
• teacher	• maestro	• mah-EHS-troh
• priest	• sacerdote	• sah-sehr-DOH-teh

OFFICER	AGENTE	
I want to help you.	*Quiero ayudarte.*	KYEH-roh ah-yoo-DAHR-teh.
Do you want to talk to someone who speaks Spanish?	*¿Quieres hablar con alguien que habla español?*	¿KYEH-rehs ah-BLAHR kohn AHL-gyehn keh AH-blah ehs-pah-NYOHL?
It's important you tell me the truth.	*Es importante que me digas la verdad.*	Ehs eem-pohr-TAHN-teh keh meh DEE-gahs lah vehr-DAHD.
Do you know the difference between the truth and a lie?	*¿Sabes cuál es la diferencia entre la verdad y la mentira?*	¿SAH-behs kwahl ehs lah dee-feh-REHN-see-ah EHN-treh lah vehr-DAHD ee lah mehn-TEE-rah?
Promise me you'll tell the truth.	*Prométeme que me vas a decir la verdad.*	Proh-MEH-teh-meh keh meh vahs ah deh-SEER lah vehr-DAHD.
Is there someone you want to be here while I talk to you?	*¿Hay alguien que quieres que esté aquí mientras hablo contigo?*	¿Ay AHL-gyehn keh KYEH-rehs keh ehs-TEH ah-KEE MYEHN-trahs AH-bloh kohn-TEE-goh?
Someone told me...	*Alguien me contó...*	AHL-gyehn meh kohn-TOH...
• what happened to you.	• *lo que te pasó.*	• loh keh teh pah-SOH.
• about that picture you drew.	• *del dibujo que hiciste.*	• dehl dee-BOO-hoh keh ee-SEES-teh.
• about that mark on your face.	• *de esa herida en la cara.*	• deh EH-sah eh-REE-dah ehn lah KAH-rah.
Can you tell me about that?	*¿Puedes hablarme de eso?*	¿PWEH-dehs ah-BLAHR-meh deh EH-soh?

C. PHYSICAL ABUSE

CHILD	NIÑO	
• My dad...	• *Mi papá...*	• Mee pah-PAH...

- My mom's boyfriend...
- My mom...
- A friend...
...hit me.

I fell.

OFFICER

What did he/she hit you with?

CHILD

He/she hit me with...
- his/her hand.
- his/her belt.
- a paddle.

He/she punched me.

AGENT

Where did this happen?

CHILD

It happened...
- in the car.
- in the house.
- in the bedroom.
- in the kitchen.
- at home.

OFFICER

Was it...outside?

- dark
- light

When did it happen?

- *El amigo de mi mamá...*
- *Mi mamá...*
- *Un amigo...*
...*me pegó.*

Me caí.

AGENTE

¿Con qué te pegó?

NIÑO

Me pegó con...
- *la mano.*
- *el cinturón.*
- *una paleta.*

Me dio un puñetazo.

AGENTE

¿Dónde ocurrió eso?

NIÑO

Ocurrió...
- *en el carro.*
- *en la casa.*
- *en la alcoba.*
- *en la cocina.*
- *en casa.*

AGENTE

¿Era...afuera?

- *de noche*
- *de día*

¿Cuándo ocurrió eso?

- Ehl ah-MEE-goh deh mee mah-MAH...
- Mee mah-MAH...
- Oon ah-MEE-goh...
...meh peh-GOH.

Meh kah-EE.

¿Kohn keh teh peh-GOH?

Meh peh-GOH kohn...
- lah MAH-noh.
- ehl seen-too-ROHN.
- OO-nah pah-LEH-tah.

Meh dee-OH oon poo-nye-TAH-soh.

¿DOHN-deh oh-koo-rree-OH EH-soh?

Oh-koo-rree-OH...
- ehn ehl KAH-rroh.
- ehn lah KAH-sah.
- ehn lah ahl-KOH-bah.
- ehn lah koh-SEE-nah.
- ehn KAH-sah.

¿EH-rah...ah-FWEH-rah?

- deh NOH-cheh
- deh DEE-ah

¿KWAHN-doh oh-koo-rree-OH EH-soh?

Do you know why this happened?	¿Por qué ha ocurrido esto?	¿Pohr KEH ah oh-koo-RREE-doh EHS-toh?
CHILD	**NIÑO**	
Because...	Porque...	POHR-keh...
• I was bad.	• me portaba mal.	• meh pohr-TAH-bah mahl.
• I was fighting with my sister.	• peleaba con mi hermana.	• peh-leh-AH-bah kohn mee ehr-MAH-nah.
• Dad was drunk.	• mi papá estaba borracho.	• mih pah-PAH ehs-TAH-bah boh-RRAH-choh.
• Mom and Dad were fighting.	• mi mamá y mi papá se peleaban.	• mee mah-MAH ee mee pah-PAH seh-peh leh-AH-bahn.
OFFICER	**AGENTE**	
Has this happened before?	¿Ha ocurrido esto antes?	¿Ah oh-koo-RREE-doh EHS-toh AHN-tehs?
When?	¿Cuándo?	¿KWAHN-doh?
Where?	¿Dónde?	¿DOHN-deh?
CHILD	**NIÑO**	
Never.	Nunca.	NOON-kah.
Yes.	Sí.	See.
Often.	A menudo.	Ah meh-NOO-doh.
At home/school/the gym.	En casa/en la escuela/ en el gimnasio.	Ehn KAH-sah/ehn lah ehs-koo-EH-lah/ehn ehl heem-NAH-syoh.

D. SEXUAL ABUSE

OFFICER	**AGENTE**	
What did he/she do?	¿Qué hizo él/ella?	¿Keh EE-soh ehl/EH-yah?
CHILD	**NIÑO**	
He/she touched me.	Me tocó donde no debía.	Meh toh-KOH DOHN-deh noh deh-BEE-ah.

OFFICER	AGENTE	
Can you tell me/show me where he/she touched you?	¿Me puedes decir dónde te tocó?	¿Meh PWE-dehs dehseer DOHN-deh teh toh-KOH?
Where did he/she touch you?	¿Dónde te tocó?	¿DOHN-deh teh toh-KOH?

CHILD	NIÑO	
He/she touched...	Me tocó...	Meh toh-KOH...
• my vagina.	• la vagina.	• lah vah-HEE-nah.
• my penis.	• el pene.	• ehl PEH-neh.
• my breasts.	• los pechos.	• lohs PEH-chohs.
• here.	• aquí.	• ah-KEE.

OFFICER	AGENTE	
Were your clothes...	¿Estabas...	¿Ehs-TAH-bahs...
• on?	• vestido?	• vehs-TEE-doh?
• off?	• desnudo?	• dehs-NOO-doh?
Did he/she touch you...	¿Te tocó...	¿Teh toh-KOH...
• over your clothes?	• por encima de la ropa?	• pohr ehn-SEE-mah deh lah ROH-pah?
• under your clothes?	• por debajo de la ropa?	• pohr deh-BAH-hoh deh lah ROH-pah?
What did he/she touch you with?	¿Con qué te tocó?	• ¿Kohn keh teh toh-KOH?

CHILD	NIÑO	
He touched me with...	Me tocó con...	Meh toh-KOH kohn...
• his/her hand.	• la mano.	• lah MAH-noh.
• his/her finger.	• el dedo.	• ehl DEH-doh.
• his/her tongue.	• la lengua.	• lah LEHN-gwa.
• his penis.	• el pene.	• ehl PEH-neh.

OFFICER	AGENTE	
Have you told anybody about this?	¿Se lo has dicho a alguien?	¿Seh loh ahs DEE-choh ah AHL-gyehn?
Who?	¿A quién?	¿Ah kyehn?

CHILD	NIÑO	
I told...	Se lo dije a...	Seh loh DEE-heh ah...
• my teacher.	• mi maestro/a.	• mee mah-EHS-troh/trah.
• my brother.	• mi hermano.	• mee ehr-MAH-noh.
• my sister.	• mi hermana.	• mee ehr-MAH-nah.
• my counselor.	• mi psicólogo/a.	• mee psee-KOH-loh-goh/ah.
• my friend.	• mi amigo/a.	• mee ah-MEE-goh/ah.
• the police.	• la policía.	• lah poh-lee-SEE-ah.

AGENT	AGENTE	
When did you tell him/her?	¿Cuándo se lo dijiste?	¿KWAHN-doh seh loh dee-HEES-teh?

CHILD	NIÑO	
I told him/her...	Se lo dije...	Seh loh DEE-heh...
• the next day.	• al día siguiente.	• ahl DEE-ah see-GYEHN-teh.
• one hour later.	• una hora más tarde.	• OO-nah OH-rah mahs TAHR-deh.
• in the morning.	• en la mañana.	• ehn lah mah-NYA-nah.
• last night.	• anoche.	• ah-NOH-cheh.

OFFICER	AGENTE	
Did the person who did this threaten you?	¿Te amenazó esta persona?	¿Teh ah-meh-nah-SOH EHS-tah pehr-SOH-nah?
How?	¿Cómo?	¿KOH-moh?

CHILD	NIÑO	
He/she said...	Me dijo que...	Meh DEE-hoh keh...
• he/she would kill me.	• me mataría.	• meh mah-tah-REE-ah.
• he/she would kill my mom.	• mataría a mi madre.	• mah tah-REE-ah ah mee MAH-dreh.

- Social Services would hurt me.

- *los Servicios Sociales me harían daño.*

- lohs Sehr-VEE-syohs Soh-SYAH-lehs meh ah-REE-ahn DAH-nyoh.

- it was our secret.

- *era nuestro secreto.*

- EH-rah NWEHS-troh seh-KREH-toh.

- no one would believe me.

- *nadie me creería.*

- NAH-dyeh meh creh-eh-REE-ah.

OFFICER

¿Has this happened to anybody else you know?

AGENTE

¿Le ha pasado esto a alguna otra persona que conoces?

¿Leh ah pah-SAH-doh EHS-toh ah ahl-GOO-nah OH-trah pehr-SOH-nah keh koh-NOH-sehs?

CHILD

To my...

NIÑO

A mi...

Ah mee...

- sister.

- *hermana.*

- ehr-MAH-nah.

- brother.

- *hermano.*

- ehr-MAH-noh.

- friend.

- *amigo/a.*

- ah-MEE-goh/gah.

OFFICER

We'll take care of you.

AGENTE

Te cuidaremos.

Teh kwee-dah-REH-mohs.

You did the right thing to tell.

Tenías razón al contar lo que pasó.

Teh-NEE-ahs rrah-SOHN ahl kohn-TAHR loh keh pah-SOH.

Everything will be fine.

Todo va a salir bien.

TOH-doh vah ah sa-LEEHR byehn.

We'll make sure he/she won't hurt you again.

No dejaremos que esto te pase otra vez.

Noh deh-hah-REH-mohs keh EHS-toh teh PAH-seh OH-trah vehs.

A doctor is going to see you.

Un médico te va a examinar.

Oon MEH-dee-koh teh vah ah ehk-sah-mee-NAHR.

I need to see...

Necesito ver...

Neh-seh-SEE-toh vehr...

- if you are hurt.

- *si estás herido/a.*

- see ehs-TAHS eh-REE-doh/dah.

• your bruises.	• *tus heridas.*	• toos eh-REE-dahs.
May I touch you?	*¿Puedo tocarte?*	¿PWEH-doh toh-KAHR-teh?
Can somebody stay in the room while I check your injuries?	*¿Puede alguien estar en el cuarto mientras veo tus heridas?*	¿PWEH-deh AHL-gyehn ehs-TAHR ehn ehl KWAHR-toh MYEHN-trahs VEH-oh toos eh-REE-dahs?

GRAMMAR NOTE ••••

DOUBLE OBJECT PRONOUNS   When the direct object pronouns *lo, la, los, las* (him, her, you, it, them) appear in the sentence with the indirect object pronoun *le, les* (to him, to her, to them, to you), *le* or *les* become *se:*

I told it to my mother (lit.: To her it I told my mother).	*Se lo dije a mi madre.*

E. TALKING TO THE SUSPECT

OFFICER	*AGENTE*	
What's your...	*¿Cuál es...*	¿KWAHL ehs...
• name?	• *su nombre?*	• soo NOHM-breh?
• address?	• *su dirección?*	• soo dee-rehk-SYOHN?
• phone number?	• *su número de teléfono?*	• soo NOO-meh-roh deh teh-LEH-foh-noh
• work address?	• *la dirección de su trabajo?*	• lah dee-rehk-SYOHN deh soo trah-BAH-hoh?

• work number?	• el número de teléfono en su trabajo?	• ehl NOO-meh-roh deh teh-LEH-foh-noh ehn soo trah-BAH-hoh?
I'm going to read you your rights.	Voy a leerle sus derechos.	Voy ah leh-EHR-leh soos deh-REH-chohs.
You are here because I'm investigating an allegation of child abuse/molestation.	Está aquí porque estoy investigando una denuncia de abuso físico/sexual a un niño.	Ehs-TAH ah-KEE POHR-keh ehs-TOY een-vehs-tee-GAHN-doh OO-nah deh-NOON-sy-ah deh ah-BOO-soh FEE-see-koh/sehk-soo-AHL ah oon NEE-nyoh.
Someone reported that you...	Alguien dijo que usted...	AHL-gyehn DEE-hoh keh oos-TEHD...
• touched this child inappropriately.	• tocó a este/a niño/a donde no debía.	• toh-KOH ah EHS-teh/tah NEE-nyoh/nyah DOHN-deh noh deh-BEE-ah.
• disciplined him/her too hard.	• lo/la disciplinó muy duro.	• loh/lah dees-see-plee-NOH mwee DOO-roh.
• hit him/her too hard.	• lo/la pegó muy fuerte.	• loh/lah peh-GOH mwee FWEHR-teh.
SUSPECT	SOSPECHOSO	
No, I didn't do that.	No, no lo hice.	Noh, noh loh EE-seh.
He's/she's lying.	Él/ella miente.	Ehl/EH-yah MYEHN-teh.
What's wrong with my kid?	¿Qué le pasa a ese niño?	¿Keh leh PAH-sah ah EH-seh NEE-nyoh?
I'll kill the bastard who did this.	Mataré al hijo de puta que hizo esto.	Mah-tah-REH ahl EE-hoh deh POO-tah keh EE-soh EHS-toh.
He's/she's confused.	Él/ella está confundido/a.	Ehl/EH-yah ehs-TAH kohn-foo-DEE-doh/dah.
I accidentally touched him/her when I was...	Sin querer lo/la toqué cuando...	Seen keh-REHR loh/lah toh-KEH KWAHN-doh...

• bathing him/her.	• lo/la bañaba.	• loh/lah bah-NYAH-bah.
• wrestling with him/her.	• jugaba con él/ella.	• hoo-GAH-bah kohn ehl/EH-yah.
• giving him/her a backrub.	• le masajeaba la espalda a él/ella.	• leh mah-sah-heh-AH-bah lah ehs-PAHL-dah ah ehl/EH-yah.
He/she spilled something and made me angry.	Él/ella derramó algo y me hizo enojar.	Ehl/EH-yah deh-rrah-MOH AHL-goh ee meh EEH-soh eh-noh-HAHR.
He/she fell.	Se cayó.	Seh kah-YOH.

OFFICER / **AGENTE**

What happened specifically?	¿Qué pasó específicamente?	¿Keh pah-SOH ehs-peh-see-fee-kah-MEHN-teh?

SUSPECT / **SOSPECHOSO**

I touched...	Le toqué...	Leh toh-KEH...
• her breasts.	• los pechos.	• lohs PEH-chohs.
• his/her genitals.	• los genitales.	• lohs heh-nee-TAH-lehs.
• his penis.	• el pene.	• ehl PEH-neh.
• his/her butt.	• las nalgas.	• lahs NAHL-gahs.
...over his/her clothes with my...	...sobre la ropa con mi...	...SOH-breh lah ROH-pah kohn mee...
• hand.	• mano.	• MAH-noh.
• finger.	• dedo.	• DEH-doh.
• mouth.	• boca.	• BOH-cah.
• tongue.	• lengua.	• LEHN-gwah.
• leg.	• pierna.	• PYEHR-nah.

OFFICER / **AGENTE**

Are you ever alone with the child?	¿Está sólo con este/a niño/a alguna vez?	¿Ehs-TAH SOH-loh kohn EHS-teh/tah NEE-nyoh/nah ahl-GOO-nah vehs?

SUSPECT	SOSPECHOSO	
Rarely.	*Raramente.*	Rah-rah-MEHN-teh.
Sometimes.	*A veces.*	Ah VEH-sehs.
Every day.	*Cada día.*	KAH-dah DEE-ah.
Never.	*Nunca.*	NOON-kah.

OFFICER	AGENTE	
Have you ever been accused of something like this before?	*¿Lo han acusado a usted de esto alguna vez?*	¿Loh ahn ah-koo-SAH-doh deh EHS-toh ahl-GOO-nah vehs?
How does this child know about sex?	*¿Cómo sabe este niño acerca de cosas sexuales?*	¿KOH-mo SAH-beh EHS-teh nee-nyoh ah-SEHR-kah deh KOH-sahs sehk-soo-AH-lehs?

SUSPECT	SOSPECHOSO	
From pornographic movies.	*Por ver películas pornográficas.*	Pohr vehr peh-LEE-koo-lahs pohr-noh-GRAH-fee-kahs.
From seeing me and my wife.	*Por vernos a mí y a mi mujer.*	Pohr VEHR-nohs ah mee ee ah mee moo-HEHR.
From friends.	*De sus amigos.*	Deh soos ah-MEE-gohs.
From school.	*De la escuela.*	Deh lah ehs-KWEH-lah.
I talked to him/her about it.	*Le hablé a él/ella de esto.*	Leh ah-BLEH ah ehl/EH-yah deh EHS-toh.

OFFICER	AGENTE	
What should happen to someone who did something like this?	*¿Qué consecuencias debe haber para alguien que ha hecho algo así?*	¿Keh kohn-seh-KWHEN-syahs DEH-beh ah-BEHR PAH-rah AHL-gyehn keh ah EH-choh AHL-goh ah-SEE?

SUSPECT	SOSPECHOSO	
Counseling.	*Consejo.*	Kohn-SEH-hoh.
Therapy.	*Terapia.*	Teh-RAH-pyah.
Jail.	*Cárcel.*	KAHR-sehl.
They should kill the _____.	*Deberían matar al _____.*	Deh-beh-RYAHN mah-TAHR ahl _____.

OFFICER	AGENTE	
¿Why did you molest this child?	¿Por qué molestó a este/a niño/a?	¿Pohr keh moh-lehs-TOH ah EHS-teh/tah NEE-nyoh/nyah?

SUSPECT	SOSPECHOSO	
I didn't.	No lo hice.	Noh loh EE-seh.
I was drunk.	Yo estaba borracho.	Yoh ehs-TAH-bah boh-RRAH-choh.
It was a mistake.	Fue un error.	Fweh oon eh-RROHR.
I thought she was my wife.	Pensé que era mi mujer.	Pehn-SEH keh EH-rah mee moo-HEHR.

OFFICER	AGENTE	
Do you know this is a crime?	¿Sabe que esto es un crimen?	¿SAH-beh keh EHS-toh ehs oon KREE-mehn?
Is there anything about this you would like me to know?	¿Hay algo que quiere que yo sepa?	¿Ay AHL-goh keh KYEH-reh keh yoh SEH-pah?

SUSPECT	SOSPECHOSO	
I'd like you to know I didn't hurt him/her.	Quiero que sepa que no le hice daño a él/ella.	KYEH-roh keh SEH-pah keh noh leh EE-seh DAH-nyoh ah ehl/EH-yah.
He/she started it.	Él/ella lo empezó.	Ehl/EH-yah/ehl loh ehm-peh-SOH.
No, I didn't know this is a crime.	No, no sabía que esto era un crimen.	Noh, noh sah-BEE-ah keh EHS-toh EH-rah oon KREE-mehn.

OFFICER	AGENTE	
You are under arrest for...	Usted está arrestado...	Oos-TEHD ehs-TAH ah-rrhes-TAH-doh...
• child abuse.	• por abuso físico de un menor.	• pohr ah-BOO-soh FEE-see-koh deh oon meh-NOHR.
• child molestation.	• por abuso sexual de un menor.	• pohr ah-BOO-soh sehk-SWAHL deh oon meh-NOHR.

GRAMMAR NOTE ••••

IRREGULAR PRETERITES   The most common irregular verbs in the preterite are listed below. While they have irregular stems, their endings follow the *-ir/-er* pattern.

to want	*querer*	I wanted	*quise*
to know	*saber*	I found out	*supe*
to do, to make	*hacer*	I did, I made	*hice*
to say	*decir*	I said	*dije*
to bring	*traer*	I brought	*traje*
to come	*venir*	I came	*vine*
to be able to	*poder*	I was able to	*pude*
to put	*poner*	I put	*puse*
to have	*tener*	I had	*tuve*
to be	*estar*	I was	*estuve*
to go	*ir*	I went	*fui*
to be	*ser*	I was	*fui*
to walk	*andar*	I walked	*anduve*
to give	*dar*	I gave	*di*

3. Sexual Assault

A. OBTAINING BASIC INFORMATION ABOUT THE CRIME

OFFICER	AGENTE	
I'm agent ____.	*Soy el agente* ____.	Soy ehl ah-HEHN-teh ____.
Are you okay?	*¿Está usted bien?*	¿Ehs-TAH oos-TEHD byehn?

VICTIM	VÍCTIMA	
No. I'm not okay.	*No. No estoy bien.*	Noh. Noh ehs-TOY byehn.
I'm...	*Estoy...*	Ehs-TOY...
• bleeding.	• *sangrando.*	• sahn-GRAHN-doh.
• scared.	• *asustada.*	• ah-soos-TAH-dah.

I'm in pain.	*Tengo dolor.*	TEHN-goh doh-LOHR.

OFFICER / *AGENTE*

Would you like someone here to help you through the interview?	*¿Quiere que alguien esté aquí para ayudarle con la entrevista?*	¿KYEH-reh keh AHL-gyehn ehs-TEH ah-KEE PAH-rah ah-yoo-DAHR-leh kohn lah ehn-treh-VEES-tah?
Did you bathe or wash yourself after the assault?	*¿Se bañó o se lavó después del asalto?*	¿Seh bah-NYOH oh seh lah-VOH dehs-PWEHS dehl ah-SAHL-toh?
Can you identify the person, if you see him again?	*¿Puede identificar a la persona si la ve otra vez?*	¿PWEH-deh ee-dehn-tee fee-KAHR ah lah pehr-SOH-nah see lah veh oh-TRAH vehs?
Are you hurt?	*¿Está herida?*	¿Ehs-TAH eh-REE-dah?
Do you know who did this to you?	*¿Sabe quién le hizo esto?*	¿SAH-beh kyehn leh HEE-soh EHS-toh?

VICTIM / *VICTIMA*

I don't know.	*No lo sé.*	Noh loh seh.
I don't know him.	*No lo conozco.*	Noh loh koh-NOHS-koh.
I've never seen him before.	*No lo he visto nunca.*	Noh loh eh VEES-toh NOON-kah.
I couldn't see his face.	*No pude ver su cara.*	Noh POO-deh vehr soo KAH-rah.
He's...	*Es...*	Ehs...
• a friend.	• *un amigo.*	• oon ah-MEE-goh.
• an acquaintance.	• *un conocido.*	• oon kohn-noh-SEE-doh.
• a neighbor.	• *un vecino.*	• oon veh-SEE-noh.
• a co-worker.	• *un compañero de trabajo.*	• oon kohn-pah-NYEH-roh deh trah-BAH-hoh.

OFFICER / *AGENTE*

What happened?	*¿Qué pasó?*	¿Keh pah-SOH?

VICTIM	**VÍCTIMA**	
He...	*Él...*	Ehl...
• raped me.	• *me violó.*	• meh vyoh-LOH.
• attacked me.	• *me atacó.*	• meh ah-tah-KOH.
• put a pillow on my face.	• *me tapó la cara con una almohada.*	• meh tah-POH lah KAH-rah kohn OO-nah ahl-moh-AH-dah.
• threatened me...	• *me amenazó...*	• meh ah-meh-nah-SOH...
• with a knife.	• *con un cuchillo.*	• kohn oon koo-CHEE-yoh.
• with a gun.	• *con una pistola.*	• kohn OO-nah pees-TOH-lah.
• yelled at me.	• *me gritó.*	• meh gree-TOH.
He said he'd kill me.	*Dijo que me mataría.*	DEE-hoh keh me mah-tah-REE-ah.

OFFICER	**AGENTE**	
• Where were you...	• *¿Dónde estaba...*	• ¿DOHN-deh ehs-TAH-bah...
• What were you doing...	• *¿Qué hacía usted...*	• ¿Keh ah-SYAH oos-TEHD...
...when this happened?	*...cuando pasó esto?*	...KWAHN-doh pah-SOH EHS-toh?

VICTIM	**VÍCTIMA**	
I was...	*Estaba...*	Ehs-TAH-bah...
• sleeping.	• *durmiendo.*	• door-MYEHN-doh.
• walking in the park.	• *caminando en el parque.*	• kah-mee-NAHN-doh ehn ehl PAHR-keh.
• jogging.	• *trotando.*	• troh-TAHN-doh.
• entering my house.	• *entrando en mi casa.*	• ehn-TRAHN-doh ehn mee KAH-sah.
• at home.	• *en mi casa.*	• ehn mee KAH-sah.
• watching TV.	• *mirando la tele.*	• mee-RAHN-doh lah teh-LEH.

• on my way home.	• *en el camino a mi casa.*	• ehn ehl kah-MEE-noh ah mee KAH-sah.
• at work.	• *en el trabajo.*	• ehn ehl trah-BAH-hoh.

B. DESCRIPTION OF THE SUSPECT

OFFICER	AGENTE	
Can you describe him?	*¿Puede describirlo?*	¿PWEH-deh deh-skree-BEER-loh?
What was he wearing?	*¿Qué ropa llevaba?*	¿Keh RHO-pah yeh-VAH-bah?

VICTIM	VÍCTIMA	
He's...	*Él es...*	Ehl ehs...
• tall.	• *alto.*	• AHL-toh.
• short.	• *bajo.*	• BAH-hoh.
• skinny.	• *gordo.*	• GOHR-doh.
• fat.	• *delgado.*	• dehl-GAH-doh.
• bald.	• *calvo.*	• KAHL-voh.
• old.	• *viejo.*	• VYEH-hoh.
• young.	• *joven.*	• HOH-vehn.
He has...	*Él tiene...*	Ehl TYEH-neh...
• black hair.	• *pelo negro.*	• PEH-loh NEH-groh.
• curly hair.	• *pelo rizado.*	• PEH-loh ree-SAH-doh.
• a moustache.	• *un bigote.*	• oon bee-GOH-teh.
• a beard.	• *una barba.*	• OO-nah BAHR-bah.
• a tattoo.	• *un tatuaje.*	• oon tah-TWAH-heh.
• a scar.	• *una cicatriz.*	• OO-nah see-kah-TREES.
He was wearing...	*Él llevaba...*	Ehl yeh-VAH-bah...
• a mask.	• *una máscara.*	• OO-nah MAHS-kah-rah.

174

• a T-shirt.	• *una camiseta.*	• OO-nah kah-mee-SEH-tah.
• jeans.	• *vaqueros.*	• vah-KEH-rohs.
• a black sweater.	• *un suéter negro.*	• oon SWEH-tehr NEH-groh.
• a ski jacket.	• *una chaqueta de esquí.*	• OON-nah chah-KEH-tah deh eh-SKEE.
• gloves.	• *guantes.*	• GWAHN-tehs.
• a long coat.	• *un abrigo largo.*	• un ah-BREE-goh LAHR-goh.

OFFICER	**AGENTE**	
What did he smell like?	*¿Recuerda su olor?*	¿Reh-KWEHR-dah soo oh-LOHR?
What did he sound like?	*¿Recuerda su voz?*	¿Reh-KWEHR-dah soo vohs?
How did he behave?	*¿Cómo se portó?*	¿KOH-moh seh pohr-TOH?

VICTIM	**VÍCTIMA**	
He smelled...	*Olía...*	Oh-LEE-ah...
• bad.	• *mal.*	• mahl.
• like alcohol.	• *a alcohol.*	• ah ahl-KOHL.
He...	*Él...*	Ehl...
• had bad breath.	• *tenía mal aliento.*	• teh-NEE-ah mahl ahl-LYEHN-toh.
• was sweaty.	• *estaba sudando.*	• ehs-TAH-bah soo-DAHN-doh.
• felt greasy.	• *estaba grasoso.*	• esh-TAH-bah grah-SOH-so.
I couldn't smell anything.	*No podía oler nada.*	Noh poh-DEE-ah oh-LEHR NAH-dah.
His voice was...	*Su voz era...*	Soo vohs EH-rah...
• low.	• *baja.*	• BAH-hah.
• sharp.	• *aguda.*	• ah-GOO-dah.
He didn't say anything.	*No dijo nada.*	Noh DEE-hoh NAH-dah.

He was violent.	*Era violento.*	EH-rah vee-oh-LEHN-toh.
He was...	*Estaba...*	Ehs-TAH-bah...
• scared.	• *asustado.*	• ah-SOOS-TAH-doh.
• calm.	• *tranquilo.*	• trahn-KEE-loh.
• polite.	• *amable.*	• ah-MAH-bleh.
• yelling.	• *gritando.*	• gree-TAHN-doh.
• threatening.	• *amenazando.*	• ah-meh-nah-SAHN-doh.
• saying obscenities.	• *diciendo palabrotas.*	• dee-SYEHN-doh pah-lah-BROH-tahs.
• cursing.	• *diciendo palabrotas/groserías.*	• dee-SYEHN-doh pah-lah-BROH-tahs/groh-seh-REE-ahs.
• laughing.	• *riéndose.*	• ree-EHN-doh-seh.
• calling me names.	• *insultándome.*	• een-sool-TAHN-doh-meh.

C. ESTABLISHING THE CIRCUMSTANCES OF THE CRIME

OFFICER	**AGENTE**	
Were you alone?	*¿Estaba sola?*	¿Ehs-TAH-bah SOH-lah?
Were there any witnesses?	*¿Había testigos?*	¿Ah-BEE-ah tehs-TEE-gohs?
Was anyone else in the house?	*¿Había alguien más en la casa?*	¿Ah-BEE-ah AHL-gyehn mahs ehn lah KAH-sah?
VICTIM	**VÍCTIMA**	
I didn't...	*No...*	Noh...
• see anybody.	• *vi a nadie.*	• vee ah NAH-dyeh.
• hear anything.	• *oí nada.*	• oh-EE NAH-dah.
I saw/heard people nearby.	*Vi/oí a gente cerca.*	Vee/oh-EE ah HEHN-teh SEHR-kah.

English	Spanish	Pronunciation
Somebody saw us and called the police.	Alguien nos vio y llamó a la policía.	AHL-gyehn nohs vee-OH ee yah-MOH ah lah POH-lee-SEE-ah.
I couldn't tell.	No sé.	Noh seh.
Nobody else was in the house.	No había nadie en la casa.	Noh ah-BEE-ah NAH-dyeh ehn lah KAH-sah.
The kids were sleeping.	Los niños estaban durmiendo.	Lohs NEE-nyohs ehs-TAH-bahn door-MYEHN-doh.
I live alone.	Vivo sola.	VEE-voh SOH-lah.

OFFICER / **AGENTE**

Were the...locked?	¿Estaban cerradas...?	¿Ehs-TAH-bahn seh-RAH-dahs...?
• doors	• las puertas	• lahs PWEHR-tahs
• windows	• las ventanas	• lahs vehn-TAH-nahs

VICTIM / **VÍCTIMA**

The doors/windows were...	Las puertas/ventanas estaban...	Lahs PWEHR-tahs/vehn-TAH-nahs ehs-TAH-bahn...
• locked.	• cerradas.	• seh-RRAH-dahs.
• open.	• abiertas.	• ah-BYEHR-tahs.
The...window was open.	La ventana...estaba abierto/a.	Lah vehn-TAH-nah...ehs-TAH-bah ah-BYEHR-toh/tah.
• living room	• del salón	• dehl sah-LOHN
• bathroom	• del baño	• dehl BAH-nyoh
• basement	• del sótano	• dehl SOH-tah-noh
• kitchen	• de la cocina	• deh lah koh-SEE-nah
The garage door was unlocked.	La puerta del garaje estaba abierta.	Lah PWEHR-tah dehl gah-RRAH-heh ehs-TAH-bah ah-BYEHR-tah.
I don't know if the door was locked.	No sé si la puerta estaba cerrada.	Noh seh see lah PWEHR-tah ehs-TAH-bah seh-RRAH-dah.

OFFICER	AGENTE	
What made him leave?	¿Qué lo hizo salir?	¿Keh loh EE-soh sah-LEER?
Did he leave anything behind?	¿Dejó alguna cosa?	¿Deh-HOH ahl-GOO-nah COH-sah?

VICTIM	VÍCTIMA	
He left when he was done.	Se fue cuando terminó.	Seh fweh KWAHN-doh tehr-mee-NOH.
I don't know what made him leave.	No sé qué lo hizo salir.	Noh seh keh loh HEE-soh sah-LEER.
I don't know. I was unconscious.	No sé. Me dejó sin sentido.	Noh seh. Meh deh-HOH seen sehn-TEE-doh.
He left...behind.	Dejó...	Deh-HOH...
• a glove	• un guante.	• oon GWAHN-teh.
• his shirt	• su camiseta.	• soo kah-mee-SEH-tah.
• his wallet	• su cartera.	• soo karh-TEH-rah.
• a sock	• un calcetín.	• oon kahl-seh-TEEN.
_____ fell from his pocket.	_____ se cayó del bolsillo.	_____ seh kah-YOH dehl bohl-SEE-yoh.

D. VICTIM INSTRUCTIONS

OFFICER	AGENTE	
Do you need to go to the hospital?	¿Necesita ir al hospital?	¿Neh-seh-SEE-tah eer ahl ohs-pee-TAHL?
Do you need help?	¿Necesita ayuda?	¿Neh-seh-SEE-tah ah-YOO-dah?

VICTIM	VÍCTIMA	
I need/don't need...	Necesito/no necesito...	Neh-seh-SEE-toh/noh neh-seh-SEE-toh...
• to go to the hospital.	• ir al hospital.	• eer ahl ohs-pee-TAHL.
• to see a doctor.	• un médico.	• oon MEH-dee-koh.
• help.	• ayuda.	• ah-YOO-dah.

I'm scared.	*Estoy asustada.*	Ehs-TOY ah-soos-TAH-dah.
OFFICER	*AGENTE*	
I'll take you home.	*La llevaré a su casa.*	Lah yeh-vah-REH ah soo KAH-sah.
Calm down.	*Cálmese.*	KAHL-mah-seh.
Everything is okay.	*Todo está bien.*	TOH-doh ehs-TAH byehn.
Can we call someone for you?	*¿Puedo llamar a alguien por usted?*	¿PWE-doh yah-MAHR ah AHL-gyehn pohr oos-TEHD?
Here is your case report number.	*Aquí tiene su informe con el número de su caso.*	Ah-KEE TYEH-neh soo een-FOHR-meh kohn ehl NOO-meh-roh deh soo KAH-soh.
Do you want to press charges?	*¿Quiere presentar cargos?*	¿KYEH-rre preh-sehn-TAHR KAHR-gohs?
Call us if...	*Llámenos si...*	YAH-meh-nohs see...
• you hear anything.	• *oye algo.*	• OH-yeh AHL-goh.
• you think of anything else.	• *piensa que hay algo más.*	• PYEHN-sah keh aye AHL-goh mahs.
Please keep the doors/windows locked.	*Por favor, mantenga las puertas/ventanas cerradas.*	Pohr fah-VOHR, mahn-TEHN-gah lahs PWEHR-tahs/vehn-TAH-nahs seh-RAH-dahs.

4. Domestic Violence

VOCABULARY ••••

FAMILY RELATIONS

relatives	parientes	pah-RYEHN-tehs
parents	padres	PAH-drehs
father	padre	PAH-dreh
mother	madre	MAH-dreh
husband	esposo, marido	ehs-POH-soh, mah-REE-doh
wife	mujer	moo-HEHR
son	hijo	EE-hoh
daughter	hija	EE-hah
children	niños	NEE-nyohs
brother	hermano	ehr-MAH-noh
sister	hermana	ehr-MAH-nah
nephew	sobrino	soh-BREE-noh
niece	sobrina	soh-BREE-nah
grandfather	abuelo	ah-BWEH-loh
grandmother	abuela	ah-BWEH-lah
uncle	tío	TEE-oh
aunt	tía	TEE-ah
cousin	primo/a	PREE-moh/mah
stepfather	padrastro	pah-DRAHS-troh
stepmother	madrastra	mah-DRAHS-trah
stepson	hijastro	ee-HAH-stroh
stepdaughter	hijastra	ee-HAH-strah
boyfriend/girlfriend	amigo/a	ah-MEE-goh/ah

CULTURE NOTE ••••

DOMESTIC VIOLENCE   When responding to a domestic call, you may find it difficult to get information from the female victim. This may be because she is afraid of retaliation from the abuser and/or because she mistrusts the intervention of an outsider. In order to obtain her cooperation, the suspected abuser must be removed from the scene, firmly but calmly, to allow him to save face in front of his wife, girlfriend, daughter, other relatives, or neighbors. The female victim may then talk more freely, especially if she has been reassured that she and her family will be protected by the police.

A. TALKING TO A CHILD REPORTING DOMESTIC TROUBLE

DISPATCHER	OPERADORA DE EMERGENCIA	
Good evening.	*Buenas noches.*	BWEH-nahs NOH-chehs.
What's your emergency?	*¿Cuál es tu emergencia?*	¿Kwahl ehs too eh-mehr-HEHN-syah?
CHILD	**NIÑO**	
My mom and dad are fighting.	*Mi madre y mi padre están peleando.*	Mee MAH-dreh ee mee PAH-dreh ehs-TAHN peh-leh-AHN-doh.
My mom's boyfriend hit her.	*El amigo de mi madre le pegó a ella.*	EHL ah-MEE-goh deh deh mee MAH-dreh leh peh-GOH ah EH-yah.
My dad hit my mom.	*Mi padre le pegó a mi madre.*	Mee PAH-dreh leh peh-GOH ah mee MAH-dreh.
My stepfather shot my mom.	*Mi padrastro le disparó a mi madre*	Mee pahd-RAHS-troh leh dees-pah-ROH ah mee MAH-dreh.

English	Spanish	Pronunciation
My mother punched my sister.	*Mi madre le dio un puñetazo a mi hermana.*	Mee MAH-dreh leh DEE-oh oon poo-nyeh-TAH-soh ah mee ehr-MAH-nah.
My mom beat my dog.	*Mi madre le pegó a mi perro.*	Mee MAH-dreh leh peh-GOH ah mee PEH-rroh.

DISPATCHER — *OPERADORA DE EMERGENCIA*

| Is anyone else there with you? | *¿Quién más está ahí contigo?* | ¿Kyehn mahs ehs-TAH ah-EE kohn-TEE-goh? |

CHILD — *NIÑO*

My...	*Mi...*	Mee...
• little sister.	• *hermana pequeña.*	• ehr-MAH-noh peh-KEH-nyah.
• older brother.	• *hermano mayor.*	• ehr-MAH-nah mah-YOHR.

DISPATCHER — *OPERADORA DE EMERGENCIA*

| How old are you? | *¿Cuántos años tienes?* | ¿KWAHN-tohs AH-nyohs TYEH-nehs? |

CHILD — *NIÑO*

| I'm ___ years old. | *Tengo ___ años.* | TEHN-goh ___ AH-nyohs. |

DISPATCHER — *OPERADORA DE EMERGENCIA*

What's your...	*¿Cuál es su...*	¿Kwahl ehs soo...
• address?	• *dirección?*	• dee-rehk-SYOHN?
• phone number?	• *número de teléfono?*	• NOO-meh-roh deh teh-LEH-foh-noh?
Does he/she have a weapon?	*¿Él/ella está armado?*	¿Ehl/EH-yah ehs-TAH ahr-MAH-doh?

CHILD — *NIÑO*

He/she has...	*Él/ella tiene...*	Ehl/EH-yah TYEH-neh...
• a knife.	• *un cuchillo.*	• oon koo-CHEE-oh.
• a gun.	• *una pistola.*	• OO-nah pees-TOH-lah.
• a hammer.	• *un martillo.*	• oon mahr-TEE-yoh.

- a baseball bat.

- a broken bottle.

No, there aren't any weapons here.

DISPATCHER

Where is the weapon now?

CHILD

He/she has it.

It's on the floor.

It's somewhere in the yard.

I don't know.

My grandma...

- picked it up.

- threw it out of the window.

- has it.

DISPATCHER

Is anyone injured?

Have your mom and dad been drinking?

CHILD

My mom/sister/ brother/father is bleeding from his/her...

- nose.

- *un palo de béisbol.*

- *una botella rota.*

No, no hay armas aquí.

OPERADORA DE EMERGENCIA

¿Dónde está el arma ahora?

NIÑO

Él/ella la tiene.

Está en el suelo.

Está en el jardín.

No sé.

Mi abuela...

- *la cogó.*

- *la tiró por la ventana.*

- *la tiene.*

OPERADORA DE EMERGENCIA

¿Hay alguien herido?

¿Tu madre y tu padre han estado bebiendo?

NIÑO

Mi madre/hermana/ hermano/padre está sangrando...

- *por la nariz.*

- oon PAH-loh deh BEHS-bohl.

- OO-nah boh-TEH-yah ROH-tah.

Noh, noh ay AHR-mahs ah-KEE.

¿DOHN-deh ehs-TAH ehl AHR-mah ah-OH-rah?

Ehl/EH-yah lah TYEH-neh.

Ehs-TAH ehn ehl SWEH-loh.

Ehs-TAH-ehn ehl hahr-DEEN.

Noh seh.

Mee ah-BWEH-lah...

- lah koh-HOH.

- lah tee-ROH pohr lah vehn-TAH-nah.

- lah TYEH-neh.

¿Ahy AHL-gyehn eh-REE-doh?

¿Too MAH-dreh ee too PAH-dreh ahn ehs-TAH-doh beh-BYEHN-doh?

Mee MAH-dreh/ehr-MAH-nah/ehr-MAH-noh/PAH-dreh ehs-tah sahn-GRAHN-doh...

- pohr lah nah-REES.

- mouth.
- *por la boca.*
- pohr lah BOH-kah.

My mom/dad/ sister/brother...

Mi madre/padre/ hermana/hermano...

Mee MAH-dreh/PAH-dreh/ehr-MAH-nah/ ehr-MAH-noh...

- is unconscious.
- *está inconsciente.*
- ehs-TAH een-kohn-SYEHN-teh.

- is screaming.
- *está gritando.*
- ehs-TAH-gree-TAHN-doh.

- has/have been drinking.
- *ha/han estado bebiendo.*
- ah/ahn ehs-TAH-doh beh-BYEHN-doh.

DISPATCHER

OPERADORA DE EMERGENCIA

Are they/is he/she still in the house?

¿Están ellos/está él/ella todavía en la casa?

¿Ehs-TAHN EH-yohs/ Ehs-TAH ehl/EH-yah toh-dah-VEE-ah ehn lah KAH-sah?

Where in the house are they/is he/she?

¿En qué parte de la casa están ellos/está él/ella?

¿Ehn keh PAHR-teh deh lah KAH-sah ehs-TAHN EH-yohs/ehs TAH ehl/EH-yah?

CHILD

NIÑO

They are...

Están...

Ehs-TAHN...

- outside.
- *afuera.*
- ah-FWEH-rah.

- in the kitchen.
- *en la cocina.*
- ehn lah koh-SEE-nah.

- in the garage.
- *en el garaje.*
- ehn ehl gah-RAH-heh.

- in the bedroom.
- *en la alcoba.*
- ehn lah ahl-KOH-bah.

He/she/they left.

Él/ella/ellos se fue/ se fueron.

Ehl/EH-yah/EH-yohs seh fweh/seh FWEH-rohn.

I don't know where he/she/they went.

No sé adónde se fue/se fueron.

Noh seh ah-DOHN-deh seh fweh/seh FWEH-rohn.

He/she/they got in the car and left.

Él/ella/ellos se fue/ fueron en el carro.

Ehl/EH-yah/EH-yohs seh fweh/FWEH-rohn ehn ehl KAH-rroh.

DISPATCHER	OPERADORA DE EMERGENCIA	
Does he/she/do they know you are calling the police?	¿Sabe él/ella/saben ellos que estás llamando a la policía?	¿SAH-beh ehl/EH-yah/ SAH-behn EH-yohs keh ehs-TAHS yah-MAHN- doh ah lah poh-lee- SEE-ah?

CHILD	NIÑO	
No. They...	No. Ellos...	Noh. EH-yohs...
• don't know I'm calling.	• no saben que estoy llamando.	• noh SAH-behn keh ehs-TOY yah- MAHN-doh.
• can't hear me.	• no pueden oírme.	• noh PWEH-dehn oh-EER-meh.
• are yelling too loud.	• están gritando.	• ehs-TAHN gree- TAHN-doh.
• are not in this room.	• no están aquí en este cuarto.	• noh ehs-TAHN ah- KEE ehn EHS-teh KWAHR-toh.
They know I'm on the phone.	Saben que estoy en el teléfono.	SAH-behn keh ehs- TOY ehn ehl teh-LEH- foh-noh.

DISPATCHER	OPERADORA DE EMERGENCIA	
What's his/her name?	¿Cómo se llama?	¿KOH-moh seh YAH-mah?
Describe him/her for me.	Descríbemelo/la.	Deh-SKREE-beh-meh- loh/lah.
Which direction did he/she take?	¿En qué dirección se fue?	¿Ehn keh dee-rehk- SYOHN seh fweh?

CHILD	NIÑO	
He/she/they went...	Él/ella/ellos se fue/fueron...	Ehl/EH-yah/EH-yohs se fweh/FWEH-rohn...
• north.	• al norte.	• ahl NOHR-teh.
• south.	• al sur.	• ahl soor.
• down the street.	• calle abajo.	• KAH-yeh ah-BAH- hoh.
I don't know which direction he/she took.	No sé en qué dirección se fue.	Noh seh ehn keh dee- rehk-SYOHN seh fweh.

| His/her name is ___. | *Se llama ___.* | Seh YAH-mah ___. |
| He/she is ___. | *Él/ella es ___.* | Ehl/EH-yah ehs ___. |

DISPATCHER	*OPERADORA DE EMERGENCIA*	
I'm sending the police right now.	*Mando a la policía ahora.*	MAHN-doh ah lah poh-lee-SEE-ah ah-OH-rah.
I'm calling an ambulance.	*Llamo a una ambulancia.*	YAH-moh ah OO-nah ahm-boo-LAHN-syah.
Calm down.	*Cálmate.*	KAHL-mah-teh.
Help is on the way.	*Alguien llega en su ayuda.*	AHL-gyehn YEH-gah ehn soo ah-YOO-dah.
I'll stay on the phone with you until the police arrive.	*Estaré en el teléfono contigo hasta que llegue la policía.*	Ehs-tah-REH ehn ehl teh-LEH-foh-noh kohn-TEE-goh AHS-tah keh YEH-geh lah poh-lee-SEE-ah.
Let the police in the door.	*Deja entrar a la policía.*	DEH-heh ehn-TRAHR ah lah poh-lee-SYAH.

Grammar Note ••••

PREPOSITIONAL PRONOUNS   The prepositional pronouns are used to clarify or to emphasize who receives the action. They are preceded by a preposition such as: *a*—to, *con*—with, *de*—of, *para*—for.

to me	*a mí*
to you	*a tí, a usted*
to him	*a él*
to her	*a ella*
to us	*a nosotros/as*
to you all	*a vosotros/as, a ustedes*
to them	*a ellos, a ellas*
He doesn't know her.	*Él no la conoce a ella.*

B. AT THE SCENE

CULTURE NOTE ••••

MACHISMO   The concept of *machismo* is an attitude. It is a reaction against control and authority, found not only in Latino societies, but in all patriarchal societies that are characterized by the unquestioned authority of the father. Obviously, not all Latino societies are patriarchal, and Latino societies are not the only patriarchal societies in the world, yet, in all male-oriented cultures, a *macho* attitude is present in varying degrees.

A *macho* is brave and fears nothing, not even death. He considers his family as an extension of himself and he will feel compelled to defend his honor or the honor of his family when any of its members are challenged, insulted, or shamed. When challenged or insulted publicly, he may feel compelled to restore his dignity no matter what it takes. When arrested, he may routinely protest verbally or fight back to "save face" *(quedar bien)*. To be embarrassed in front of others may be more painful than the arrest itself, for most Latinos have great difficulty with feelings of *vergüenza* (shame). Sometimes a *macho* attitude may cause a Latino to blame his wife or daughter in the event she is raped or beaten. Some, but by no means all or even a majority, may abuse women physically or verbally. If that is the case, many Latino women may not want to press charges, because the female ideal is to be delicate, sensitive, nonaggressive, and submissive to the man. The woman may consider it her duty to stand by her man no matter what happens.

OFFICER	AGENTE	
Good evening.	*Buenas noches.*	BWEH-nahs NOH-chehs.
Somebody called 911.	*Alguien llamó al nueve uno uno.*	AHL-gyehn yah-MOH ahl NWEH-veh OO-noh OO-noh.
Who lives here?	*¿Quién vive aquí?*	¿Kyehn VEE-veh ah-KEE?

WITNESS/VICTIM	TESTIGO/VÍCTIMA	
Me and my...live here.	*Mi/mis...y yo vivimos aquí.*	Mee/mees...ee yoh vee-VEE-mohs ah-KEE.
• family	• *familia*	• fah-MEE-lyah
• husband	• *marido*	• mah-REE-doh
• children	• *niños*	• NEE-nyohs
• boyfriend/girlfriend	• *amigo/a*	• ah-MEE-goh/gah
• wife	• *mujer*	• moo-HEHR

OFFICER	AGENTE	
What's going on here?	*¿Qué pasa aquí?*	¿Keh PAH-sah ah-KEE?

WITNESS/VICTIM	TESTIGO/VÍCTIMA	
Nothing is happening here.	*No pasa nada aquí.*	Noh PAH-sah NAH-dah ah-KEE.
My husband hit...	*Mi marido...*	Mee mah-REE-doh...
• me.	• *me pegó.*	• meh peh-GOH.
• the children.	• *le pegó a los niños.*	• leh peh-GOH ah lohs NEE-nyohs.
• the dog.	• *le pegó al perro.*	• leh peh-GOH ahl PEH-rroh.
• my mother.	• *le pegó a mi madre.*	• leh peh-GOH ah mee MAH-dreh.
• my sister/brother.	• *le pegó a mi hermano/a.*	• leh peh-GOH ah mee ehr-MAH-noh/nah.

OFFICER	AGENTE	
Is anyone...	*¿Hay alguien...*	¿Ahy AHL-gyehn...
• hurt?	• *herido?*	• eh-REE-doh?

• bleeding?	• *sangrando/a?*	• sahn-GRAHN-doh/dah?
• in pain?	• *lastimado/a?*	• lahs-tee-MAH-doh/dah?
How did...get hurt?	*¿Cómo se lastimó...?*	¿KOH-moh seh lahs-tee-MOH...?
• you	• *usted*	• oos-TEHD?
• your son/daughter	• *su hijo/a*	• soo EE-hoh/hah
• your dog	• *su perro*	• soo PEH-rroh
• your mother	• *su madre*	• soo MAH-dreh

WITNESS/VICTIM — *TESTIGO/VÍCTIMA*

He hit him/her/me with...	*Él le/me/hirió con...*	Ehl leh/meh/ee-ree-OH kohn...
• a knife.	• *un cuchillo.*	• oon koo-CHEE-yoh.
• his fist.	• *el puño.*	• ehl POO-nyoh.
• his hand.	• *la mano.*	• lah MAH-noh.
• a gun.	• *una pistola.*	• OO-nah pees-TOH-lah.
• a broken bottle.	• *una botella rota.*	• OO-nah boh-TEH-yah ROH-tah.
• a baseball bat.	• *un palo de béisbol.*	• oon PAH-loh deh BEH-ees-bohl.

OFFICER — *AGENTE*

Where is your...	*¿Dónde está su...*	¿DOHN-deh ehs-TAH soo...
• wife?	• *mujer?*	• moo-HEHR?
• husband?	• *marido?*	• mah-REE-doh?
• father?	• *padre?*	• PAH-dreh?
• stepfather?	• *padrastro?*	• pah-DRAHS-troh?
• mother?	• *madre?*	• MAH-dreh?
• stepmother?	• *madrastra?*	• mah-DRAHS-trah?
• boyfriend/girlfriend?	• *amigo/a?*	• ah-MEE-goh/gah?
Is he/she in a vehicle?	*¿Está en un carro?*	¿Ehs-TAH ehn oon KAH-rroh?
Take me there.	*Lléveme allí.*	YEH-veh-meh ah-YEH.

WITNESS/VICTIM	TESTIGO/VÍCTIMA	
He's/she's gone.	Él/ella se fue.	Ehl/EH-yah seh fweh.
He's/she's...	Él/ella está...	Ehl/EH-yah ehs-TAH...
• in the kitchen.	• en la cocina.	• ehn lah koh-SEE-nah.
• in the bedroom.	• en el cuarto.	• ehn ehl KWAHR-toh.
• in the garage.	• en el garaje.	• ehn ehl gah-RAH-heh.
• upstairs.	• arriba.	• ah-REE-bah.
• downstairs.	• abajo.	• ah-BAH-hoh.
• hiding somewhere.	• escondido por ahí.	• ehs-kohn-DEE-doh pohr ah-EE.
• in a pick-up truck.	• en una camioneta.	• ehn OO-nah ka-mee-oh-NEH-tah.
• in a van.	• en una camioneta.	• ehn OO-nah kah-myoh-NEH-tah.
• over there.	• allí.	• ah-YEE.
OFFICER	AGENTE	
May I come in?	¿Puedo pasar?	¿PWEH-doh pah-SAHR?
Stop talking/yelling.	Pare de hablar/gritar.	PAH-reh deh ah-ah-BLAHR/gree-TAHR.
Speak one at a time.	Hablen uno a la vez.	AH-blehn OO-noh ah lah vehs.
Who else is in the house?	¿Quién más está en la casa?	¿Kyehn mahs ehs-TAH ehn lah KAH-sah?
WITNESS/VICTIM	TESTIGO/VÍCTIMA	
Nobody else.	Nadie más.	NAH-dyeh mahs.
Just me and my children.	Sólo los niños y yo.	SOH-loh lohs NEE-nyohs ee yoh.
My mother.	Mi madre.	Mee MAH-dreh.
A friend.	Un amigo/una amiga.	Oon ah-MEE-goh/OO-nah ah-MEE-gah.

190

OFFICER	AGENTE	
Do you want to report this matter?	*¿Quiere usted poner una denuncia?*	¿KYEH-reh oos-TEHD poh-NEHR OO-nah deh-NOON-syah?
Do you want to talk to a counselor?	*¿Quiere usted hablar con un consejero?*	¿KYEH-reh oos-TEHD ah-BLAHR kohn oon kohn-seh-HEH-roh?
I don't see any visible sign of abuse.	*No veo señales visibles de abuso.*	Noh VEH-oh seh-NYAH-lehs vee-SEE-blehs deh ah-BOO-soh.
I can only attend to this matter if you want to report this.	*Sólo puedo ayudarle en este asunto si quiere poner una denuncia.*	SOH-loh PWEH-doh ah-yoo-DAHR-leh ehn EHS-teh ah-SOON-toh see KYEH-reh poh-NEHR OO-ah deh-NOON-syah.
Go with this officer while I speak to him/her.	*Vaya con este agente mientras le hablo a él/ella.*	Vah-yah kohn EHS-teh ah-HEHN-teh MYEHN-trahs leh ah-BLAH ah ehl/EH-yah.
Do you want a restraining order?	*¿Quiere usted una orden de restricción?*	¿KYEH-reh oos-TEHD OO-nah OHR-dehn deh rehs-treek-SYOHN?
It is the law to arrest the offender when obvious signs of injuries are present.	*Es la ley arrestar al ofensor cuando la señal de daño físico es evidente.*	Ehs lah LEH-ee ah-rrehs-TAHR ahl oh-fehn-SOHR KWAHN-doh lah seh-NYAHL deh DAH-nyoh FEE-see-koh ehs eh-vee-DEHN-teh.
Police departments are forced to document all domestic violence incidents.	*Los departamentos de policía están obligados a documentar todos los casos de violencia doméstica.*	Lohs deh-pahr-tah-MEHN-tohs deh poh-lee-SEE-ah ehs-TAHN oh-blee-GAH-dohs ah doh-koo-mehn-TAHR TOH-dohs lohs KAH-sohs deh vee-oh-LEHN-see-ah doh-MEHS-tee-kah.

WITNESS/VICTIM	TESTIGO/VÍCTIMA	
I want to report this.	*Quiero poner una denuncia.*	KYEH-roh poh-NEHR OO-nah deh-NOON-syah.
I don't want to report this.	*No quiero poner una denuncia.*	Noh KYEH-roh poh-NEHR OO-nah deh-NOON-syah.

C. TALKING TO THE SUSPECTED ABUSER

GRAMMAR NOTE ••••

REFLEXIVES Reflexive pronouns are used with reflexive verbs. Verbs are reflexive when the subject and the object of the verb are the same. Reflexive pronouns stand between the subject pronoun and the verb, or are attached to an affirmative command.

myself	*me*
yourself (inf. sing.)	*te*
himself/herself/yourself (form.)/ itself/yourselves/themselves	*se*
ourselves	*nos*
yourselves (inf. pl.)	*os*

I'm bathing (myself).	*Yo me baño.*
How are you feeling (yourself)?	*¿Cómo se siente usted?*
Sit (yourself) down!	*¡Siéntese!*

OFFICER	AGENTE	
I'm Officer ＿＿ from ＿＿ Police Department.	*Soy el agente ＿＿ del departamento de policía de ＿＿.*	Soy ehl ah-HEHN-teh ＿＿ dehl deh-pahr-tah-MEHN-toh deh poh-lee-SEE-ah deh ＿＿.

Drop your...	Suelte...	SWEHL-teh...
• gun.	• la pistola.	• lah pees-TOH-lah.
• knife.	• el cuchillo.	• ehl koo-CHEE-yoh.
• weapon.	• el arma.	• ehl AHR-mah.
What happened here?	¿Qué ha pasado aquí?	¿Keh ah pah-SAH-doh ah-KEE?

OFFENDER / **OFENSOR**

Nothing.	Nada.	NAH-dah.
Just a little argument.	Una pequeña plática.	OO-nah peh-KEH-nyah PLAH-tee-kah.
None of your business.	No es asunto suyo.	Noh ehs ah-SOON-toh SOO-yoh.
This is a family matter.	Esto es cosa nuestra.	EHS-toh ehs KOH-sah NWEHS-trah.

OFFICER / **AGENTE**

Stay where you are!	¡Quédese quieto!	¡KEH-deh-seh KYEH-toh!
Hands up!	¡Manos arriba!	¡MAH-nohs ah-RREE-bah!
Get up!	¡Levántese!	¡Leh-VAHN-teh-seh!
Turn around!	¡Voltéese!	¡Vohl-TEH-eh-seh!
I'm going to search you for weapons.	Voy a registrarlo para ver si acaso lleva armas.	Voy ah reh-HEES-trahr-loh PAH-rah VEHR see ah-KAH-soh YEH-vah AHR-mahs.
Spread your feet!	¡Separe las piernas!	¡Seh-PAH-reh lahs PYEHR-nahs!
How did your...get hurt?	¿Cómo se lastimó su...	¿KOH-moh seh lahs-tee-MOH soo...
• wife	• mujer?	• moo-HEHR?
• girlfriend	• amiga?	• ah-MEE-gah?
• son	• hijo?	• EE-hoh?
• daughter	• hija?	• EE-hah?
• mother-in-law	• suegra?	• SWEH-grah?

OFFENDER / *OFENSOR*

She/he fell in the kitchen.	*Se cayó en la cocina.*	Seh kah-YOH ehn lah koh-SEE-nah.
I don't know.	*No sé.*	Noh seh.
I slapped the bitch around.	*Le di una cachetada a la puta.*	Leh dee OO-nah kah-cheh-TAH-dah ah lah POO-tah.
What do you care?	*¿Qué le importa a usted?*	¿Keh leh eem-POHR-tah ah oos-TEHD?
None of your business.	*No es asunto suyo.*	Noh ehs ah-SOON-toh SOO-yoh.
Get out of my house!	*¡Salga de mi casa!*	¡SAHL-gah deh mee KAH-sah!

OFFICER / *AGENTE*

Calm down!	*¡Cálmese!*	¡KAHL-meh-seh!
Have you been...	*¿Ha estado...*	¿Ah ehs-TAH-doh...
• drinking?	• *bebiendo?*	• beh-BYEHN-doh?
• taking drugs?	• *tomando drogas?*	• toh-MAHN-doh DROH-gahs?

OFFENDER / *OFENSOR*

Yes, one or two drinks.	*Sí, uno o dos tragos.*	See, OO-noh oh dohs TRAH-gohs.
No, I have not...	*No, no he...*	Noh, noh eh...
• been drinking.	• *estado bebiendo.*	• ehs-TAH-doh beh-BYEHN-doh.
• been taking drugs.	• *tomando drogas.*	• toh-MAHN-doh DROH-gahs.

OFFICER / *AGENTE*

Your wife/daughter/ son says you...	*Su mujer/hija/hijo dice que usted...*	Soo moo-HEHR/EE-hah/EE-hoh DEE-seh keh oos-TEHD...
• hit her/him.	• *le pegó.*	• leh peh-GOH.
• threatened her/him with a gun/knife.	• *le amenazó con una pistola/un cuchillo.*	• leh ah-mehn-nah-SOH kohn OO-nah pees-TOH-lah/oon koo-CHEE-yoh.

- hit your son/
  daughter.

- *le pegó a su hijo/a.*

- leh peh-GOH ah soo
  EE-hoh/hah.

OFFENDER

OFENSOR

He's/she's lying.

Él/ella miente.

Ehl/EH-yah MYEHN-
teh.

That's not true.

No es verdad.

Noh ehs vehr-DAHD.

I didn't beat anyone.

No le pegué a nadie.

Noh leh peh-GEH ah
NAH-dyeh.

I just yelled at her/him.

Sólo le grité.

SOH-loh leh gree-TEH.

He/she wouldn't
behave.

No se portaba bien.

Noh seh pohr-TAH-
bah byehn.

Sorry officer, I
lost control.

*Lo siento, perdí
el control.*

Loh SYEHN-toh, pehr-
DEE ehl kohn-TROHL.

I was mad at
her/him.

*Estaba enojado
con él/ella.*

Eh-TAH-bah eh-noh-
HAH-doh kohn ehl/
EH-yah.

She threatened me with
a knife/gun.

*Me amenazó con un
cuchillo/una pistola.*

Meh ah-meh-nah-SOH
kohn oon koo-CHEE-
yoh OO-nah pees-
TOH-lah.

I punched her in self-
defense.

*La golpeé en defensa
propia.*

Lah gohl-peh-EH ehn
deh-FEHN-sah PROH-
pee-ah.

OFFICER

AGENTE

You are under arrest.

Está arrestado.

Ehs-TAH ah-rrehs-
TAH-doh.

I have to arrest you
for ____.

*Tengo que arrestarlo
por ____.*

TEHN-goh keh ah-
rrehs-TAHR-loh
pohr ____.

Calm down!

¡Cálmese!

¡KAHL-meh-seh!

Do you want to talk
to a counselor?

*¿Quiere hablar
con un consejero?*

¿KYEH-reh ah-BLAHR
kohn oon kohn-seh-
HEH-roh?

You can talk to your
wife now if you
promise to remain
calm.

*Puede hablar con
su mujer ahora si
promete mantener
la calma.*

PWEH-deh ah-BLAHR
kohn soo moo-HEHR
see proh-MEH-teh
mahn-teh-NEHR lah
KAHL-mah.

You should come outside with me to calm down.	*Debe salir afuera conmigo para calmarse.*	DEH-beh sah-LEER ah-FWEH-rah kohn-MEE-goh PAH-rah kahl-MAHR-seh.
Your wife/husband signed a restraining order, you have to leave.	*Su esposa/esposo firmó una orden de restricción. Tiene que irse.*	Soo ehs-POH-sah/ehs-poh-soh feer-MOH OO-nah OHR-dehn deh rehs-treek-SYOHN. TYEH-neh keh EER-seh.
Take enough clothes for a few days.	*Traiga bastante ropa para varios días.*	TRAH-ee-gah bahs-TAHN-teh ROH-pah pah-rah VAH-ree-ohs DEE-ahs.
You can only come back with a police escort.	*Usted puede volver sólo con una escolta de policía.*	Oos-TEHD PWEH-deh vohl-VEHR SOH-loh kohn OO-nah ehs-KOHL-tah deh poh-lee-SYAH.
If you come back alone, you will go to jail.	*Si vuelve solo, irá a la cárcel.*	See VWEHL-veh SOH-loh, ee-RAH ah lah KAHR-sehl.

5. Victim Assistance

COUNSELOR	*CONSEJERO/A*	
I'm here to...	*Estoy aquí para...*	Ehs-TOY ah-KEE PAH-rah...
• help you.	• *ayudarlo/la.*	• ah-yoo-DAHR-loh/lah.
• be with you.	• *estar con usted.*	• ehs-TAHR kohn oos-TEHD.
• assist you.	• *atenderlo/la.*	• ah-tehn-DEHR-loh/lah.
• help you understand what's going on.	• *ayudarlo/la a comprender lo que pasa.*	• ah-yoo-DAHR-loh/lah ah kohm-prehn-DEHR loh keh PAH-sah.

If you have any questions, let me know.	*Si tiene preguntas, dígamelo.*	See TEYH-neh preh-GOON-tahs, DEE-gah-meh-loh.
I'm...	*Soy...*	Soy...
• a psychologist.	• *psicólogo/a.*	• see-KOH-loh-goh/gah.
• a counselor.	• *consejero/a.*	• kohn-seh-HEH-roh/rah.
I'm not a police officer.	*No soy policía.*	Noh soy pohl-lee-SEE-ah.
I'm sorry this has happened to you.	*Siento mucho por lo que le ha pasado.*	SYEHN-toh MOO-choh pohr loh keh leh ah pah-SAH-doh.
Do you need anything?	*¿Necesita algo?*	¿Neh-seh-SEE-tah AHL-goh?
Do you want to speak to someone who speaks Spanish?	*¿Quiere hablar con alquien que hable español?*	¿KYEH-reh ah-BLAHR kohn AHL-gyehn keh AH-bleh ehs-pah-NYOHL?

VICTIM — *VÍCTIMA*

Yes, I need...	*Sí, necesito...*	See, neh-seh-SEE-toh...
• water.	• *agua.*	• AH-gwah.
• something to eat.	• *algo de comer.*	• AHL-goh deh koh-MEHR.
• a blanket.	• *una cobija.*	• OO-nah koh-BEE-hah.
• to lie down.	• *acostarme.*	• ah-koh-STAHR-meh.
• a translator.	• *un traductor.*	• oon trah-dook-TOHR.
• an interpreter.	• *un intérprete.*	• oon een-TEHR-preh-teh.
• someone who speaks Spanish.	• *alguien que hable español.*	• AHL-gyehn kehy AH-bleh ehs-pah-NYOHL.

COUNSELOR — *CONSEJERO/A*

Are you in pain?	*¿Tiene dolor?*	¿TYEH-neh doh-LOHR?

| Does anything hurt? | ¿Le duele algo? | ¿Leh DWEH-leh AHL-goh? |
| Are you hurt? | ¿Está herido/a? | ¿Ehs-TAH eh-REE-doh/dah? |

VICTIM — **VÍCTIMA**

My…hurts.	Me duele…	Meh DWEH-leh…
• arm	• el brazo.	• ehl BRAH-soh.
• head	• la cabeza.	• lah kah-BEH-sah.
• stomach	• el estómago.	• ehl ehs-TOH-mah-goh.
• back	• la espalda.	• lah ehs-PAHL-dah.
• neck	• el cuello.	• ehl KWEH-yoh.
• chest	• el pecho.	• ehl PEH-choh.
• leg	• la pierna.	• lah PYEHR-nah.

COUNSELOR — **CONSEJERO/A**

Do you want me to call…	¿Quiere que llame…	¿KYEH-reh keh YAH-meh…
• a doctor?	• al médico?	• ahl MEH-dee-koh?
• the paramedics?	• a los paramédicos?	• ah lohs pah-rah-MEH-dee-kohs?
• an abulance?	• una ambulancia?	• OO-nah ahm-boo-LAHN-syah?
• a taxi?	• un taxi?	• oon TAHK-see?
Do you want something for your pain?	¿Quiere algo para el dolor?	¿KYEH-reh AHL-goh PAH-rah ehl doh-LOHR?
Do you want to have… here with you?	¿Quiere tener a… aquí con usted?	¿KYEH-reh teh-NEHR ah…ah-KEE kohn oos-TEHD?
• a friend	• a un amigo/a	• ah oon ah-MEE-goh/gah
• your family	• a su familia	• ah soo fah-MEE-lyah
Would you like me to call him/her/them?	¿Quiere que lo/la/los/las llame?	¿KYEH-reh keh loh/lah/lohs/lahs YAH-meh?

| Does he/she/do they speak English? | ¿Habla/hablan inglés? | ¿AH-blah/AH-blahn een-GLEHS? |

VICTIM — **VÍCTIMA**

Yes, I need my...	Sí, necesito...	See, neh-seh-SEE-toh...
• family.	• a mi familia.	• ah mee fah-MEE-lyah.
• friends.	• a mis amigos/as.	• ah mees ah-MEE-gohs/gahs.
I don't have family/ friends here.	No tengo familia/ amigos/as aquí.	Noh TEHN-goh fah-MEE-lyah/ah-MEE-gohs/gahs ah-KEE.
Please call this person.	Por favor, llame a esta persona.	Pohr fah-VOHR, YAH-meh ah EHS-tah pehr-SOH-nah.
They don't speak English.	Ellos no hablan inglés.	EH-yohs noh AH-blahn een-glehs.
They only speak Spanish.	Solamente hablan español.	Soh-lah-MEHN-teh AH-blahn ehs-pah-NYOHL.
I don't need anybody, thank you.	No necesito a nadie, gracias.	Noh neh-seh-SEE-toh ah NAH-dyeh, GRAH-syahs.

COUNSELOR — **CONSEJERO/A**

Do you have children?	¿Tiene niños?	¿TYEH-neh NEE-nyohs?
Have they heard/seen anything?	¿Han oído/visto algo?	¿Ahn oh-EE-doh/VEES-toh ahl-goh?
Are they...	¿Están...	¿Ehs-TAHN...
• upset?	• perturbados?	• pehr-toor-BAH-dohs?
• disturbed?	• agitados?	• ah-hee-TAH-dohs?
• afraid?	• asustados?	• ah-soos-TAH-dohs?
• angry?	• enojados?	• ehn-oh-HAH-dohs?
How are you feeling?	¿Cómo se siente usted?	¿KOH-moh seh SYEHN-teh oos-TEHD?

VICTIM	VÍCTIMA	
My children are...	Mis niños están...	Mees NEE-nyohs ehs-TAHN...
• fine.	• bien.	• byehn.
• shaken.	• nerviosos.	• nehr-VYOH-sohs.
• scared.	• asustados.	• ah-soos-TAH-dohs.
We are all fine.	Todos estamos bien.	TOH-dohs ehs-TAH-mohs byehn.
Don't worry about us.	No se preocupe por nosotros.	Noh seh preh-oh-KOO-peh pohr noh-SOH-trohs.
We will be okay.	Estaremos bien.	Ehs-tah-REH-mohs byehn.
I'm...	Tengo...	TEHN-goh...
• afraid.	• miedo.	• myeh-doh.
• in pain.	• dolor.	• doh-LOHR.
I'm...	Estoy...	Ehs-TOY...
• worried.	• preocupado/a.	• preh-oh-koo-PAH-doh/dah.
• angry.	• enojado/a.	• eh-no-HAH-doh/dah.
I think I'm going to...	Creo que voy a...	KREH-yoh key voy ah...
• faint.	• desmayarme.	• dehs-mah-YAHR-meh.
• get sick.	• ponerme enfermo/a.	• poh-NEHR-meh ehn-FEHR-moh/ah.
• throw up.	• vomitar.	• voh-mee-TAHR.
COUNSELOR	CONSEJERO/A	
Let me know if your...	Dígame si su/sus...	DEE-gah-meh see soo/soos...
• chest begins to hurt.	• pecho comienza a dolerle.	• PEH-choh koh-MYEHN-sah ah doh-LEHR-leh.
• arms/legs feel numb.	• brazos/piernas se le duermen.	• BRAH-sohs/PYER-nahs seh leh DWEHR-mehn.

Help is on the way.	*Ya vienen a ayudarle.*	Yah VYEH-nehn ah ah-yoo-DAHR-leh.
Lie down.	*Acuéstese.*	Ah-KWEHS-teh-seh.
Sit down.	*Siéntese.*	SYEHN-teh-seh.
Calm down.	*Cálmese.*	KAHL-meh-seh.
No need to cry.	*No necesita llorar.*	Noh neh-seh-SEE-tah yoh-RAHR.
It's okay to cry.	*Está bien que llore.*	Ehs-TAH byehn keh YOH-reh.

Vocabulary ····

MEDICAL TERMS

cramps	*calambres*	kah-LAHM-brehs
labor pains	*contracciones*	kohn-trahk-SYOH-nehs
blood pressure	*presión de la sangre*	preh-SYOHN deh lah SAHN-greh
blood type	*tipo de sangre*	TEE-poh deh SAHN-greh
insurance company	*compañía de seguros*	kohm-pah-NYEE-ah deh seh-GOO-rohs
policy number	*número de póliza*	NOO-meh-roh deh POH-lee-sah
allergies	*alergias*	ahl-lehr-HEE-ahs
illness	*enfermedad*	ehn-fehr-mee-DAHD
emotional problems	*problemas emocionales*	proh-BLEH-mah seh-moh-syoh-NAH-lehs
good health	*buena salud*	BWEH-nah sah-LOOD

(cont'd.)

Medical Terms *(cont'd.)*

bad health	*mala salud*	mah-la deh sah-LOOD
heart problems	*problemas de corazón*	proh-BLEH-mahs deh koh-rah-SOHN
• emergency	• *emergencia*	• eh-mehr-HEHN-syah
• operating	• *operaciones*	• oh-peh-rah-SYOH-nehs
• recovery	• *recuperación*	• reh-koo-peh-rah-SYOHN
• waiting	• *espera*	• ehs-PEH-rah
...room	*la sala de...*	lah SAH-lah deh...
burns	*quemaduras*	keh-mah-DOO-rahs
poisoning	*envenenamiento*	ehn-veh-neh-nah-MYEHN-toh
splint	*cabestrillo*	kah-behs-TREE-yoh
medication	*medicamento*	meh-dee-kah-MEHN-toh
pain	*dolor*	doh-LOHR
Take a deep breath!	*¡Respire profundamente!*	¡Reh-SPEE-reh proh-foon-dah-MEHN-teh!
Relax!	*¡Relájese!*	¡Reh-LAH-heh-seh!
Don't move!	*¡No se mueva!*	¡Noh seh MWEH-vah!
Calm down!	*¡Cálmese!*	¡KAHL-meh-seh!
Close your eyes!	*¡Cierre los ojos!*	¡See-EH-rreh lohs OH-hohs!
Push!	*¡Empuje!*	¡Ehm-POO-heh!
Pull!	*¡Jale!*	¡HAH-leh!
Rest!	*¡Descanse!*	¡Dehs-KAHN-seh!
Grab my hand!	*¡Agárreme la mano!*	¡Ah-GAH-rreh-meh lah MAN-noh!
Stay awake!	*¡No se duerma!*	¡Noh seh DWEHR-mah!

6. Drug-Related Crimes

OFFICER	AGENTE	
Have you…any drugs?	¿Ha…drogas?	¿Ah…DROH-gahs?
• taken	• tomado	• toh-MAH-doh
• swallowed	• tragado	• trah-GAH-doh
What kind of drugs have you taken/ swallowed?	¿Qué tipo de drogas ha tomado/ tragado?	¿Keh TEE-poh deh DROH-gahs ah toh-MAH-doh/trah-GAH-doh?

SUBJECT	SUJETO	
I swallowed…	He tragado…	Eh trah-GAH-doh…
• "chiva."	• chiva.	• CHEE-vah.
• heroin.	• heroína.	• eh-roh-EE-nah.
• marijuana.	• marijuana.	• mah-ree-WAH-nah.
• "weed."	• yerba.	• YEHR-bah.
I took…	Tomé…	Toh-MEH…
• cocaine.	• cocaína.	• koh-kah-EE-nah.
• ecstasy.	• éxtasy.	• EKS-tah-see.
• acid.	• ácido.	• AH-see-do.
• poppers.	• pastillas.	• pahs-TEE-yahs.
• crack.	• crack.	• krahk.

OFFICER	AGENTE	
How was it packaged?	¿Cómo estaba envuelta?	¿KOH-moh ehs-TAH-bah ehn-VWEHL-tah?
What was the amount?	¿En qué cantidad?	¿Ehn keh kahn-tee-DAHD?

SUBJECT	SUJETO	
In a balloon.	En un globo.	Ehn oon GLOH-boh.
I swallowed/ purchased…	Yo tragué/compré…	Yoh trah-GEH/ kohm-PREH…
• a deck.	• un paquete.	• oon pah-KEH-teh
• a quarter of a gram.	• un cuarto de gramo.	• oon KWAHR-toh deh GRAH-moh.

• a half of a gram.	• *medio gramo.*	• MEH-dyoh GRAH-moh.
• a gram.	• *un gramo.*	• oon GRAH-moh.
• an ounce.	• *una onza.*	• OO-nah OHN-sah.
• a kilo.	• *un kilo.*	• oon KEE-loh.
• a nickle bag.	• *una bolsita de a cinco.*	• OO-nah bohl-SEE-tah deh ah SEEN-koh.
• a dime bag.	• *una bolsita de a diez.*	• OO-nah bohl-SEE-tah de ah DEE-ehs.

OFFICER	AGENTE	
We have to go to the hospital.	*Tenemos que ir al hospital.*	Teh-NEH-mohs keh eer ahl ohs-pee-TAHL.
If the balloon breaks you may die.	*Si el globo se rompe usted se puede morir.*	See ehl GLOH-boh seh ROHM-peh oos-TEHD PWEH-deh moh-REER.
How did you get the drugs?	*¿Cómo consiguió las drogas?*	¿KOH-moh kohn-see-GYOH lahs DROH-gahs?
Who supplied the drugs to you?	*¿Quién le ha proporcionado las drogas?*	¿KYEHN leh ah proh-pohr-syoh-NAH-doh lahs DROH-gahs?
Who is your source?	*¿Quién es su conexión?*	¿Kyehn ehs soo koh-nehk-SYOHN?

SUBJECT	SUJETO	
I can't tell you.	*No puedo decirle.*	Noh PWEH-doh deh-SEER-leh.
I can't tell you because...	*No puedo decírselo porque...*	Noh PWEH-doh deh-SEER-seh-loh pohr-KEH...
• he'll kill me.	• *me mataría.*	• meh mah-tah-REE-ah.
• he's a relative.	• *es un pariente.*	• ehs oon pah-RYEHN-teh.
• he's a friend.	• *es un amigo.*	• ehs oon ah-MEE-goh.
• he's my boss.	• *es mi jefe.*	• ehs mee-HEH-feh.
• he knows where I live.	• *sabe dónde vivo.*	• SAH-beh DOHN-deh VEE-voh.

• he's watching us now.

• *nos está mirando.*

• nohs ehs-TAH mee-RAHN-doh.

A friend asked me to...

Un amigo me pidió que...

Oon ah-MEE-goh meh pee-DYOH keh...

• watch the package.

• *le vigilara el paquete.*

• leh vee-hee-LAH-rah ehl pah-KEH-teh.

• keep the package for him.

• *le guardara el paquete.*

• leh gwahr-DAH-rah ehl pah-KEH-teh.

OFFICER

AGENTE

Do you...

¿Usted...

¿Oos-TEHD...

• have more than one source of supply?

• *tiene más de un proveedor?*

• TYEH-neh mahs deh oon proh-veh-eh-DOHR?

• know other customers of your source?

• *conoce a otros clientes de su conexión?*

• koh-NOH-seh ah OH-trohs KLYEHN-tehs deh soo koh-nehk-SYOHN?

What's...

¿Cuál es...

¿Kwahl ehs...

• his/her address?

• *su dirección?*

• soo dee-rehk-SYOHN?

• his/her phone number?

• *su número de teléfono?*

• soo NOO-meh-roh deh teh-LEH-foh-noh?

• his/her pager number?

• *su número de busca personas/biper?*

• soo NOO-meh-roh deh BOOS-kah pehr-soh-nahs/BEE-pehr?

How long have you dealt with him/her?

¿Por cuánto tiempo ha hecho negocio con él/ella?

¿Pohr KWAHN-toh TYEHM-poh ah EH-choh neh-GOH-syoh kohn ehl/EH-yah?

How much did you purchase in the past?

¿Cuánto le ha comprado en el pasado?

¿KWAHN-toh leh ah kohm-PRAH-doh ehn ehl pah-SAH-doh?

Are you...

¿Está usted...

¿Ehs-TAH oos-TEHD...

• selling these drugs?

• *vendiendo estas drogas?*

• vehn-DYEHN-doh EHS-tahs DROH-gahs?

• using these drugs yourself?	• usando estas drogas usted mismo?	• oos-AHN-doh EHS-tahs DROH-gahs oos-TEHD MEES-moh?
Who are you selling them to?	¿A quién se las está vendiendo?	¿Ah kyehn seh las ehs-TAH vehn-DYEHN-doh?
How much are you...	¿Cuánto está...	¿KWAHN-toh ehs-tah...
• selling?	• vendiendo?	• vehn-DYEHN-doh?
• buying?	• comprando?	• kohm-PRAHN-doh?
• using?	• usando?	• oos-AHN-doh?
How do you pay for your habit?	¿Cómo paga usted por su hábito?	¿KOH-moh PAH-gah pohr soo AH-bee-toh?
How were you recruited?	¿Cómo fue reclutado?	¿KOH-moh fweh reh-kloo-TAH-doh?
Will you make a buy for me?	¿Me hará una compra?	¿Meh ah-RAH OO-nah KOHM-prah?
If you cooperate with the police...	Si usted coopera con la policía...	See oos-TEHD koh-oh-PEH-rah kohn lah poh-lee-SEE-ah...
• we will recommend you to the district attorney's office.	• le recomendaremos a la oficina del fiscal.	• leh reh-koh-mehn-dah-REH-mohs ah lah oh-fee-SEE-nah dehl fees-KAHL.
• we will give you assistance.	• le ayudaremos a usted.	• leh ah-yoo-dah-REH-mos ah oos-TEHD.

SUBJECT

How can you protect me?	¿Cómo pueden protegerme?	¿KOH-moh PWEH-dehn proh-teh-HEHR-meh?
I won't say anything without my lawyer.	No diré nada sin mi abogado/a.	Noh dee-REH NAH-dah seen mee ah-boh-GAH-doh/dah.
I want to speak to a lawyer.	Quiero hablar con un abogado/a.	KYEH-roh ah-BLAHR kohn oon ah-boh-GAH-doh/dah.

VOCABULARY ••••

DRUG-RELATED TERMS

acid	*ácido*	AH-see-doh
amphetamine	*anfetas, anfetaminas*	ahn-FEH-tahs/ahn-feh-tah-MEEH-nahs
angel dust	*polvo de ángel*	POHL-voh deh AHN-hehl
booze	*licor, vino, pisto*	lee-KOHR, VEE-noh, PEES-toh
cocaine	*coca, cocaína, périco*	KOH-kah, koh-kah-EE-nah, PEH-ree-koh
crack	*crack*	krahk
downers	*diablos*	DYAH-blohs
drugs	*drogas*	DROH-gahs
heroin	*chiva, heroína, manteca, tecata*	CHEE-vah, eh-roh-EE-nah, mahn-TEH-kah, teh-KAH-tah
marijuana	*mota, yerba, grifa, marijuana*	MOH-tah, YEHR-bah, GREE-fah, mah-ree-HOO-ah-nah
mushrooms	*hongos, sombrillas*	HOHN-gohs, sohm-BREE-yahs
pills	*píldoras*	PEEL-doh-rahs
speedball	*"chute"*	"choo-teh"
tranquilizer	*tranquilizante, calmante*	trahn-kee-lee-SAHN-teh, kahl-MAHN-teh
drug runner, mule	*camello, burro, mula, correo de drogas*	kah-MEH-yoh, BOO-rroh, MOO-lah, koh-RREOH deh DROH-gahs
drug dealer	*narcotraficante*	NAHR-koh trah-fee-KAHN-teh

(cont'd.)

Drug-Related Terms *(cont'd.)*

deal	*"dil"*	deel
drug addict	*drogadicto*	droh-gah-DEEK-toh
informant	*chivato, rata, chota*	chee-VAH-toh, RAH-tah, CHOH-tah
uppers	*anfetaminas, acceleradores, blancas, diablos*	AHN-feh-tah-MEE-nahs, AH-seh-leh-rah-DOH-rehs, BLAHN-kahs, dee-AH-blohs.
ecstasy	*éxtasy*	EKS-tah-see
poppers	*píldoras, pastillas*	PEEL-doh-rahs, pahs-TEE-yahs
downers	*barbitúricos, rojas, diablos, colorados*	bahr-bee-TOO-ree-kohs, ROH-has, dee-AH-blohs, koh-loh-RAH-dohs
to drink	*"pistiar"*	"pees-TYAHR"
to get high	*agarrar onda, curarse*	ah-gah-RRAHR OHN-dah, kooh-RAHR-seh
hit	*calada*	kah-LAH-dah
to inject oneself	*picarse, curarse*	pee-KAHR-seh, kooh-RAHR-seh
to kick the habit	*salirse*	sah-LEER-seh
needle	*aguja*	ah-GOO-hah
pipe	*pipa*	PEE-pah
roach	*cucaracha, colilla*	koo-kah-RAH-chah, koh-LEE-yah
shit	*mierda*	MYEHR-dah
to smoke	*fumar*	foo-MAHR
syringe	*jeringa, los trabajos*	heh-REEN-gah, lohs trah-BAH-hohs

(cont'd.)

Drug-Related Terms *(cont'd.)*

to be stoned	*estar en onda, estar curado*	ehs-TAHR ehn OHN-dah, ehs-TAHR koo-RAH-doh
straight	*derecho, limpio*	deh-REH-choh, LEEM-pee-oh
supplier	*proveedor, conexión*	proh-veh-eh-DOHR, koh-nehks-YOHN
trip	*viaje*	vee-AH-heh
bindle	*papelito, bolsita*	pah-peh-LEE-toh, bohl-SEE-tah
brick	*ladrillo, pedazo, kilo, aparato*	lah-DREE-yoh, peh-DAH-soh, KEE-loh, ah-pah-RAH-toh
can	*lata*	LAH-tah
dime bag	*bolsita de a diez, bolsa*	bohl-SEE-tah deh ah dyehs, BOHL-sah
kilo	*kilo*	KEE-loh
nickel bag	*bolsita de a cinco*	bohl-SEE-tah deh ah SEEN-koh
deck	*paquete*	pah-KEH-teh
gram, half gram	*gramo, medio gramo*	GRAH-moh, MEH-dyoh GRAH-moh
joint	*porro, leño, pitillo, toque, tabaco*	POH-rroh, LEH-nyoh, pee-TEE-yoh, TOH-keh, tah-BAH-koh
lid	*tapa*	TAH-pah
spoon	*cuchara*	koo-CHAH-rah
ounce	*onza*	OHN-sah
one ounce piece	*cacho una onza*	KAH-choh OO-nah OHN-sah
quarter ounce	*un cuarto de onza*	oon KWAHR-toh deh OHN-sah
half ounce	*media onza*	MEH-dyah OHN-sah

7. Gang-Related Crimes

CULTURE NOTE ····

GANGS A gang is defined as a group of three or more individuals who have a common identifying name, symbol, and organizational structure, and engage in a pattern of criminal activity that creates an atmosphere of fear and intimidation within the community. Gangs are territorial and live to protect their turf in the *barrios,* as well as their peers.

The primary reason for becoming a gang member is to belong to a family or a group. Generally speaking, gang candidates come from dysfunctional families and seek emotional and social support, guidance, and consistent norms and rules. Belonging to a gang is like living with a surrogate family that offers recognition, respect, protection, and loyalty. Another factor contributing to gang appeal is the lifestyle and economic gain that drug dealing and other criminal activity can provide.

Most gangs share a lack of respect for authority. Gangs are cohesive and loyal to one another. Members vow never to betray another gang member. Latino gangs openly engage in territorial disputes with rival gang members without concern for their own physical safety. They will confront anybody interfering with their business or intruding on their turf, even police officers. Hispanic gangs speak "Calo," which is a combination of English and Spanish. This jargon allows gang members to communicate among themselves without being understood by outsiders. They utilize hand signals and tattoos that identify them as members of a specific subgroup. Gang-related criminal activity seems to concentrate on drug trafficking and vehicle theft, as well as other connected crimes.

A. OBTAINING GENERAL INFORMATION

OFFICER	AGENTE	
Stop!	¡Alto!	¡AHL-toh!
I stopped you for ____.	Te paré por ____.	Teh pah-REH pohr ____.
I'm doing a routine check.	Hago una parada de rutina.	AH-goh OO-nah pah-RAH-dah deh roo-TEE-nah.
I'm investigating a crime.	Estoy investigando un crimen.	Ehs-TOY een-vehs-tee-GAHN-doh oon KREE-mehn.

GANG MEMBER	PANDILLERO	
What do you want?	¿Qué quiere?	¿Keh KYEH-reh?
What did I do wrong?	¿Qué hice yo de malo?	¿Keh EE-seh yoh deh MAH-loh?
I wasn't doing anything wrong.	No hacía nada malo.	Noh ah-SEE-ah NAH-dah MAH-loh.
What?	¿Qué?	¿Keh?
I don't understand.	No comprendo.	Noh kohm-PREHN-doh.
I don't speak English.	No hablo inglés.	Noh AH-bloh een-GLEHS.

OFFICER	AGENTE	
What were you doing...	¿Qué hacías...	¿Keh ah-SEE-ahs...
• in the dark?	• en la oscuridad?	• ehn lah ohs-koo-ree-DAHD?
• behind that building?	• detrás de ese edificio?	• deh-TRAHS deh EH-seh eh-dee-FEE-syoh?
• in this alley?	• en este callejón?	• ehn EHS-teh kah-yeh-HOHN?
What's your name?	¿Cómo te llamas?	¿KOH-moh teh YAH-mahs?
Do you have a nickname?	¿Tienes un apodo?	¿TYEH-nehs oon ah-POH-doh?
May I see...	¿Puedo ver...	¿PWEH-doh vehr...

English	Spanish	Pronunciation
• some identification?	• alguna identificación?	• ahl-GOO-nah ee-dehn-tee-fee-kah-SYOHN?
• your driver's license?	• tu licencia de manejar?	• too lee-SEHN-syah deh mah-neh-HAHR?
• proof of insurance?	• prueba del seguro?	• PRWEH-bah del seh-GOO-roh?
• your vehicle's registration?	• el registro del vehículo?	• ehl reh-HEES-troh dehl veh-EE-koo-loh?
GANG MEMBER	**PANDILLERO**	
My name is ____.	Mi nombre es ____.	Mee NOHM-breh ehs ____.
It's on the driver's license.	Está en la licencia.	Ehs-TAH ehn lah lee-SEHN-syah.
I don't have…	No tengo…	Noh TEHN-goh…
• a driver's license.	• licencia de manejar.	• lee-SEHN-syah deh mah-neh-HAHR.
• insurance.	• seguro.	• seh-GOO-roh.
I lost my license.	Perdí mi licencia.	Pehr-DEE me lee-SEHN-syah.
I can't find my insurance papers.	No encuentro mi papel del seguro.	Noh ehn-KWEHN-troh mee pah-PEHL dehl seh-GOO-roh.
Here, man.	Aquí está, oiga.	Ah-KEE ehs-TAH, OY-gah.
Okay. Can I go now?	Bien. ¿Me puedo ir ya?	Byehn. ¿Meh PWEH-doh eer yah?
OFFICER	**AGENTE**	
Repeat your full name, please.	Repite tu nombre y apellidos, por favor.	Reh-PEE-teh too NOHM-breh ee ah-peh-YEE-dohs, pohr fah-VOHR.
Where do you live?	¿Dónde vives?	¿DOHN-deh VEE-vehs?

Is this your correct address?	¿Es esta tu dirección correcta?	¿Ehs EHS-tah too dee-rehk-SYOHN koh-REHK-tah?
Do you have another address?	¿Tiene otra dirección?	¿TYEH-neh OH-trah dee-rehk-SYOHN?
Repeat it, please.	Repítela, por favor.	Reh-PEE-teh-lah, pohr fah-VOHR.
Who is the owner of this car?	¿Quién es el dueño de este carro?	¿Kyehn ehs ehl DWEH-nyoh deh EHS-teh KAH-rroh?

GANG MEMBER	PANDILLERO	
My address is ____.	Mi dirección es ____.	Mee dee-rehk-SYOHN ehs ____.
I don't need to tell you.	No necesito decírselo.	Noh neh-seh-SEE-toh deh-SEER-seh-loh.
Leave us alone.	Déjenos en paz.	DEH-heh-nohs en pahs.
This is my...	Este es...	EHS-teh ehs...
• car.	• mi carro.	• mee KAH-rroh.
• friend's car.	• el carro de mi amigo/a.	• ehl KAH-rroh deh mee ah-MEE-goh/gah.
• old man's car.	• el carro de mi viejo.	• ehl KAH-rroh deh mee VYEH-hoh.

GRAMMAR NOTE ••••

THE IMPERFECT OF *IR* (TO GO)

iba	íbamos
ibas	íbais
iba	iban

When were you going to buy drugs? ¿Cuándo ibas a comprar drogas?

Where was he going? ¿Adónde iba?

OFFICER	AGENTE	
How did you get here?	¿Cómo llegaste aquí?	¿KOH-moh yeh-GAHS-teh ah-KEE?
Where were you going?	¿Adónde ibas?	¿Ah-DOHN-deh EE-bahs?
What are you doing around here?	¿Qué hacías por aquí?	¿Keh ah-SEE-ahs pohr ah-KEE?
You're not from this area.	No es de aquí.	Noh ehs deh ah-KEE.

GANG MEMBER	PANDILLERO	
Why do you care?	¿Qué le importa a usted?	¿Keh leh eem-POHR-tah ah oos-TEHD?
That's none of your business.	No es asunto suyo.	Noh ehs ah-SOON-toh SOO-yoh.
I'm hanging out, man.	Daba una vuelta, no más.	DAH-bah OO-nah VWEHL-tah, noh mahs.
What's with you?	¿Qué le pasa a usted?	¿Keh leh PAH-sah ah oos-STEHD?
Are you looking for trouble?	¿Anda buscando pelea?	¿AHN-dah boos-KAHN-doh peh-LEH-ah?

GRAMMAR NOTE ••••

DEMONSTRATIVE ADJECTIVES AND PRONOUNS

The demonstrative adjectives and pronouns point out people and things. Demonstrative adjectives accompany a noun, demonstrative pronouns stand by themselves. The pronouns show an accent mark when they are not followed by a noun. *Este/esta/estos/estas* refer to people or things that are near the speaker. *Ese/esa/esos/esas* refer to people or things that are near the listener and away from the speaker. *Aquel/aquella/aquellos/aquellas* are further away from the speaker and the listener.

	M.SG.	F.SG.
this	*este*	*esta*
that	*ese*	*esa*
that over there	*aquel*	*aquella*

	M.PL.	F.PL.
these	*estos*	*estas*
those	*esos*	*esas*
those over there	*aquellos*	*aquellas*

Those men over there are suspects.	*Aquellos hombres son sospechosos.*
Who is this?	*¿Quién es éste?*

B. SEARCHING FOR WEAPONS

OFFICER	AGENTE	
Are you armed?	*¿Estás armado?*	¡Ehs-TAHs ahr-MAH-doh?

GANG MEMBER	PANDILLERO	
Of course not!	*¡Por supuesto que no!*	¡Pohr soo-PWEHS-toh keh noh!

I have no weapons, man.	No tengo armas, hombre.	Noh TEHN-goh AHR-AHR-mahs, OHM-breh.
Yes, I have a...	Sí, tengo un...	See, TEHN-goh oon...
• gun.	• cuete.	• KWEH-teh.
• knife.	• cuchillo.	• koo-CHEE-yoh.

OFFICER	**AGENTE**	
Get out of the vehicle.	Sal del carro.	Sahl dehl KAH-rroh.
I'm going to search your car.	Voy a registrar tu carro.	Voy ah reh-hees-TRAHR too KAH-rroh.
Keep your hands visible.	Mantén las manos visibles.	Mahn-TEHN lahs MAH-nohs vee-SEE-blehs.
Raise your hands above your head.	Levanta las manos por encima de la cabeza.	Leh-VAHN-tah lahs MAH-nohs pohr ehn-SEE-mah deh lah kah-BEH-sah.
I'm going to handcuff you for your safety.	Voy a ponerte las esposas por tu seguridad.	Voy ah poh-NEHR-teh lahs ehs-POH-sahs pohr too seh-goo-ree-DAHD.
I'm going to hand pat your body in case you carry weapons.	Voy a palparte el cuerpo para ver si llevas armas.	Voy ah pahl-PAHR-teh ehl KWEHR-poh pah-rah vehr see YEH-vahs AHR-mahs.
Do you have any needles that may stick me?	¿Tienes agujas que puedan pincharme?	¿TYEH-nehs ah-GOO-hahs keh PWEH-dehn peen-CHAHR-meh?
Do you have HIV/AIDS?	¿Tienes el SIDA?	¿TYEH-nehs ehl SEE-dah?
Where is your...	¿Dónde está tu...	¿DOHN-dah ehs-TAH too...
• gun?	• cuete?	• KWEH-teh?
• knife?	• cuchillo?	• koo-CHEE-yoh?

GANG MEMBER	**PANDILLERO**	
I told you I don't have weapons.	*Le dije que no tengo armas.*	Leh DEE-heh keh noh TEHN-goh AHR-mahs.
My gun is in the car.	*Mi cuete está en el carro.*	Mee KWEH-teh ehs-TAH ehn ehl KAH-rroh.
Go fuck yourself!	*¡Vete al carajo!*	¡VEH-teh ahl kah-RAH-hoh!

OFFICER	**AGENTE**	
Do you have any other weapons with you?	*¿Tienes otras armas contigo?*	¿TYEH-nehs OH-trahs AHR-mahs kohn-tee-goh?
Is anything else in the car?	*¿Hay algo más en el carro?*	Ahy AHL-goh mahs ehn ehl KAH-rroh?

GANG MEMBER	**PANDILLERO**	
There are no other weapons in the car.	*No hay otras armas en el carro.*	Noh ahy OH-trahs AHR-mahs ehn ehl KAH-rroh.
Yes, there are some more weapons in the trunk.	*Sí, hay algunas armas en la cajuela.*	See, ay ahl-GOO-nahs AHR-mahs ehn lah kah-HWEH-lah.

OFFICER	**AGENTE**	
Where did you get the weapons?	*¿De dónde sacaste las armas?*	¿Deh DOHN-deh sah-KAHS-teh lahs AHR-mahs?
What are you doing with these weapons?	*¿Qué haces con estas armas?*	¿Keh AH-sehs kohn EHS-tahs AHR-mahs?

C. SEARCHING FOR DRUGS

> # CULTURE NOTE ••••
>
> **OBTAINING INFORMATION**   Latinos usually prefer to resolve their differences and conflicts among themselves. Loyalty to their group does not allow them to easily confide in the police about someone who may have broken the law. "Ratting" (*chivarse*) on a friend is a serious offense to honor, duty, and friendship. Some who may want to help the police may not do so for fear of retaliation. Therefore, it is often best to try and get information through the grapevine from a trusted member of the community such as a priest, a teacher, or a coach.

GANG MEMBER	PANDILLERO	
There is/there are drugs...	*Hay drogas...*	Ay DROH-gahs...
• in the trunk.	• *en la cajuela.*	• ehn lah kah-HWEH-lah.
• under the passenger's seat.	• *debajo del asiento del pasajero.*	• deh-BAH-hoh dehl ah-SYEHN-toh dehl pah-sah-HEH-roh.
• in the glove compartment.	• *en la guantera.*	• ehn lah gwahn-TEH-rah.

OFFICER	AGENTE	
How did you get the drugs?	*¿De dónde sacaste las drogas?*	¿Deh DOHN-deh sah-KAHS-teh lahs DROH-gahs?
Are there any more drugs?	*¿Tienes más drogas?*	¿TYEH-nehs mahs DROH-gahs?

Are these drugs for you?	¿Son para ti estas drogas?	¿Sohn PAH-rah tee EHS-tahs DROH-gahs?
Are you "slinging?"	¿Vendes?	¿VEHN-dehs?
Are you selling?	¿Vendes?	¿VEHN-dehs?
What other drugs are you dealing?	¿Qué otras drogas vendes?	¿Keh OH-trahs DROH-gahs VEHN-dehs?

GANG MEMBER — *PANDILLERO*

I can't tell you.	No puedo decirle.	Noh PWEH-doh deh-SEER-leh.
I'm not a snitch.	No soy un chivato.	Noh soy oon chee-VAH-toh.
If I told you I would get killed.	Si se lo dijera me matarían.	See seh loh dee-HEH-rah meh mah-tah-REE-ahn.
I don't deal with drugs.	No vendo drogas.	Noh VEHN-doh DROH-gahs.
I deal a little bit.	Tráfico sólo un poquito.	Trah-FEE-koh SOH-loh oon poh-KEE-toh.
I bought some drugs.	Compré algunas drogas.	Kohm-PREH ahl-GOO-nahs DROH-gahs.
I have some ____.	Tengo algo de ____.	TEHN-goh AHL-goh deh ____.
No big deal, man.	Poca cosa, hombre.	POH-kah KOH-sah, OHM-breh.
I have to make a living.	Tengo que ganarme la vida.	TEHN-goh keh gahn-AHR-meh lah VEE-dah.
That's it.	Eso es todo.	EH-soh ehs TOH-doh.
I don't have any more.	No tengo más.	Noh TEHN-goh mahs.

D. SPECIFIC QUESTIONS ABOUT GANG ACTIVITIES

OFFICER — *AGENTE*

| Are you in a gang? | ¿Andas con una pandilla? | ¿AHN-dahs kohn oon-ah pahn-DEE-yah? |

GANG MEMBER	PANDILLERO	
Are you kidding?	¿Habla en serio?	¿AH-blah ehn SEH-ryoh?
Who, me?	¿Quién? ¿Yo?	¿Kyehn? ¿Yoh?
What do you mean?	¿Qué quiere decir?	¿Keh KYEH-reh deh-SEER?
Why do you ask that?	¿Por qué me pregunta eso?	¿Pohr keh meh preh-GOON-tah EH-soh?
Yes, I am in a gang.	Sí, ando con una "ganga."	See, AHN-doh kohn OO-nah "GAHN-gah."

OFFICER	AGENTE	
What gang do you belong to?	¿A qué "ganga" perteneces?	¿Ah keh "GAHN-gah" pehr-teh-NEH-sehs?
Who are your...	¿Quiénes son tus...	¿KYEH-nehs sohn toos...
• friends?	• amigos?	• ah-MEE-gohs?
• associates?	• compradres?	• kohm-PAH-drehs?
Do you have any tattoos?	¿Tienes tatuajes?	¿TYEH-nehs tah-TWAH-hehs?
Show them to me.	Enséñame los tatuajés.	Ehn-SEH-nyah-meh lohs tah-TWAH-hehs.

GANG MEMBER	PANDILLERO	
Yes, I have a tattoo...	Sí, tengo un tatuaje en...	See, TEHN-goh oon tah-TWAH-heh ehn...
• on my stomach.	• el estómago.	• ehl ehs-TOH-mah-goh.
• on my calf.	• la pantorrilla.	• lah pahn-toh-RREE-yah.
• across my shoulder blades.	• la espalda entre los hombros.	• lah ehs-PAHL-dah EHN-treh lohs OHM-brohs.
• between my toes.	• entre los dedos del pie.	• EHN-treh lohs DEH-dohs dehl pyeh.
Would you like to see/touch it?	¿Quiere verlo/tacarlo?	¿KYEH-reh VEHR-loh/toh-KAHR-loh?

No, I don't have any tattoos.	No, no tengo tatuajes.	Noh, noh TEHN-goh tah-TWAH-hehs.

OFFICER — *AGENTE*

May I see your tattoo?	¿Puedo ver tu tatuaje?	¿PWEH-doh vehr too tah-TWAH-heh?
I need to see your tattoo.	Tengo que ver tu tatuaje.	TEHN-goh keh vehr too tah-TWAH-heh.
I am going to photograph your tatoo.	Voy a fotografiar tu tatuaje.	Voy ah foh-to-grah-fee-AHR too tah-TWAH-heh.

OFFICER — *AGENTE*

What does this tattoo mean?	¿Qué quiere decir ese tatuaje?	¿Keh KYEH-reh deh-SEER EH-seh tah-TWAH-heh?

GANG MEMBER — *PANDILLERO*

What?	¿Qué?	¿Keh?
It means I belong to ____.	Quiere decir que pertenezco a ____.	KYEH-reh deh-SEER keh pehr-teh-NEHS-koh ah ____.
It doesn't mean anything.	No quiere decir nada.	Noh KYEH-reh deh-SEER NAH-dah.
It's just a tattoo.	Sólo es un tatuaje.	SOH-loh ehs oon tah-TWAH-heh.

OFFICER — *AGENTE*

Where are you from?	¿De dónde eres?	¿Deh DOHN-deh EH-rehs?

GANG MEMBER — *PANDILLERO*

I'm from ____.	Soy de ____.	Soy deh ____.
• here.	• aquí.	• ah-KEE.
• El Salvador.	• El Salvador.	• El Sahl-vah-DOHR.
• Mexico.	• México.	• MEH-hee-koh.

OFFICER — *AGENTE*

Are you on…	¿Estás en libertad…	¿Ehs-TAHS ehn lee-behr TAHD…
• parole?	• provisional?	• proh-vee-syoh-NAHL?

• probation?	• *condicional?*	• kohn-dee-SYOH-nahl?
GANG MEMBER	*PANDILLERO*	
I'm/I'm not ___.	*Estoy/no estoy* ___.	Ehs-TOY/noh ehs-TOY ___.
OFFICER	*AGENTE*	
Who's your...	*¿Quién es tu...*	¿Kyehn ehs too...
• parole agent?	• *agente de libertad provisional?*	• ah-HEHN-teh deh lee-behr-TAHD proh-vee-syoh-NAHL?
• probation officer?	• *agente de libertad vigilada?*	• ah-HEHN-teh deh lee-behr-TAHD vee-hee-LAH-dah?
Do you know the conditions of your parole?	*¿Sabes las condiciones de tu libertad provisional?*	¿SAH-behs lahs kohn-dee-SYOHN-ehs deh too lee-behr-TAHD proh-vee-syoh-NAHL?

IF THE SUSPECT IS TALKING WITH HIS PARTNER OR IF THE SUSPECTS ARE GIVING SIGNS TO EACH OTHER

OFFICER	*AGENTE*	
Shut up!	*¡Cállate!*	¡KAH-yah-teh!
Look the other way!	*¡Mira para el otro lado!*	¡Mee-rah PAH-rah ehl OH-troh LAH-doh!
Don't look at each other!	*¡No se miren!*	¡Noh seh MEE-rehn!
You! Face that way!	*¡Tú! ¡Mira para allá!*	¡Too! ¡MEE-rah PAH-rah ah-YAH!

VOCABULARY ••••

SLANG

beer	cerveza	sehr-VEH-sah
binge	borrachera	boh-rrah-CHEH-rah
blasted	borracho	boh-RRAH-choh
booze	pisto	PEES-toh
to drink	tomar, "pistiar"	toh-MAHR, "pees-TYAHR"
drunk	tomado, borracho	toh-MAH-doh, boh-RRAH-choh
fucked up	borracho	boh-RRAH-choh
hangover	cruda, mona, resaca	KRUH-dah, MOH-nah, reh-SAH-kah
to be loaded	borracho	boh-RRAH-choh
shit-faced	pedo	PEH-doh
balls	huevos	HWEH-vohs
What a bummer!	¡Qué gacho!	¡Keh GAH-choh!
cocksucker	lambiscón	lahm-bees-KOHN
damned	pinche	PEEN-cheh
darn	híjole	EE-hoh-leh
fuck	carajo, joder	kah-RAH-hoh, hoh-DEHR
jeez	híjole	EE-hoh-leh
man	híjole	EE-hoh-leh
shit	mierda	MYEHR-dah
son of a bitch	hijo de puta, hijo de la chingada	EE-hoh deh POO-tah, EE-hoh deh lah cheen-GAH-dah
asshole	pendejo, huevón	pehn-DEH-hoh, hweh-VOHN

(cont'd.)

Slang *(cont'd.)*

bastard	*cabrón, hijo de puta*	kah-BROHN, EE-hoh deh POO-tah
butch	*marimacho*	mah-ree-MAH-choh
creep	*pendejo*	pehn-DEH-hoh
cunt	*cabrona*	kah-BROH-nah
dick-head	*pendejo*	pehn-DEH-hoh
dumb shit	*pendejo*	pehn-DEH-hoh
fag	*joto*	HOH-toh
fart	*pedo*	PEH-doh
Go fuck yourself!	*¡Chinga tu madre!*	¡CHEEN-gah too MAH-dreh!
kiss-ass	*lameculos*	lah-meh-KOO-lohs
motherfucker	*hijo de la chingada*	EE-hoh deh lah cheen-GAH-dah
queer	*maricón*	mah-ree-KOHN
scumbag	*huevón*	hweh-VOHN
slut	*puta*	POO-tah
wimp	*pendejo*	pehn-DEH-hoh
to check his lily	*ir a hacer pis*	eer ah ah-SEHR pees
crap	*cagada*	kah-GAH-dah
to take a dump/shit	*ir a cagar*	eer ah kah-GAHR
to do number one	*ir a hacer pis*	eer ah ah-SEHR pees
to be on the rag...	*tener la regla...*	teh-NEHR lah REH-glah...
ass	*culo*	KOO-loh
balls	*huevos, cojones*	HWEH-vohs, koh-HOH-nehs
boobs	*tetas, chichis*	TEH-tahs, CHEE-chees
to give a blow job	*chupar la punta*	choo-PAHR lah POON-tah

(cont'd.)

Slang *(cont'd.)*

bush	*coño*	KOH-nyoh
butt	*nalgas, cachetes*	NAHL-gahs, kah-CHEH-tehs
cock	*pene*	PEH-neh
cunt	*vagina*	vah-HEE-nah
to ejaculate	*terminar, correrse*	tehr-mee-NAHR, koh-RREHR-seh
hard-on	*erección*	eh-rehk-SYOHN
to finger fuck	*meter mano*	meh-TEHR MAH-noh
to fuck	*joder, coger, culear*	hoh-DEHR, koh-HEHR, koo-leh-AHR
to get laid	*chingar, culear*	cheen-GAHR, koo-leh-AHR
hickey	*chupón*	choo-POHN
to make out	*acariciar*	ah-kah-ree-SYAHR
nuts	*testículos*	tehs-TEE-koo-lohs
peepee	*pene*	PEH-neh
pussy	*vagina*	vah-HEE-nah
stroke	*acariciar*	ah-kah-ree-SYAHR
gang	*pandilla*	pahn-DEE-yah
police	*"jara," "placa"*	"HAH-rah," "PLAH-kah"
tattoo	*"placa," tatuaje*	"PLAH-kah," tah-TWAH-heh
shoes	*"calcos"*	KAHL-kohs
senior gang member	*veterano*	veh-teh-RAH-noh
spaced out	*cruzado, firoláis, fumado*	kroo-SAH-doh, fee-roh-LAH-ees, foo-MAH-doh

COMMUNITY SERVICE

CULTURE NOTE ••••

THE IMAGE OF THE POLICE   In some Latin American countries the police are badly trained, badly paid, and low on morale, and many police departments are ruled by corruption and fear. The police have a very bad reputation, and most individuals do not trust them and avoid contact at all cost. Many aliens perceive United States police officers in the same light, and may overreact or even turn to physical or verbal abuse when confronted with a police officer. Such a reaction should not be taken personally, but seen as the fearful reaction of an individual that may not be familiar with American customs. It is best to react firmly but calmly, and make sure that the individual understands that you are not there to harm, but to help.

1. Lost Person or Runaway

OFFICER	AGENTE	
I want to help you.	*Quiero ayudarte/le.*	KYEH-roh ah-yoo-DAHR-teh/leh.
I'm here to help you.	*Estoy aquí para ayudarte/le.*	Ehs-TOY ah-KEE PAH-rah an-yoo-DAHR-teh/leh.
Don't be afraid.	*No tentas/tenga miedo.*	Noh TEHN-gahs/tehn-gah MYEH-doh.
Everything is alright.	*Todo está bien.*	TOH-doh ehs-TAH byehn.
What's your name?	*¿Cómo te llamas/se llama?*	¿KOH-moh teh YAH-mahs/seh YAH-mah?
What's...	*¿Cuál es...*	¿Kwahl ehs...
• your address?	• *tu/su dirección?*	• too/soo dee-rek-SYOHN?
• your phone number?	• *tu/su número de teléfono?*	• too/soo NOO-meh-roh deh teh-LEH foh-noh?
Are you lost?	*¿Está perdido?*	¿EHS-tah pehr-DEE-doh?
Where do you live?	*¿Dónde vives/vive?*	¿DOHN-deh VEE-vehs/VEE-veh?
What's the name of the city where you live?	*¿Cuál es el nombre de la ciudad donde vives/vive?*	¿Kwahl ehs ehl NOHM-breh deh lah syoo-dahd DOHN-deh VEE-vehs/VEE-veh?
Do you have...	*¿Tienes/tiene...*	¿TYEH-nehs/TYEH-neh...
• an ID?	• *identificación?*	• ee-dehn-tee-fee-kah-SYOHN?
• a driver's license?	• *licencia de manejar?*	• lee-SEHN-see-ah deh mah-neh-HAHR?
SUBJECT	SUJETO	
I don't have...with me.	*No tengo...conmigo.*	Noh TEHN-goh... kohn-MEE-goh.

- an ID
- *identificación*
- ee-dehn-tee-fee-kah-SYOHN

- a driver's license
- *licencia de manejar*
- lee-SEHN-cee-ah deh mah-neh-HAHR

I left it at home.	*La dejé en casa.*	Lah deh-HEH ehn KAH-sah.
I lost it.	*La perdí.*	Lah pehr-DEE.
Yes, I have a driver's license from _____.	*Sí, tengo una licencia de manejar de _____.*	See, TEHN-goh OO-nah lee-SEHN-syah deh mah-neh-HAHR de _____.

OFFICER — *AGENTE*

| Where did you come from? | *¿De dónde vienes/viene?* | ¿Deh DOHN-deh VEE-eh-nehs/VEE-eh-neh? |
| How did you get here? | *¿Cómo llegaste/llegó aquí?* | ¿KOH-moh yeh-GAHS-teh/yeh-GOH ah-KEE? |

SUBJECT — *SUJETO*

I'm lost.	*Me perdí.*	Meh pehr-DEE.
I can't find my way home.	*No puedo encontrar el camino.*	Noh PWE-doh ehn-kohn-TRAHR ehl kah-MEE-noh.
I'm visiting and don't know my way around.	*Estoy de visita y no conozco la ciudad.*	Ehs-toy deh vee-SEE-tah ee noh koh-NOHS-koh lah syoo-DAHD.

SUBJECT — *SUJETO*

My name is _____.	*Mi nombre es _____.*	Mee NOHM-breh ehs _____.
I don't know...	*No sé...*	Noh seh...
• my address.	• *mi dirección.*	• mee dee-rek-SYOHN.
• my phone number.	• *mi número de teléfono.*	• mee NOO-meh-roh deh teh-LEH-foh-noh.

OFFICER — *AGENTE*

| What's near where you live? | *¿Qué hay cerca de dónde vives/vive?* | ¿Keh ay SEHR-kah deh DOHN-deh VEE-vehs/VEE-veh? |

I want to help you find your home.	Quiero ayudarte/le a encontrar tu/su casa.	KYEH-roh ah-yoo-DAHR-teh/leh ah ehn-kohn-TRAHR too/soo KAH-sah.
What are your parents' names?	¿Cómo se llaman tus/sus padres?	¿KOH-moh seh-YAH-mahn toos/soos PAH-drehs?
Where are your friends/relatives?	¿Dónde están tus/sus amigos/parientes?	¿DOHN-deh eshs-TAHN toos/soos ah-MEE gohs/pah-RYEHN-tehs?
Who lives in your house?	¿Quién vive en tu/su casa?	¿Kyehn VEE-veh ehn too/soo KAH-sah?
Can I call someone to...	¿Puedo llamar a alguien para que...	¿PWEH-doh yah-MAHR ah AHL-gyehn PAH-rah keh...
• help you?	• venga a ayudarte/le?	• VEHN-gah ah ah-yoo-dahr-teh/leh?
• pick you up?	• te/lo/la venga a recoger?	• teh/loh/lah VEHN-gah ah rreh-koh-HEHR?

SUBJECT — *SUJETO*

You can call my...	Puede llamar a mi...	PWE-deh yah-MAHR ah mee...
• friend.	• amigo.	• ah-MEE-goh.
• cousin.	• primo.	• PREE-moh.
• uncle.	• tío.	• TEE-oh.
• boss.	• jefe.	• HEH-feh.

OFFICER — *AGENTE*

May I...you?	¿Puedo...a ti/a usted?	¿PWEH-doh...ah tee/ah oos-TEHD?
• check	• registrar/te/lo/la	• reh-hees-TRAHR/teh/loh/lah
• touch	• tocarte/lo/la	• toh-KAHR-teh/loh/lah
Turn around.	Voltéate/Voltéese.	Vohl-TEH-ah-teh/Vohl-TEH-eh-seh.

Put your hands on your head.	*Ponga las manos en la cabeza.*	POHN-gah lahs MAH-nohs ehn lah kah-BEH-sah.
I need to check your...	*Necesito mirar en tu/tus/su/sus...*	Neh-seh-SEE-toh mee-RAHR ehn too/toos/soo/soos...
• backpack.	• *mochila.*	• moh-CHEE-lah.
• pockets.	• *bolsillos.*	• bohl-SEE-yohs.
• bag.	• *bolsa.*	• bohl-sah.

OFFICER / ***AGENTE***

Do you have any medical problems?	*¿Tienes/tiene problemas médicos?*	¿TYEH-nehs/TYEH-neh proh-BLEH-mahs MEH-dee-kohs?

SUBJECT / ***SUJETO***

I'm...	*Soy...*	Soy...
• a diabetic.	• *diabético/a.*	• dee-ah-BEH-tee-koh/kah.
• an epileptic.	• *epiléptico/a.*	• eh-PEE-LEHP-tee-koh/kah.
I don't want to go back home.	*No quiero volver a casa.*	Noh KYEH-roh vohl-vehr ah KAH-sah.
I can't go back home.	*No puedo volver a casa.*	Noh PWEH-doh vohl-vehr ah KAH-sah.
I have nowhere to go.	*No tengo adónde ir.*	Noh TEHN-goh ah-DOHN-deh eer.

OFFICER / ***AGENTE***

Why don't you come with me to the station?	*¿Por qué no vienes/viene a la estación de policía conmigo?*	¿POHR-keh noh VYEH-nehs/VYEH-neh ah lah ehs-tah-SYON deh poh-lee-SEE-ah kohn-MEE-goh?
We'll talk there.	*Allá podemos hablar.*	Ah-YAH poh-DEH-mohs ah-BLAHR.

2. Missing Persons

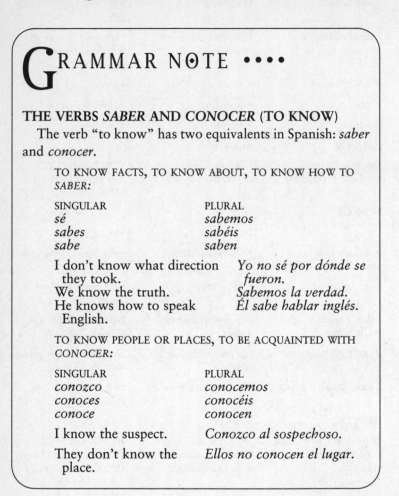

GRAMMAR NOTE ••••

THE VERBS *SABER* AND *CONOCER* (TO KNOW)

The verb "to know" has two equivalents in Spanish: *saber* and *conocer*.

TO KNOW FACTS, TO KNOW ABOUT, TO KNOW HOW TO
SABER:

SINGULAR	PLURAL
sé	*sabemos*
sabes	*sabéis*
sabe	*saben*

I don't know what direction they took.	*Yo no sé por dónde se fueron.*
We know the truth.	*Sabemos la verdad.*
He knows how to speak English.	*Él sabe hablar inglés.*

TO KNOW PEOPLE OR PLACES, TO BE ACQUAINTED WITH
CONOCER:

SINGULAR	PLURAL
conozco	*conocemos*
conoces	*conocéis*
conoce	*conocen*

I know the suspect.	*Conozco al sospechoso.*
They don't know the place.	*Ellos no conocen el lugar.*

A. OBTAINING IDENTIFYING INFORMATION

PARENT	*PADRE/MADRE*	
My child has not come back from school.	*Mi hijo/a no ha regresado de la escuela.*	Mee EE-hoh/hah noh ah reh-greh-SAH-doh deh lah ehs-KWEH-lah.

| I went to school to pick up my child and he/she wasn't there. | Fui a la escuela a buscar a mi hijo/a y no estaba allí. | FWEE ah lah ehs-KWEH-lah ah boos-KAHR ah mee EE-hoh/hah ee noh ehs-TAH-bah ah-YEE. |

OFFICER / *AGENTE*

| How long has he/she been missing? | ¿Por cúanto tiempo ha estado perdido? | ¿Pohr KWAHN-toh TYEHM-poh ah ehs-TAH-doh pehr-DI-doh? |

PARENT / *PADRE/MADRE*

For six hours.	Por seis horas.	Pohr SEH-ees OH-rahs.
All afternoon.	Toda la tarde.	TOH-dah la TAHR-deh.
All day.	Todo el día.	TOH-doh ehl DEE-ah.

OFFICER / *AGENTE*

Did you call...to see if he/she is there?	¿Ha llamado...para ver si está allí?	¿Ah yah-MAH-doh... PAH-rah vehr see ehs-TAH ah-YEE?
• his/her friends	• a sus amigos	• ah soos ah-MEE-gohs
• your family	• a su familia	• ah soo fah-MEE-LYAH
• the neighbors	• a sus vecinos	• ah soos veh-SEE-nohs
• the school	• a la escuela	• ah lah ehs-KWEH-lah
Are his/her friends home?	¿Están sus amigos en casa?	¿Ehs-TAHN soos ah-MEE-gohs ehn KAH-sah?
Does he/she get along with his/her friends?	¿Se lleva bien con sus amigos?	¿Seh YEH-vah byehn kohn soos ah-MEE-gohs?
Did somebody see him/her after school?	¿Lo/la vio alguien después de la escuela?	¿Loh/lah vee-OH AHL-gyehn dehs-PWEHS deh lah ehs-KWEH-lah?

PARENT / *PADRE/MADRE*

| Yes, I called _____. | Sí, ya he llamado _____. | See, yah eh yah-MAH-doh. |

English	Spanish	Pronunciation
No one has seen him/her.	*Nadie lo/la ha visto.*	NAH-dyeh loh/lah ah-VEES-toh.
I didn't call anyone.	*No llamé a nadie.*	Noh yah-MEH ah NAH-dyeh.
I don't speak English.	*No hablo inglés.*	Noh AH-bloh een-GLEHS.

OFFICER / ***AGENTE***

English	Spanish	Pronunciation
How does he/she get home from school?	*¿Cómo regresa de la escuela normalmente?*	¿KOH-moh rreh-GREH-sah deh lah ehs-KWEH-lah nohr-mahl-MEHN-teh?
Does he/she...	*¿Él/ella...*	¿Ehl/EH-yah...
• walk alone?	• *camina solo/a?*	• kah-MEE-nah SOH-loh/lah?
• take the bus?	• *toma el autobús?*	• TOH-mah ehl aoo-to-BOOS?
• get a ride?	• *le dan un viaje?*	• leh dahn oon vee-AH-heh?
What time does he/she usually come home?	*¿A qué hora llega a casa?*	¿Ah keh OH-rah YEH-gah ah KAH-sah?

PARENT / ***PADRE/MADRE***

English	Spanish	Pronunciation
I pick him/her up.	*Yo lo/la recojo.*	YOH loh/lah rreh-KOH-hoh.
Sometimes he/she...	*A veces él/ella...*	Ah VEH-sehs ehl/EH-yah...
• walks.	• *camina.*	• kah-MEE-nah.
• takes the bus.	• *toma el autobús.*	• TOH-mah ehl au-toh-BOOS.
• gets a ride with a friend.	• *lo trae un amigo.*	• loh TRAH-eh oon ah-MEE-goh.

OFFICER / ***AGENTE***

English	Spanish	Pronunciation
What route does he/she take?	*¿Qué dirección toma?*	¿Keh dee-rehk-SYOHN TOH-mah?
Does he/she come home...	*¿Pasa por...*	¿PAH-sah pohr...
• through populated areas?	• *lugares concurridos?*	• loo-GAH-rehs kohn-koo-REE-dohs?

- through deserted areas?
- by lakes?
- by ditches?
- by parks?

PARENT

I don't know.

Yes, there's a…on his way home.

- lake
- river
- ditch
- construction site

OFFICER

Describe the child.

What was he/she wearing?

What was he/she carrying?

PARENT

He/she is…
- tall.
- short.

He/she has…
- long hair.
- short hair.

He/she was wearing…
- jeans.
- a T-shirt.
- a dress.

- *lugares desiertos?*
- *lagos?*
- *regueras?*
- *parques?*

PADRE/MADRE

No sé.

Sí, hay un…de camino a su casa.

- *lago*
- *río*
- *reguera*
- *lugar en construcción*

AGENTE

Describe al niño.

¿Qué ropa llevaba?

¿Qué objetos llevaba?

PADRE/MADRE

Es…
- *alto/a.*
- *bajo/a.*

Tiene…
- *pelo largo.*
- *pelo corto.*

Llevaba…
- *vaqueros.*
- *una camiseta.*
- *un vestido.*

- loo-GAH-rehs deh-SYEHR-tohs?
- LAH-gohs?
- reh-GWEH-rahs?
- PAHR-kehs?

Noh SEH.

See, ahy oon…deh kah-MEE-noh ah soo KAH-sah.

- LAH-goh
- REE-oh
- reh-GWEH-rah
- loo-GAHR ehn cohns-trook-SYON

Dehs-KREE-bah ahl NEE-nyoh.

¿Keh RROH-pah yeh-BAH-bah?

¿Keh obh-HEH-tohs yeh-VAH-bah?

Ehs…
- AHL-toh/tah.
- BAH-hoh/hah.

TYEH-neh…
- PEH-loh LAHR-goh.
- PEH-loh KOHR-toh.

Yeh-BAH-bah…
- va-KEH-rohs.
- OO-nah kah-mee-SEH-tah.
- oon vehs-TEE-doh.

He/she was carrying...	Llevaba...	Yeh-BAH-bah...
• a skate board.	• un patín.	• oon pah-TEEN.
• a backpack.	• una mochila.	• OO-nah moh-CHEE-lah.
• a ball.	• una pelota.	• OO-nah peh-LOH-tah.
• a baseball bat.	• un palo de béisbol.	• oon PAH-loh deh BEH-ees-bohl.

OFFICER — **AGENTE**

Was he/she alone?	¿Estaba sólo/a?	¿Ehs-TAH-bah soh-loh/lah?
With whom was he/she?	¿Con quién estaba?	¿Kohn kyehn ehs-TAH-bah?
Where was he/she going?	¿Adónde iba?	¿Ah-DOHN-deh ee-bah?

PARENT — **PADRE/MADRE**

He/she was going toward...	Iba hacia...	EE-bah AH-syah...
• the mall.	• el centro comercial.	• ehl SEHN-troh koh-mehr-SYAHL.
• downtown.	• el centro.	• ehl SEHN-troh.
• the river.	• el río.	• ehl REE-oh.
• the street.	• la calle.	• lah KAH-yeh.
• the ice cream shop.	• la heladería.	• lah heh-lah-deh REE-ah.

He/she was...	Estaba...	Ehs-TAH-bah...
• with an adult.	• con un adulto.	• kohn oon ah-DOOL-toh.
• alone.	• sólo/a.	• SOH-loh/lah.
• with other kids.	• con otros niños.	• kohn OH-trohs NEE-nyohs.

OFFICER — **AGENTE**

Do you think he/she might have gone with another relative?	¿Cree usted que se fue con otro pariente?	¿KREH-eh OOS-tehd ke seh fweh kohn OH-troh pah-RYEHN-teh?

PARENT	PADRE/MADRE	
No, our relatives live in another state/city.	No, *nuestros parientes viven en otro estado/otra ciudad.*	Noh, NWEHS-trohs pah-RYEHN-tehs VEE-vehn OH-troh ehs-TAH-doh/oh-trah syoo-DAHD.
No, I already called them.	No, *ya los llamé.*	Noh, yah lohs yah-MEH.

B. OBTAINING INFORMATION REGARDING THE FAMILY BACKGROUND

CULTURE NOTE ••••

FAMILY VALUES Family ties are highly valued in Latino culture. Grandparents often live with their children and grandchildren, provide support, and exercise a strong influence within the family. Family members are openly affectionate with one another. Therefore, crimes against children and the elderly are not very common. The mother is considered the "heart" of the household, while the father is the official head of his family with unquestioned authority.

OFFICER	AGENTE	
Do both parents live together?	¿Viven juntos los padres?	¿VEE-vehn HOON-tohs lohs PAH-drehs?

PARENT	PADRE/MADRE	
Yes, we live together.	Sí, vivimos juntos.	See, vee-VEE-mohs HOON-tohs.

No, his/her mother/father lives in another…	No, su madre/padre vive en otro…	Noh, soo MAH-dreh/ PAH-dreh VEE-veh ehn OH-troh…
• state.	• estado.	• ehs-TAH-doh.
• city.	• ciudad.	• SYOO-dahd.
• neighborhood.	• barrio.	• BAH-rryoh.

OFFICER — **AGENTE**

Do you think his/her mom/dad could have picked up the child?	¿Cree que su padre/madre vino a recogerlo/la?	¿KREH-eh keh soo PAH-dreh/MAH-dreh VEE-noh ah rreh-koh-HEHR-loh/lah?
Are there custody orders for your child?	¿Hay órdenes para la custodia de su hijo/a?	¿Ahy ah-RREH-glohs deh koos-toh-DEE-ah PAH-rah soo EE-hoh/hah?
Do you and your ex-husband/ex-wife get along?	¿Se lleva bien con su ex-esposo/a?	¿Seh YEH-vah byehn kohn soo eks ehs-POH-soh/sah?

PARENT — **PADRE/MADRE**

Yes, we get along.	Sí, nos llevamos bien.	See, nohs yehh-VAH-mohs byehn.
No, we don't get along.	No, no nos llevamos bien.	Noh, noh nohs yeh-VAH-mohs byehn.
I have custody.	Tengo la custodia.	TEHN-goh lah koos-TOH-dyah.
We have joint custody.	Compartimos la custodia.	Kohm-pahr-TEE-mohs lah koos-TOH-dyah.

OFFICER — **AGENTE**

Does he/she get along with his parents/ siblings?	¿Se lleva bien con sus padres/hermanos?	¿Seh YEH-vah bee-EHN kohn soos PAD-drehs/ehr-MAH-nohs?
Have you observed any particular or unusual behavior lately?	¿Ha observado algo diferente en su actitud últimamente?	¿Ah ohb-sehr-VAH-doh AHL-goh dee-feh-REHN-teh ehn soo ahk-tee-TOOD OOL-tee-mah-MEHN-teh?

PARENT — **PADRE/MADRE**

He was…lately.	Estaba…últimamente.	Ehs-TAH-bah…OOL-tee-mah-MEHN-teh.

- moody
- withdrawn
- quiet

• de mal humor	• deh mahl oo-MOHR
• callado	• kah-YAH-doh
• callado	• kah-YAH-doh

OFFICER

Has he/she ever run away?

Has he/she ever been missing before?

Where did he/she go before?

AGENTE

¿Se ha escapado alguna vez?

¿Ha estado perdido alguna vez?

¿Adónde fue?

¿Seh ah ehs-kah-PAH-doh ahl-GOO-nah vehs?

¿Ah ehs-TAH-dah pehr-DEE-doh ahl-GOO-nah vehs?

¿Ah-DOHN-deh fweh?

PARENT

He/she...
- went to a friend's house.

- hid in the garage for hours.

PADRE/MADRE

Él/ella se...
- fue a la casa de sus amigos.

- escondió en el garaje por horas.

Ehl/EY-ah seh...
- fweh ah lah KAH-sah deh soos ah-MEE-gohs.

- ehs-kohn-dee-OH ehn ehl gah-RAH-heh pohr OH-rahs.

OFFICER

Is anybody out looking for him/her now?

AGENTE

¿Hay alguien buscándolo/la ahora?

¿Ahy ahl-GYEHN boos-KAHN-doh-loh/lah ah-oh-RAH?

PARENT

Yes, the neighbors/ friends.

PADRE/MADRE

Sí, los vecinos/amigos.

See, lohs veh-SEE-nohs/ ah-MEE-gohs.

OFFICER

What's the child's name?

Is he/she afraid of the police?

How old is the child?

Does the child have any medical problems?

AGENTE

¿Cómo se llama el niño/la niña?

¿Tiene miedo de la policía?

¿Cuántos años tiene?

¿Tiene problemas médicos?

¿KOH-moh seh YAH-mah ehl nee-NYOH/ lah nee-NYAH?

¿TYEH-neh mee-EH-doh deh lah poh-lee-SEE-ah?

¿KWAHN-tohs AH-nyohs TYEHN-eh?

¿TYEH-neh proh-BLEH-mahs MEH-dee-kohs?

Has he/she done this before?	¿Ha hecho esto alguna vez?	¿Ah EH-cho EHS-toh ahl-GOO-nah vehs?
PARENT	*PADRE/MADRE*	
He/she does/does not have medical problems.	*Tiene/no tiene problemas médicos.*	TYEH-neh/noh TYEH-neh proh-BLEH-mahs MEH-dee-kohs.
He/she is...	*Es...*	Ehs...
• epileptic.	• *epiléptico/a.*	• eh-pee-LEHP-tee-koh/ah.
• diabetic.	• *diabético/a.*	• dee-ah-BEH-tee-koh/ah.
• handicapped.	• *impedido/a.*	• eem-peh-DEE-doh/ah.
• retarded.	• *retrasado/a mental.*	• reh-trah-SAH-doh/ah mehn-TAHL.

C. OBTAINING INFORMATION FOR A GUIDED SEARCH

OFFICER	*AGENTE*	
Have you looked...	¿Ha buscado...	¿Ah boos-kah-doh...
• everywhere?	• *en todas partes?*	• ehn TOH-dahs PAHR-tehs?
• in the house?	• *en la casa?*	• ehn lah KAH-sah?
• in the yard?	• *en el jardín?*	• ehn ehl hahr-DEEN?
• in the car?	• *en el carro?*	• ehn ehl KAH-rroh?
• in the bushes?	• *en los arbustos?*	• ehn lohs ahr-BOOS-tohs?
• in the basement?	• *en el sótano?*	• ehn ehl SOH-tah-noh?
May I come in and search?	¿Puedo entrar a registrar?	¿PWEH-doh ehn-TRAHR ah reh-hees-TRAHR?
PARENT	*PADRE/MADRE*	
Go ahead.	*Como guste.*	KOH-moh GOOS-teh.
Come in, please.	*Entre, por favor.*	EHN-treh, pohr fah-VOHR.

| I have already looked everywhere. | Ya busqué por todas partes. | Yah boohs-KEH pohr TOH-dahs PAHR-tehs. |

OFFICER · **AGENTE**

| Are there any clothes/things missing from his/her bedroom? | ¿Faltan ropa/cosas de su cuarto? | ¿FAHL-tahn RROH-pah/KOH-sahs deh soo KWAR-toh? |

PARENT · **PADRE/MADRE**

| Only the clothes he's/she's wearing. | Sólo la ropa que lleva puesta. | SOH-loh lah RRO-pah ke YEH-vah PWEHS-tah. |

OFFICER · **AGENTE**

| If he/she gets scared or angry is there a place for him/her to hide? | Si se asusta o se enoja, ¿hay algún lugar dónde se esconde? | See seh ah-SOOS-tah oh seh eh-noh-hah, ¿ahy ahl-GOON loo-GAHR DOHN-deh seh ehs-KOHN-deh? |

PARENT · **PADRE/MADRE**

He/she locks himself/ herself up in…	Se esconde en…	Seh ehs-KOHN-deh ehn…
• the bathroom.	• el baño.	• ehl BAH-nyoh.
• his room.	• su cuarto.	• soo KWAHR-toh.
• the basement.	• el sótano.	• ehl SOH-tah-noh.

OFFICER · **AGENTE**

| Are there stores in the area he/she likes to visit? | ¿Hay tiendas que frecuenta? | ¿Ahy TYEHN-dahs keh freh-KWEHN-tah? |
| Does he/she have any new friends? | ¿Tiene amigos/as nuevos/as? | ¿TYEH-neh ah-MEE-gohs/gahs NWEH-vohs/vahs? |

PARENT · **PADRE/MADRE**

| Yes. He/she likes to go to ___. | Sí. Le gusta ir a ___. | See. Leh GOOS-tah eer ah___. |
| I'm not aware of any new friends. | No creo que haya amigos nuevos. | Noh KREH-oh keh AH-yah ah-MEE-gohs NWE-vohs. |

OFFICER	AGENTE	
Is there...missing from the house?	¿Le falta...de su casa?	¿Leh FAHL-tah... deh soo KAH-sah?
• money	• dinero	• dee-NEH-roh
• credit cards	• tarjetas de crédito	• tahr-HEE-tah deh KREH-dee-toh
• anything	• alguna cosa	• ahl-GOO-nah KOH-sah
How much money do you think he/she has?	¿Cuánto dinero cree que él/ella tiene?	¿KWAHN-toh dee-NEH-roh KREH-eh KEH ehl/EH-yah TYEH-neh?
Does he/she have a vehicle?	¿Tiene un vehículo?	¿TYEH-neh oon veh-EE-koo-loh?
Describe the vehicle.	Describa el vehículo.	Dehs-KREE-bah ehl veh-EE-koo-loh.
What's the license plate number?	¿Cuál es el número de su placa?	¿Kwahl ehs ehl NOO-meh-roh deh soo PLAH-kah?
Do you have a picture we could use?	¿Tiene una foto que podemos usar?	¿TYEH-neh OO-nah FOH-toh keh poh-DEH-mohs oo-SAHR?
Here is our phone number.	Aquí tiene nuestro número de teléfono.	Ah-KEE TYEH-neh NWES-troh NOO-meh-roh deh teh-LEH-foh-noh.
Call immediately when you find out where he/she is.	Llámenos inmediatamente cuando sepa dónde está.	YAH-meh-nohs een-meh-dee-ah-tah-MEHN-teh KWAHN-doh SEH-pah DOHN-deh ehs-TAH.
We'll call you shortly to see if he/she has come back home.	Lo/la llamaré para ver si ya ha regresado.	Loh yah-mah-REH PAH-rah vehr see yah ah reh-greh-SAH-doh.
We'll do our best to find him/her.	Haremos lo que podamos para encontrarlo.	Ah-REH-mohs loh keh poh-DAH-mohs PAH-rah ehn-kohn-TRAHR-loh.

| We have to wait ___ hours before we can start an official search, but we'll keep our eyes open. | Tenemos que esperar ___ horas antes de empezar una búsqueda oficial, pero mantendremos los ojos abiertos. | Teh-NEH-mohs keh ehs-peh-RAHR ___ OH-rahs AHN-tehs deh ehm-peh-SAHR OO-nah BOOS-keh-dah oh-fee-SYAHL, PEH-roh mahn-tehn-DREH-mohs lohs OH-hohs ah-BYEHR-tohs. |

3. Dealing with the Homeless

OFFICER	**AGENTE**	
Hello!	¡Hola!	¡OH-lah!
What's your name?	¿Cómo se llama?	¿KOH-moh seh YAH-mah?
HOMELESS PERSON	**VAGABUNDO**	
Hello!	¡Hola!	¡OH-lah!
My name is ___.	Me llamo ___.	Meh YAH-moh ___.
OFFICER	**AGENTE**	
Do you have an ID?	¿Tiene identificación?	¿TYEH-neh ee-dehn-tee-fee-kah-SYOHN?
HOMELESS PERSON	**VAGABUNDO**	
I don't have an ID.	No tengo identificación.	Noh TEHN-goh ee-dehn-tee-fee-kah-SYOHN.
I lost it.	La perdí.	Lah pehr-DEE.
OFFICER	**AGENTE**	
What's your address?	¿Cual es su dirección?	¿Kwahl ehs soo dee-rehk-SYOHN?
HOMELESS PERSON	**VAGABUNDO**	
I don't have an address.	No tengo una dirección.	Noh TEHN-goh dee-rehk-SYOHN.
OFFICER	**AGENTE**	
When did you last have a home?	¿Cuándo tiempo hace que no tiene casa?	¿KWAHN-toh TYEHM-poh AH-seh keh no TYEH-neh KAH-sah?

HOMELESS PERSON	VAGABUNDO	
Last week.	Hace una semana.	AH-seh OO-nah seh-MAH-nah.
A month ago.	Hace un mes.	AH-seh OON mehs.
A few days ago.	Hace unos días.	AH-seh OO-nohs DEE-ahs.
Years ago.	Hace unos años.	AH-seh OO-nohs AH-nyohs.
I don't remember.	No recuerdo.	No reh-KWEHR-doh.

OFFICER	AGENTE	
Where was it?	¿Dónde estaba?	¿DOHN-deh ehs-TAH-bah?

HOMELESS PERSON	VAGABUNDO	
It was...	Estaba...	Ehs-TAH-bah...
• in (city) _____.	• en (ciudad) _____.	• ehn (syoo-DAHD) _____.
• on _____ street.	• en la calle _____.	• ehn lah KAH-yeh _____.
• in (state) _____.	• en (estado) _____.	• ehn (ehs-TAH-doh) _____.

OFFICER	AGENTE	
Are you working?	¿Trabaja usted?	¿Trah-BAH-hah oos-TEHD?
Where do you work?	¿Dónde trabaja usted?	¿DOHN-deh trah-BAH-hah oos-TEHD?
What type of work do you do?	¿Qué tipo de trabajo hace usted?	¿Keh TEE-poh deh trah-BAH-hoh AH-seh oos-TEHD?

HOMELESS PERSON	VAGABUNDO	
No, I don't...	No, no...	Noh, noh...
• work right now.	• trabajo ahorita.	• trah-BAH-hoh ah-oh-REE-tah.
• have a job.	• tengo trabajo.	• TEHN-goh trah-BAH-hoh.
Yes, I work...	Sí, trabajo...	See, trah-BAH-hoh...

• in construction.	• *en la construcción.*	• ehn lah kohn-strook-SYOHN.
• as a temporary laborer.	• *de obrero temporero.*	• deh oh-BREH-roh tehm-poh-REH-roh.

OFFICER

AGENTE

Where did you sleep last night?	*¿Dónde durmió anoche?*	¿DOHN-deh door-MYOH ah-NOH-cheh?

HOMELESS PERSON

VAGABUNDO

I don't remember.	*No recuerdo.*	No rreh-KWEHR-doh.
I sleep wherever I can.	*Duermo donde puedo.*	DWEHR-moh DOHN-deh PWEH-doh.
At a friend's house.	*En casa de un amigo.*	Ehn KAH-sah deh oon ah-MEE-goh.
In a motel.	*En un motel.*	Ehn oon moh-TEHL.
In a shelter.	*En un refugio.*	Ehn oon reh-FOO-hyoh,

OFFICER

AGENTE

You cannot stay here.	*No puede quedarse aquí.*	Noh PWEH-deh keh-DAHR-seh ah-KEE.
You need to leave.	*Tiene que marcharse.*	TYEH-neh keh mahr-CHAR-seh.

HOMELESS PERSON

VAGABUNDO

I don't know where to go.	*No sé adónde ir.*	No seh ah-DOHN-dah eer.
Let me sleep here one more night.	*Déjeme dormir aquí una noche más.*	DEH-heh-meh dohr-MEER ah-KEE OO-nah NOH-cheh mahs.

OFFICER

AGENTE

Do you have any drugs/alcohol with you?	*¿Tiene drogas/alcohol con usted?*	¿TYEH-neh DROH-gahs/AHL-kohl kohn oos-TEHD?
Can I check your bags/things?	*¿Puedo registrar sus bolsas/cosas?*	¿PWEH-doh reh-hees-TRAHR soos BOHL-sahs/KOH-sahs?
I need to search you.	*Necesito registrarlo.*	Neh-seh-SEE-toh reh-hees-TRAHR-loh.

HOMELESS PERSON

VAGABUNDO

Sure. Go ahead.

Sí. ¿Cómo no?

See. ¿KOH-moh noh?

I got nothing to hide.

No tengo nada que ocultar.

Noh TEHN-goh NAH-dah oh-kool-TAHR.

No problem.

No hay problema.

Noh ahy proh-BLEH-mah.

OFFICER

AGENTE

Turn around.

Voltéese.

Vohl-TEH-eh-seh.

Put your hands together on your head.

Ponga las manos juntas en la cabeza.

POHN-gah lahs MAH-nohs HOON-tahs ehn lah kah-BEH-sah.

Have you ever been arrested?

¿Lo han arrestado alguna vez?

¿Loh ahn ah-rrhes-TAH-doh ahl-GOO-nah vez?

Where?

¿Dónde?

¿DOHN-deh?

When?

¿Cuándo?

¿KWAHN-doh?

Why?

Por qué?

¿Pohr keh?

You have to go to a shelter.

Debe ir al refugio.

DEH-beh eer ahl reh-FOO-hyoh.

Can I take you...

¿Puedo llevarlo...

¿PWEH-doh yeh-VAHR-loh...

• somewhere?

• *a algún sitio?*

• ah ahl-GOON SEE-tyoh?

• to a shelter?

• *al refugio?*

• ahl reh-FOO-hyoh?

I have to give you a ticket for...

Tengo que ponerle una multa por...

TEHN-goh poh-NEHR-leh OO-nah MOOL-tah pohr...

• trespassing.

• *pasar a una zona prohibida.*

• pah-SAHR ah OO-nah SOH-nah proh-ee-BEE-dah.

• urinating in public.

• *orinar en público.*

• oh-ree-NAHR ehn POO-blee-koh.

• carrying an open alcohol container.

• *llevar una botella de alcohol abierta.*

• yeh-VAHR OO-nah boh-TEH-yah deh ahl-KOHL ah-BYEHR-tah.

• drug possession.

• *posesión de drogas.*

• poh-seh-SYOHN deh DROH-gahs.

I have to check your identity.	Tengo que comprobar su identidad.	TEHN-goh keh kohm-proh-BAHR soo ee-dehn-tee-DAHD.
You have to come with me to the station...	Tiene que venir conmigo a la estación...	TYEH-neh keh vehn-EER kohn-MEE-go ah lah ehs-tah-SYOHN...
• until you're sober.	• hasta que esté sobrio.	• AHS-tah keh ehs-TEH SOH-bree-oh.
• for questioning.	• para el interrogatorio.	• PAH-rah ehl een-teh-rroh-gah-TOH-ryoh.
• so I can check your identity.	• para comprobar su identidad.	• PAH-rah kohm-pro-BAHR soo ee-dehn-tee-DAHD.

Grammar Note ••••

THE VERB *HACER* (TO DO/TO MAKE) WITH EXPRESSIONS OF TIME The structure *hace* + period of time + *que* + verb in the preterite is equivalent to the simple English "ago" + past tense. It indicates that an event happened some time ago.

> *Hace una hora que ocurrió el accidente.*
> The accident happened one hour ago.

If the word order is reversed, *que* is dropped.

> *El accidente ocurrió hace una hora.*
> The accident happened one hour ago.

The structure *hace* + period of time + *que* + the verb in the present is equivalent to the English "since" + present perfect continuous, and it indicates how long an action has been taking or going on.

> *Hace una semana que no tengo casa.*
> It has been a week since I don't have a home.

4. Nonarrest Contact

> # CULTURE NOTE ••••
>
> **THE LEGAL SYSTEM**   The United States legal system
> assumes "innocence until proven guilty." The Latin
> American approach is just the opposite: you are "guilty until
> proven innocent." Many Latinos feel that in Latin America
> civil rights are routinely ignored, because they have wit-
> nessed unjust jailings, random abuse or even killings in the
> name of authoritarian regimes. Obviously this does not
> result in a strong belief in law and order. Many Latinos feel
> that fair laws should be flexible, and should be interpreted
> according to relevant particular circumstances. Some may
> try to talk their way out of a citation or an arrest, as this is
> accepted practice in some Latin American countries. Do not
> consider this as an act of disrespect, but calmly explain that
> in the U.S. laws cannot be interpreted by a police officer, but
> must be strictly enforced. An interpretation of the law must
> be left up to a trial and a jury.

OFFICER	*AGENTE*	
Stop!	*¡Alto!*	¡AHL-toh!
Police!	*¡Policía!*	¡Poh-lee-SEE-ah!
I'm Officer ____.	*Soy el agente ____.*	Soy ehl ah-HEHN-teh ____.
Your driver's license or other form of identification, please.	*Su licencia de manejar u otro tipo de identificación, por favor.*	Soo lee-SEHN-see-ah deh mah-neh-HAHR oo OH-troh TEE-poh deh ee-dehn-tee-fee-kah-SYOHN, pohr fah-VOHR.

Why are you…	¿Por qué anda por…	¿Pohr KEH ahn-dah pohr…
• out so late?	• la calle tan tarde?	• lah KAH-yeh tahn TAHR-deh?
• in this area?	• esta zona?	• EHS-tah SOH-nah?
SUBJECT	**SUJETO**	
Because…	Porque…	POHR-keh…
• I couldn't sleep.	• no podía dormir.	• noh poh-DEE-ah dohr-MEER.
• I'm going to work.	• voy a trabajar.	• voy ah trah-bah-HAR.
• I'm going home.	• voy a casa.	• voy ah KAH-sah.
• my wife kicked me out.	• mi mujer me echó de casa.	• mee moo-HEHR meh eh-CHOH deh KHA-sah.
• I live here.	• vivo aquí.	• VEE-voh ah-KEE.
• I work here.	• trabajo aquí.	• trah BAH-hoh ah-KEE.
• I'm lost.	• estoy perdido.	• ehs-TOY pehr-DEE-doh.
OFFICER	**AGENTE**	
Do you realize that this is…	¿No sabe usted que ésta es…	¿Noh SAH-beh oos-TEHD keh EHS-tah ehs…
• a dangerous area?	• una zona peligrosa?	• OO-nah SOH-nah peh-lee-GROH-sah?
• private property?	• propiedad privada?	• proh-pyeh-DAHD pree-VAH-dah?
• a crime scene?	• la escena de un crimen?	• lah ehs-SEH-nah deh oon KREE-mehn?
Do you need…	¿Necesita…	¿Neh-seh-SEE-tah…
• a ride somewhere?	• que lo lleve a alguna parte?	• keh loh YEH-veh ah ah ahl-GOO-nah PAHR-teh?
• assistance?	• ayuda?	• ah-YOO-dah?
SUBJECT	**SUJETO**	
No, thank you.	No, gracias.	Noh, GRAH-syahs.

Yes, please.	Sí, por favor.	See, pohr fah-VOHR.
• I live	• Vivo	• VEE-voh
• I work	• Trabajo	• Trah-BAH-hoh
...nearby.	...cerca.	...SEHR-kah.
My car...	Mi carro...	Mee KAH-rroh...
• is just over there.	• está allí.	• ehs-TAH ah-YEE.
• broke down.	• está descompuesto.	• ehs-TAH dehs-kohm-PWEHS-toh.
Would you give me a ride...	¿Me podría llevar...	¿Meh poh-DREE-ah yeh-VAHR...
• home?	• a casa?	• ah KAH-sah?
• to work?	• al trabajo?	• ahl trah-BAH-hoh?
• to this address?	• a esta dirección?	• ah EHS-tah dee-rehk-SYOHN?
Would you call a cab for me?	¿Me podría llamar a un taxi?	¿Meh poh-DREE-ah yah-MAHR ah oon TAHK-see?

OFFICER	**AGENTE**	
You should...	Debe...	DEH-beh...
• go home.	• irse a su casa.	• EER-seh ah soo KAH-sah.
• leave this area.	• salir de este lugar.	• sah-LEER deh EHS-teh loo-GAHR.
• get in your car.	• entrar en su carro.	• ehn-TRAHR ehn soo KAH-rroh.
• turn around.	• salir de aquí.	• sah-LEER deh ah-KEE.
You are drunk.	Está borracho.	Ehs-TAH boh-RRAH-choh.
You cannot...	No puede...	Noh PWEH-deh...
• drive.	• manejar.	• mah-neh-HAHR.
• walk home by yourself.	• caminar a casa.	• kah-mee-NAHR ah KAH-sah.

I have to make sure that you...	Tengo que asegurarme que...	TEHN-goh keh ah-seh-goo-RAHR-meh kee...
• get home safe.	• llega a casa bien.	• YEH-gah ah KAH-sah byehn.
• will find your way home.	• va a encontrar su casa.	• vah ah ehn-kohn-TRAHR soo KAH-sah.
Please come to the station with me so I can...	Por favor, venga a la estación conmigo para...	Pohr fah-VOHR, VEHN-gah ah lah ehs-tah-SYOHN kohn-MEE-goh PAH-rah...
• check your ID.	• comprobar su identificación.	• kohm-pro-BAHR soo ee-dehn-tee-fee-kah-SYOHN.
• call your family.	• llamar a su familia.	• yah-MAHR ah soo fah-MEE-lee-ah.
• give you a ride home.	• llevarlo a su casa.	• yeh VAHR loh ah soo KAH-sah.

5. Curfew Violations

OFFICER	AGENTE	
Stop! Come here.	¡Alto! Vengan aquí.	¡AHL-toh! VEHN-gahn ah-KEE.

CHILDREN	NIÑOS	
We are not doing anything wrong.	No hacemos nada malo.	Noh ah-SEH-mohs NAH-dah MAH-loh.
Is there something wrong?	¿Cuál es el problema?	¿Kwal ehs ehl proh-BLEH-mah?

OFFICER	AGENTE	
You look too young to be out this late.	Ustedes parecen muy jóvenes para andar por la calle a estas horas.	Oos-TEH-dehs pah-REH-sehn mwee HOH-veh-nehs PAH-rah AHN-dahr pohr lah KAH-yeh ah EHS-tahs OH-rahs.

Do you know what time it is?	¿Saben qué hora es?	¿SAH-behn keh OH-rah ehs?
Give me your...	Denme sus...	DEHN-meh soos...
• names.	• nombres.	• NOHM-brehs.
• birthdates.	• fechas de nacimiento.	• FEH-chahs deh nah-see-MYEHN-to.
• addresses.	• direcciones.	• dee-rehk-SYOH-nehs.
Who is driving this car?	¿Quién maneja este carro?	¿Kyehn mah-NEH-hah EHS-teh KAH-rroh?
May I see your driver's license?	¿Puedo ver tu licencia de manejar?	¿PWEH-doh vehr too lee-SEHN-see-ah deh mah-neh-HAHR?
How old are you?	¿Cuántos años tienes?	¿KWAHN-tohs AH-nyohs TYEH-nehs?

CHILDREN — **NIÑOS**

I don't have a driver's license.	No tengo licencia de manejar.	Noh TEHN-goh lee-SEHN-see-ah deh mah-neh-HAHR.
I have a permit.	Tengo un permiso.	TEHN-goh oon pehr-MEE-soh.
I'm getting my license in a week.	Voy a tener mi licencia en una semana.	Voy ah teh-NEHR mee lee-SEHN-see-ah ehn OO-nah seh-MAH-nah.
Here is my license.	Aquí está mi licencia.	Ah-KEE ehs-TAH mee lee-SEHN-see-ah.

OFFICER — **AGENTE**

Where were you going?	¿Adónde iban?	¿Ah-DOHN-deh EE-bahn?

CHILDREN — **NIÑOS**

We were not going anywhere.	No íbamos a ninguna parte.	Noh EE-bah-mohs ah neen-GOO-nah PAHR-teh.
We were just hanging out.	Estábamos por aquí.	Ehs-TAH-bah-mohs pohr ah-KEE.
We were going...	Íbamos...	Ee-BAH-mohs...

• to a friend's house.	• *a casa de un/una amigo/a.*	• ah lah KAH-sah deh OON/OO-nah ah-MEE-goh/gah.
• to my house.	• *a mi casa.*	• ah mee KAH-sah.

OFFICER / *AGENTE*

Do you have any drugs/alcohol on you?	*¿Tienen drogas/alcohol con ustedes?*	¿TYEH-nehn DROH-gahs/ahl-KOHL kohn oos-TEH-dehs?
I have to search...	*Tengo que registrar...*	TEHN-goh kee reh-hees-TRAHR...
• you.	• *los.*	• lohs.
• your backpack.	• *la mochila.*	• lah moh-CHEE-lah.
• your bags.	• *las bolsas.*	• lahs BOHL-sahs.
• your pockets.	• *los bolsillos.*	• lohs bohl-SEE-yohs.
• your car.	• *el carro.*	• ehl KAH-rroh.

CHILDREN / *NIÑOS*

Great!	*¡Fantástico!*	¡Fahn-TAHS-tee-koh!
Yeah!	*¡Ya!*	¡Yah!
Go ahead!	*¡Adelante!*	¡Ah-deh-LAHN-teh!
Whatever!	*¡Como quiera!*	¡KOH-moh KYEH-rah!
No way!	*¡De ninguna manera!*	¡Deh neen-GOO-nah mah-NEH-rah!
I want a lawyer.	*Quiero un abogado.*	KYEH-roh oon ah-boh-GAH-doh.
I want to call my father/mother.	*Quiero llamar a mi padre/madre.*	KYEH-roh yah-MAHR ah mee PAH-dreh/MAH-dreh.
Call my mother/father, if you don't believe me.	*Llame a mi madre/padre, si no me cree.*	YAH-meh ah mee MAH-dreh/PAH-dreh, see noh meh KREH-eh.

OFFICER / *AGENTE*

I'm going to...	*Voy a...*	Voy ah...
• call your parents.	• *llamar a sus padres.*	• yah-MAHR ah soos PAH-drehs.

- take you home.

- take you to your
  friend's house.

Do your parents
speak English?

Tell your parents to
come to headquarters.

I have to
make sure that...

- you get home safe.

- you are not lost.

I'm going to give
you a ticket for...

- curfew violation.

- driving without a
  license.

- drug possession.

Get in the car.

Give me your
car keys.

I'm going to impound
this vehicle.

- *llevarlos/las a casa.*

- *llevarlos/las a la casa
  de su amigo/a.*

*¿Hablan inglés
sus padres?*

*Dígale/Dile a sus/tus
padres que vengan a
la estación.*

*Tengo que
asegurarme que...*

- *lleguen a casa bien.*

- *no están perdidos.*

*Voy a darles una
multa por...*

- *violar el toque de
  queda.*

- *manejar
  sin licencia.*

- *posesión de drogas.*

Suban al carro.

*Denme las llaves
de su carro.*

*La grua va a llevarse
este vehículo.*

- yeh-VAHR-lohs/lahs
  ah KAH-sah.

- yeh-VAHR-lohs/lahs
  ah lah KAH-sah deh
  soo ah-MEE-goh/gah.

¿AH-blahn een-GLEHS
soos PAH-drehs?

DEE-gah-leh/DEE-leh
ah soos/toos PAH-drehs
keh vehn-gahn ah lah
ehs-tah-SYOHN.

TEHN-goh keh ah-seh-
goo-RAHR-meh keh...

- YEH-gehn ah KAH-
  sah byehn.

- noh ehs-TAHN pehr-
  dee-dohs.

Voy ah DAHR-lehs
OO-nah MOOL-tah
pohr...

- vee-oh-LAHR ehl
  TOH-keh deh KEH-
  dah.

- mah-neh-HAHR seen
  lee-SEHN-see-ah.

- poh-seh-SYOHN deh
  DROH-gahs.

SOO-bahn ahl KAH-
rroh.

DEHN-meh lahs YAH-
vehs deh soo KAH-rroh.

Lah GROO-ah vah ah
yeh-VAHR-seh EHS-
teh veh-EE-koo-loh.

6. Noise Complaints

A. ESTABLISHING THE NATURE OF THE COMPLAINT

OFFICER

AGENTE

Good evening. I'm Officer _____.

Buenas noches. Soy el agente _____.

BWEH-nahs NOH-chehs. Soy ehl ah-HEHN-teh _____.

Someone called the police.

Alguien llamó a la policía.

AHL-gyehn YAH-moh ah lah poh-lee-SEE-ah.

What's the problem?

¿Cuál es el problema?

¿Kwahl ehs ehl proh-BLEH-mah?

COMPLAINANT

DEMANDANTE

The neighbors...

Los vecinos...

Lohs veh-SEE-nohs...

• are making too much noise.

• *están haciendo mucho ruido.*

• ehs TAHN ah SYEHN-doh MOO-choh RWEE-doh.

• won't turn their music down.

• *no bajan el sonido de la música.*

• noh BAH-hahn ehl soh-NEE-doh deh lah MOO-see-kah.

The neighbor's dog won't stop barking.

El perro del vecino no para de ladrar.

Ehl PEH-rroh dehl veh-SEE-noh noh PAH-rah deh lah-DRAHR.

The neighbor's TV is too loud.

La tele del vecino está demasiado alta.

Lah teh-LEH dehl veh-SEE-noh ehs-TAH deh-mah-see-AH-doh AHL-tah.

The couple...is fighting.

La pareja...está peleando.

Lah pah-REH-hah... ehs-TAH peh-leh-AHN-doh.

• next door

• *del piso de al lado*

• dehl PEE-soh deh ahl LAH-doh

• upstairs

• *de arriba*

• deh ah-RREE-bah

• downstairs

• *de abajo*

• deh ah-BAH-hoh

The child next door has been crying for a long time.	*El niño del piso de al lado ha estado llorando por mucho tiempo.*	Ehl NEE-nyoh dehl PEE-soh deh ahl LAH-doh ah ehs-TAH-doh yoh-RAHN-doh pohr MOO-choh TYEHM-poh.

B. LOCATING THE PROBLEM

OFFICER	*AGENTE*	
Where does the noise come from?	*¿De dónde viene el ruido?*	¿Deh DOHN-deh VYEH-neh ehl RWEE-doh?
COMPLAINANT	*DEMANDANTE*	
It comes from...	*Viene...*	VYEH-neh...
• upstairs.	• *de arriba.*	• deh ah-RREE-bah.
• downstairs.	• *de abajo.*	• deh ah-BAH-hoh.
• next door.	• *de al lado.*	• deh ahl LAH-doh.
• the first floor.	• *del primer piso.*	• dehl pree-MEHR PEE-soh.
• the basement.	• *del sótano.*	• dehl SOH-tah-noh.
• apartment #A.	• *del apartamento A.*	• dehl ah-pahr-tah-MEHN-toh ah.
• the house across the street.	• *de la casa al otro lado de la calle.*	• deh lah KAH-sah ahl OH-troh LAH-doh deh lah KAH-yeh.
I don't know where the noise is coming from.	*No sé de dónde viene el ruido.*	Noh seh deh DOHN-deh VYEH-neh ehl-RWEE-doh.
OFFICER	*AGENTE*	
Do you know who lives...	*¿Sabe quién vive...*	¿SAH-beh kyehn VEE-veh...
• in that house?	• *en esa casa?*	• ehn EH-sah KAH-sah?
• in that apartment?	• *en ese apartamento?*	• ehn EH-seh ah-pahr-tah-MEHN-toh?
• next door?	• *al lado?*	• ahl LAH-doh?

English	Spanish	Pronunciation
• below you?	• *debajo de usted?*	• deh-BAH-hoh deh oos-TEHD?
• there?	• *allí?*	• ah-YEEH?
COMPLAINANT	***DEMANDANTE***	
Yes, I do.	*Sí, lo sé.*	See, loh seh.
A man called ____.	*Un hombre que se llama ____.*	Oon OHM-breh keh seh YAH-mah ____.
A young couple.	*Una pareja joven.*	OO-nah pah-REH-hah HOH-vehn.
Two men.	*Dos hombres.*	Dohs OHM-brehs.
College students.	*Estudiantes universitarios.*	Ehs-too-DYAHN-tehs oo-nee-vehr-see-TAH-ryohs.
I don't know their names.	*No sé cómo se llaman.*	Noh seh KOH-moh seh YAH-mahn.
OFFICER	***AGENTE***	
Have you...	*¿Ha...*	¿Ah...
• had this problem before?	• *tenido este problema alguna vez?*	• teh-NEE-doh EHS-teh proh-BLEH-mah ahl-GOO-nah vehs?
• asked the neighbors to keep it down?	• *pedido a los vecinos que no hagan ruido?*	• peh-DEE-doh ah lohs veh-SEE-nohs keh noh AH-gahn RWEE-doh?
COMPLAINANT	***DEMANDANTE***	
No, this is the first time.	*No, esta es la primera vez.*	Noh, EHS-tah ehs lah pree-MEH-rah vehz.
Yes, this happens all the time.	*Sí, esto pasa todo el tiempo.*	See, EHS-toh PAH-sah TOH-doh ehl TYEHM-poh.
No, I don't talk to them.	*No, no hablo con ellos.*	Noh, noh AH-bloh kohn EH-yohs.
Yes, I've called twice, but they don't listen to me.	*Sí, les he hablado dos veces pero no me hacen caso.*	See, lehs eh ah-BLAH-doh dohs VEH-sehs PEH-roh noh meh AH-sehn KAH-soh.

OFFICER	AGENTE	
Let me talk to them.	*Déjeme hablar con ellos.*	DEH-heh-meh ah-BLAHR kohn EH-yohs.
Would you like to sign a complaint?	*¿Quiere firmar una queja?*	¿KYEH-reh FEER-mahr OO-nah KEH-hah?
I'll talk to them and issue a warning.	*Les voy a hablar y les voy a dar un aviso.*	Lehs voy ah ah-BLAHR ee lehs voy ah dahr oon ah-VEE-soh.

COMPLAINANT	DEMANDANTE	
Thanks, officer.	*Gracias, agente.*	GRAH-syahs, ah-HEN-teh.
A warning?	*¿Un aviso?*	¿Oon ah-VEE-soh?
I want to press charges.	*Quiero presentar una denuncia.*	KYEH-roh preh-sehn-TAHR OO-nah deh-NOON-syah.

OFFICER	AGENTE	
Have you filed a complaint before?	*¿Ha presentado una denuncia antes?*	¿Ah preh-sehn-TAH-doh OO-nah deh-NOON-syah AHN-tehs?

COMPLAINANT	DEMANDANTE	
No, never.	*No, nunca.*	Noh, NOON-kah.
Yes, once before.	*Sí, una vez antes.*	See, OO-nah vehs AHN-tehs.
Many times.	*Muchas veces.*	MOO-chahs VEH-sehs.

C. DEALING WITH THE PROBLEM

OFFICER	AGENTE	
Good evening. I'm Officer ____.	*Buenas noches. Soy el agente ____.*	BWEH-nahs NOH-chehs. Soy ehl ah-HEHN-teh ____.
One of your neighbors complained about...	*Uno de sus vecinos se quejó acerca...*	OO-noh deh soos veh-SEE-nohs seh keh-HOH ah-SEHR-cah...

• loud music.	• *del volumen de la música.*	• dehl voh-LOO-mehn deh lah MOO-see-kah.
• loud voices.	• *del volumen de las voces.*	• dehl voh-LOO-mehn deh lahs VOH-sehs.
• a loud stereo/TV.	• *del volumen del estéreo/de la tele.*	• dehl voh-LOO-mehn dehl ehs-TEH-reh-oh/ deh lah teh-leh.
• a child crying.	• *de un niño llorando.*	• deh oon NEE-nyoh yoh-RAHN-doh.
• people fighting.	• *de gente peleando.*	• deh HEHN-teh peh-leh-AHN-doh.
I'm here…	*Estoy aquí para…*	Ehs-toy ah-KEE PAH-rah…
• to ask you to turn down the music/TV.	• *pedirles que bajen el volumen de la música/tele.*	• peh-DEER-lehs keh BAH-hehn ehl voh-LOO-mehn deh lah MOO-see-kah/TEH-leh.
• to ask you to keep your voices down.	• *pedirles que bajen la voz.*	• peh-DEER-lehs keh BAH-hehn lah vohs.
• to check if everything is alright.	• *comprobar que todo está en orden.*	• kohm-proh-BAHR keh TOH-doh ehs-TAH ehn OHR-dehn.
• to check if we can assist you.	• *ver si podemos ayudarles en algo.*	• vehr see poh-DEH-mohs ah-yoo-DAHR-lehs ehn AHL-goh.
Are you the owner of this house/apartment?	*¿Es usted el dueño de esta casa/este apartamento?*	¿Ehs oos-TEHD ehl DWE-nyoh deh EHS-tah KAH-sah/EHS-teh ah-pahr-tah-MEHN-toh?

NEIGHBOR	*VECINO*	
Yes, I'm the owner of this apartment house.	*Sí, soy el dueño de este apartamento/esta casa.*	See, soy ehl DWEH-nyo deh EHS-teh ah-pahr-tah-MEHN-toh/EHS-tah KAH-sah.
I'm sorry, officer.	*Lo siento, agente.*	Loh SYEHN-toh, ah-HEN-teh.

We didn't realize that...	No sabíamos que...	Noh sah-BEE-ah-mohs keh...
• the music/TV was so loud.	• la música/tele estaba tan alta.	• lah MOO-see-kah/ teh-LEH ehs-TAH-bah tahn AHL-tah.
• we could be heard.	• que podían oírnos.	• keh poh-DEE-ahn-oh-EER-nohs.
We'll turn it down.	Bajaremos el volumen de la música.	Bah-hah-REH-mohs ehl voh-LOO-mehn deh lah MOO-see-kah.
Who complained about us?	¿Quién se quejó de nosotros?	¿Kwyehn se keh-HOH deh noh-SOH-trohs?
OFFICER	**AGENTE**	
Your neighbor from...	Su vecino...	Soo veh-SEE-noh...
• across the street.	• del otro lado de la calle.	• dehl OH-troh LAH-doh deh lah KAH-yeh.
• next door.	• de al lado.	• deh ahl LAH-doh.
• upstairs.	• de arriba.	• deh ah-RREE-bah.
• downstairs.	• de abajo.	• deh ah-BAH-hoh.
• the basement.	• del sótano.	• dehl SOH-tah-noh.
I understand that...	He sabido que...	Eh sah-BEE-doh keh...
• this has happened before.	• esto ha ocurrido antes.	• ehs-toh ah oh-koo-RREE-doh AHN-tehs.
• your neighbor asked you to be quiet.	• su vecino les pidió que no hicieran ruido.	• soo veh-SEE-noh lehs pee-dee-OH keh noh ee-SYEH-rahn RWEE-doh.
Your neighbor asked us to...	Su vecino nos pidió...	Soo veh-SEE-noh nohs pee-dee-OH...
• issue a warning.	• que les demos una advertencia.	• keh lehs DEH-mohs OO-nah ahd-vehr-TEHN-syah.
• press charges.	• que pusiéramos una denuncia.	• keh poo-see-EH-rah-mohs OO-nah deh-NOON-see-ah.

Please tell me…	*Por favor, dígame…*	Pohr fah-VOHR, DEE-gah-meh…
• your name.	• *su nombre.*	• soo NOHM-breh.
• your phone number.	• *su número de teléfono.*	• soo NOO-meh-roh deh teh-LEH-foh-noh.
• where you work.	• *dónde trabaja.*	• DOHN-deh trah-BAH-hah.
Please show me a form of identification.	*Por favor, enséñeme su identificación.*	Pohr FAH-vohr, ehn-SEH-nyeh-meh soo ee-dehn-tee-fee-kah-SYOHN.

NEIGHBOR	*VECINO*	
Okay. You don't have to press charges.	*Bien. No necesita poner una denuncia.*	Byehn. Noh neh-seh-SEE-tah poh-nehr OO-nah deh-NOON-see-ah.
We'll turn off the music/TV.	*Apagaremos la música/ la tele.*	Ah-pah-gah-REH-mohs lah MOO-see-kah/lah teh-LEH.
We'll keep the noise down.	*Bajaremos el volumen.*	Bah-hah-REH-mohs ehl voh-LOO-mehn.
That neighbor…	*Ese/a vecino/a…*	EH-seh/ah veh-SEE-noh/ah…
• doesn't get along with us.	• *no se lleva bien con nosotros.*	• noh seh YEH-vah byehn kohn noh-SOH-trohs.
• complains about everybody in the building.	• *se queja de todo el mundo en este edificio.*	• seh KEH-hah deh TOH-doh ehl MOON-doh ehn EHS-teh eh-dee-FEE-syoh.
• won't leave us alone.	• *no nos deja en paz.*	• noh nohs DEH-hah ehn pahs.
• is crazy.	• *está loco/a.*	• ehs-TAH LOH-koh/kah.
I can't find my ID.	*No puedo encontrar mi identificación.*	No PWEH-doh ehn-kohn-TRAHR mee ee-dehn-tee-fee-kah-SYOHN.

Here is my ID.	*Aquí está mi identificación.*	Ah-KEE ehs-TAH mee ee-dehn-tee-fee-kah-SYOHN.
I live here.	*Vivo aquí.*	VEE-voh ah-KEE.
Why do you need my ID?	*¿Por qué necesita mi identificación?*	¿Pohr KEH neh-seh-SEE-tah mee ee-dehn-TEE-fee-kah-SYOHN?

OFFICER   **AGENTE**

Okay. This time I'll issue you a warning.	*Bien. Esta vez les doy una advertencia.*	Byehn. EHS-tah vehs lehs doy oon-ah ad-vehr-TEHN-syah.
But you can't make any noise after 10 P.M.	*Pero no puede hacer ruido después de las diez.*	PEH-roh noh PWEH-deh hah-SEHR RWEE-doh dehs-PWEHS deh lahs DEE-ehs.
Sorry, I have to give you a ticket.	*Lo siento, tengo que darles una multa.*	Loh SYEHN-toh, TEHN-goh keh darh-lehs OO-nah MOOL-tah.
Sign here, please.	*Firme aquí, por favor.*	FEER-meh ah-KEE, pohr FAH-vohr.
Keep the noise down.	*No hagan ruido.*	Noh AH-gahn RWEE-doh.
You should break up the party now.	*Deben parar la fiesta ahora.*	DEH-behn pah-RAHR lah FYEHS-tah ah-OH-rah.
Good night.	*Buenas noches.*	BWEH-nahs NOH-chehs.
If I have to come back, you will be arrested.	*Si tengo que volver lo arrestaré.*	See TEHN-goh keh vohl-VEHR loh ah-RREHS-tah-REH.
The party is over.	*La fiesta se ha terminado.*	La fee-EHS-tah seh ah tehr-mee-NAH-doh.
Everyone must leave.	*Deben marcharse todos.*	DEH-behn mahr-CHAHR-seh TOH-dohs.

7. Delivering Bad News to Family and Friends

OFFICER	AGENTE	
Good evening.	*Buenas noches.*	BWEH-nahs NOH-chehs.
I'm Officer _____.	*Soy el agente _____.*	Soy ehl ah-HEHN-teh _____.
Is this Mr./Mrs. _____?	*¿Es usted el señor/la señora _____?*	¿Ehs oos-TEHD ehl seh-NYOHR/lah seh-NYOH-rah?
I'm sorry to tell you that your...	*Siento decirle que su...*	SYEHN-toh deh-SEER-leh keh soo...
• daughter	• *hija*	• EE-hah
• son	• *hijo*	• EE-hoh
• husband	• *marido*	• mah-REE-doh
• father	• *padre*	• PAH-dreh
• mother	• *madre*	• MAH-dreh
• brother	• *hermano*	• Ehr-MAH-noh
• sister	• *hermana*	• Ehr-MAH-nah
• has been arrested.	• *ha sido arrestado.*	• ah SEE-doh ah-rrehs-TAH-doh.
• was involved in a car accident.	• *ha tenido un accidente de coche.*	• ah teh-NEE-doh oon ahk-see-DEHN-teh deh KOH-cheh.
• had...	• *ha sufrido...*	• ah soo-FREE-doh...
• a heart attack.	• *un ataque al corazón.*	• oon ah-TAH-keh ahl coh-rah-SOHN.
• a stroke.	• *un ataque cerebral.*	• oon ah-TAH-keh seh-reh-BRAHL.
• is in the hospital.	• *está en el hospital.*	• ehs-TAH ehn ehl ohs-pee-TAHL.
• got lost.	• *está perdido/a.*	• ehs-TAH pehr-DEE-doh/dah.
• is injured.	• *está herido/a.*	• ehs-TAH eh-REE-doh/dah.

• is dead.	• está muerto/a.	• ehs-TAH MWEHR-toh/tah.
• can't find his/her way.	• no puede encontrar su camino.	• noh PWEH-deh ehn-kohn-TRAHR soo kah-MEE-noh.

RELATIVE / **PARIENTE**

What happened?	¿Qué pasó?	¿Keh pah-SOH?
When did this happen?	¿Cuándo ocurrió estó?	¿KWAHN-doh oh-kuh-rree-OH EHS-toh?
What do I have to do?	¿Qué se debe hacer?	¿Keh seh DEH-beh ah SEHR?
Can I see my...	¿Puedo ver a mi...	¿PWEH-doh vehr ah mee...
• daughter?	• hija?	• EE-hah?
• son?	• hijo?	• EE-hoh?
• husband?	• marido?	• mah-REE-doh?
• father?	• padre?	• PAH-dreh?

OFFICER / **AGENTE**

You need to...	Usted necesita...	Oos-TEHD neh-seh-SEE-tah...
• come down to the station.	• venir a la estación.	• veh-NEER ah lah ehs-tah-SYOHN.
• go to the hospital.	• ir al hospital.	• eer ahl ohs-pee-TAHL.
• go to the morgue.	• ir al depósito de cadáveres.	• eer ahl deh-POH-see-toh deh cah-DAH-veh-rehs.
• identify the body.	• identificar el cuerpo.	• ee-dehn-tee-fee-KAHR ehl KWEHR-poh.
We'd like to ask you a few questions at the station.	Queremos hacerle unas preguntas en la estación de policía.	Keh-REH-mohs ah-SEHR-leh OO-nahs preh-GOON-tahs ehn lah ehs-tah-SYOHN deh poh-lee-SEE-ah.

RELATIVE / **PARIENTE**

How do I get there?	¿Cómo voy allí?	¿KOH-moh voy ah-YEE?

| Can someone come to pick me up? | ¿Puede alguien venir a recogerne? | ¿PWEH-deh AHL-gyehn veh-NEER ah reh-koh-HER-neh? |
| I need a ride. | Necesito un aventón. | Neh-seh-SEE-toh oon ah-vehn-TOHN. |

OFFICER	**AGENTE**	
Someone will pick you up.	Alguien vendrá a recogerlo/a.	AHL-gyehn vehn-DRAH ah reh-coh-HEHR-loh/lah.
Are you okay?	¿Está bien?	¿Ehs-TAH byehn?
Do you need help?	¿Necesita ayuda?	¿Neh-seh-SEE-tah ah-YOO-dah?
Would you like to see a counselor?	¿Quiere ver a un consejero?	¿KYEH-reh vehr ah oon koh-seh-HEH-roh?
Can we call someone for you?	¿Podemos llamar a alguien para usted?	¿Poh-DEH-mohs yah-MAHR ah AHL-gyehn PAH-rah oos-TEHD!

REFERENCE

1. Glossary of Grammatical Terms

active voice—*voz activa:* a verb form in which the actor (agent) is expressed as the grammatical subject. The girl ate the orange—*La chica comió la naranja.*

adjective—*adjetivo:* a word that describes a noun; e.g., pretty—*bonita.*

adverb—*adverbio:* a word that describes a verb, an adjective, or another adverb; e.g., quickly—*rápidamente.*

agreement—*concordancia:* the modification of words so that they match the words they describe or relate to.

auxiliary verb—*verbo auxiliar:* a helping verb used with another verb to express some facet of tense or mood.

compound—*compuesto:* verb forms composed of two parts, an auxiliary and a main verb.

conditional—*potencial simple:* the mood used for hypothetical (depending on a possible condition or circumstance) statements and questions. I would eat if...—*Comería si...*

conjugation—*conjugación:* the formation of verbs with their endings; i.e., the finite forms (vs. nonfinite forms such as the infinitive or participle).

conjunction—*conjunción:* a word that connects other words and phrases; e.g., and—*y*.

definite article—*artículo definido:* a word linked to a noun indicating it is specific; e.g., the—*el* (masculine singular).

demonstrative—*demonstrativo:* a word that indicates or highlights something referred to; e.g., this book—*este libro*, this—*este* is a demonstrative adjective.

diphthong—*diptongo:* a sequence of two vowels that glide together and act as a single sound in English. In Spanish, they are two separate sounds; e.g., *co-mió, cuán-do.*

direct object—*objeto directo:* the person or thing that receives the action of a verb (accusative).

ending—*desinencia:* the suffix added to the stem that indicates subject, tense, etc.

gender—*género:* grammatical categories for nouns, loosely related to physical gender and/or word ending; Spanish has two, masculine and feminine; e.g., *el chico* (m.), *la chica* (f.).

imperative—*imperativo:* the command form.

imperfect—*imperfecto:* the past tense used for ongoing or habitual actions or states; useful for description.

impersonal verb—*verbo impersonal:* a verb in which the person, place, or thing affected is expressed as the indirect object rather than the subject. To like (to be pleasing to)—*gustar:* I like chicken—*Me gusta el pollo* (the chicken is pleasing to me).

indefinite article—*artículo indefinido:* a word linked to a noun indicating that it is nonspecific; e.g., a/an—*un* (masculine singular).

indicative—*indicativo:* the mood used for factual or objective statements and questions.

indirect object—*objeto indirecto:* the person or thing that receives the action of the direct object and/or is the object of a preposition (dative).

infinitive—*infinitivo:* the basic form of a verb found in the dictionary which does not specify the subject (person or number), tense, or mood; e.g., to speak—*hablar.*

intransitive verb—*verbo intransitivo:* a verb that does not take a direct object; e.g., to live—*vivir.*

mood—*modo:* the attitude toward what is expressed by the verb.

noun—*sustantivo:* a word referring to a person, place, or thing; e.g., house—*casa.*

number—*número:* the distinction between singular and plural.

participle—*participio:* an unconjugated, unchanging verb form often used with auxiliary verbs to form compound verb forms; e.g., present and past participles: eating/eaten—*comiendo/comido.*

passive voice—*voz pasiva:* a verb form in which the recipient of the action is expressed as the grammatical subject. The orange was eaten by the girl—*La naranja fue comida por la chica.*

perfect—*perfecto:* verb forms used for actions or states that are already completed. I have eaten—*He comido* (present perfect).

person—*persona:* the grammatical category that distinguishes between the speaker (first person), the person spoken to (second person), and the people and things spoken about (third person); often applies to pronouns and verbs.

pluperfect—*pluscuamperfecto:* the past perfect in Spanish that uses the imperfect of *haber*—to have (in either the indicative or the subjunctive) plus the past participle; e.g., *Había comido*—I had eaten.

possessive—*posesivo:* indicates ownership; e.g., my—*mi* is a possessive pronoun (genitive).

predicate—*predicado:* the part of the sentence containing the verb and expressing the action or state of the subject.

preposition—*preposición:* a word (often as part of a phrase) that expresses spatial, temporal, or other relationships; e.g., on—*en.*

preterite—*pretérito:* the past tense used for completed actions or states; useful for narration of events.

progressive—*progresivo:* verb form used for actions that are ongoing; continuous. I am eating—*Estoy comiendo* (present progressive).

pronoun—*pronombre:* a word taking the place of a noun; e.g., personal or demonstrative.

reflexive verb—*verbo reflexivo:* a verb whose action reflects back to the subject; e.g., to wash oneself—*lavarse.*

simple—*simple:* one-word verb forms conjugated by adding endings to a stem.

stem or **root**—*raíz:* the part of the infinitive that does not change during the conjugation of regular verbs, formed by dropping *-ar, er,* or *-ir;* e.g., *habl-* in *hablar.*

subject—*sujeto:* the person, place, or thing performing the action of the verb or being in the state described by it (nominative).

subjunctive—*subjuntivo:* the mood used for nonfactual or subjective statements or questions.

tense—*tiempo:* the time of an action or state, i.e., past, present, future.

transitive verb—*verbo transitivo:* a verb that takes a direct object; e.g., to send—*mandar.*

verb—*verbo:* a word expressing an action or state; e.g., (to) walk—*caminar.*

2. Grammar Summary

• THE DEFINITE ARTICLE—*EL ARTÍCULO DEFINIDO* •

	SINGULAR	PLURAL
MASCULINE	*el*	*los*
FEMININE	*la*	*las*

• THE INDEFINITE ARTICLE—*EL ARTÍCULO INDEFINIDO* •

	SINGULAR	PLURAL
MASCULINE	*un*	*unos*
FEMININE	*una*	*unas*

• GENDER—*GÉNERO* •

All Spanish nouns are either masculine or feminine. Some types of words can be grouped by gender, but there are exceptions, and it is best to learn the word with its appropriate article.

Masculine words: nouns that end in *-o, -r, -n,* and *-l;* names of items in nature (e.g., mountains); days of the week and months; words of Greek origin ending in *-ma, -pa,* or *-ta;* verbs, adjectives, etc. used as nouns.

Feminine words: nouns that end in *-a, -dad, -tad, -tud, -ción, -sión, -ez, -umbre,* and *-ie;* names of cities and towns.

• PLURAL FORMATION—*FORMACIÓN DEL PLURAL* •

To form the plural for words ending in a vowel, add *-s.*
For words ending in a consonant or a stressed *í* or *ú,* add *-es.*
Nouns ending in *z* change to *c* in the plural; e.g., *niños felices*—happy children.

• ADJECTIVES AND AGREEMENT—
ADJETIVOS Y CONCORDANCIA •

All adjectives must agree in number and gender with the nouns they modify or describe.

For use with plural nouns, add *-s* to the adjective, or *-es* if it ends in a consonant.

When an adjective ends in *-o* (in its masculine form), its ending changes into *-a* when it modifies a feminine noun, e.g., *la mujer rica*—the rich woman. For most adjectives ending in a consonant (or a vowel other than *-o*) in the masculine form, simply use the same form for both genders. However, for adjectives ending in *-dor, -ón,* or *-án,* and for adjectives of nationality that end in a consonant, add *-a* to make the feminine form. For example: *la mujer francesa*—the French woman. Adjectives that end in *-e* do not change for masculine or feminine gender. For example: *un hombre inteligente, una mujer inteligente.*

• PRONOUNS—*PRONOMBRES* •

SUBJECT PRONOUNS

I	*yo*
you (familiar)	*tú*
he	*él*
she	*ella*
you (polite)	*usted (Ud.)* *
we	*nosotros, nosotras*
you (familiar)	*vosotros, vosotras*
you (polite)	*ustedes (Uds.)*
they	*ellos, ellas*

Note: Subject pronouns are often omitted in Spanish since the verbal endings show who or what the subject is.

Other pronouns, listed according to their corresponding subject pronoun, are:

	yo	*tú*	*él/ella/ Ud.*	*nosotros, -as*	*vosotros, -as*	*ellos/ ellas/ Uds.*
DIRECT OBJECT:	*me*	*te*	*lo/la*	*nos*	*os*	*los/las*
INDIRECT OBJECT:	*me*	*te*	*le*	*nos*	*os*	*les*
REFLEXIVE:	*me*	*te*	*se*	*nos*	*os*	*se*
POSSESSIVE:	*mi*	*tu*	*su*	*nuestro/a*	*vuestro/a*	*su*

Use the subject pronouns as objects of prepositions, except instead of *yo* and *tú*, use *mí* and *ti*. In sentences with reflexive pronouns, an optional prepositional phrase (*a* + *mí/ti/sí/nosotros,-as/vosotros,-as/sí* + *mismo/a*[*s*]) may be used

---

* *Usted* and *ustedes* are treated as if they were third person pronouns, though in meaning, they are second person (addressee) pronouns. In Latin America, *ustedes* is used as both familiar and polite, and *vosotros/as* is not used.

for emphasis (*mismo* = same). Note: *con* + *mí/ti/sí* becomes *conmigo/contigo/consigo.*

The possessive pronouns (adjectives) listed are used before the noun, as in *mi libro*—my book. The *nosotros/vosotros* forms agree in number and gender with the noun they pertain to, and the others only agree in number. Longer forms used after the noun for emphasis differ only in the *mi, tu,* and *su* forms: they are *mío, tuyo,* and *suyo.* They also show agreement in both gender and number, as in *Los libros míos están en la mesa*—My books are on the table. When these long forms are preceded by the appropriate definite article, they represent the noun and stand alone. For example: *Los libros míos están en la mesa, pero los tuyos están en tu cuarto*—My books are on the table, but yours are in your room.

• DEMONSTRATIVE ADJECTIVES AND PRONOUNS— *ADJETIVOS Y PRONOMBRES DEMOSTRATIVOS* •

DEMONSTRATIVE ADJECTIVES

this, these	*este, esta, estos, estas*
that, those	*ese, esa, esos, esas*
that, those (farther removed)	*aquel, aquella, aquellos, aquellas*

To form the pronouns, simply add an accent to the first *e* in the word, as in *No me gusta éste*—I don't like this one. There are also neuter pronouns used for general ideas or situations: *esto, eso, aquello.* When the demonstrative pronouns are followed by a noun, they do not have an accent. For example: *Yo quiero este coche*—I want this car.

• ADVERBS—*ADVERBIOS* •

Form adverbs simply by adding *-mente* (which corresponds to -ly in English) to the feminine form of an adjective, as in *obviamente*—obviously.

● NEGATION—*NEGACIÓN* ●

Form negative sentences by adding *no* before the conjugated verb and any pronouns, as in *No lo tengo*—I don't have it.

Many other negative constructions require two negative words. For example: *No tengo nada*—I don't have anything/I have nothing. (*Nada*—nothing; *algo*—something/anything.)

● COMPARISON—*COMPARACIÓN* ●

Form comparative expressions using *más*—more and *menos*—less with adjectives and adverbs. For example: *Juan es más grande que Pepe*—Juan is bigger than Pepe/*Juan corre más rápidamente que Pepe*—Juan runs faster than Pepe/*Juan es menos famoso*—Juan is less famous. Use *de* instead of *que* to mean "than" before numbers.

To make equal comparisons, use the expressions *tan...como* (before adjectives and adverbs) and *tanto...como* (before nouns, with which *tanto* must agree). For example: *Juan es tan grande como Pepe*—Juan is as big as Pepe/*Juan tiene tanto dinero como Pepe*—Juan has as much money as Pepe.

Form superlatives by using an article (a definite article that shows agreement for adjectives, *lo* for adverbs) with the comparative expressions. For example: *Juan es el más grande*—Juan is the biggest/*Ella es la menos grande del grupo*—She is the least big in the group/*Juan corre lo más rápidamente*—Juan runs the fastest.

The "absolute superlative" form is *-ísimo/a: hermosísimo*—very/most beautiful; *frecuentísimamente*—very/most frequently.

Irregular comparative words:

ADJECTIVE	ADVERB	COMPARATIVE
bueno—good	*bien*—well	*mejor*—better
malo—bad	*mal*—badly	*peor*—worse
mucho—much	*mucho*—much	*más*—more
poco—little	*poco*—little	*menos*—less

grande—great, big

pequeño—small

más grande—bigger
BUT mayor—older

más pequeño—smaller
BUT menor—younger

• RELATIVE PRONOUNS—*PRONOMBRES RELATIVOS* •

that, who, which	*que*
who(m)	*quien, quienes*
who, which	*el/la cual, los/las cuales*
who, which, the one(s) that/who	*el/la/los/las que*
what, which (refers to an entire idea)	*lo que*
whose (relative adjective)	*cuyo, -a, -os, -as*

• CONTRACTIONS—*CONTRACCIONES* •

de + el = del
a + el = al

3. Tense Formation Guide

The endings will always be presented according to subject person and number in the following order: *yo, tú, él/ella/usted, nosotros/-as, vosotros/-as, ellos/ellas/ustedes.*

• THE SIMPLE VERB FORMS •

1. To form the **present indicative**—*presente indicativo* of regular verbs, add the following endings to the stem of the infinitive*:

FOR -*AR* VERBS: -*o, -as, -a, -amos, -áis, -an*
FOR -*ER* VERBS: -*o, -es, -e, -emos, -éis, -en*
FOR -*IR* VERBS: -*o, -es, -e, -imos, -ís, -en*

---

* The stem is formed by dropping the infinitival endings -*ar*, -*er*, and -*ir*.

2. To form the **preterite**—*pretérito* of regular verbs, add the following endings to the stem of the infinitive:

FOR -*AR* VERBS: -*é, -aste, -ó, -amos, -ásteis, -aron*
FOR -*ER* AND -*IR* VERBS: -*í, -iste, -ió, -imos, -ísteis, -ieron*

Several verbs that are irregular in the preterite follow a pattern. Conjugate them in the following manner:

tener—to have: *tuve, tuviste, tuvo, tuvimos, tuvisteis, tuvieron*
estar—to be: *estuve...*
andar—to walk: *anduve...*
haber—to have: *hube...*
poder—to be able: *pude...*
poner—to put: *puse...*
saber—to know: *supe...*
caber—to fit: *cupe...*
querer—to want: *quise...*
venir—to come: *vine...*
hacer—to do, make: *hice, hiciste, hizo...*
decir—to say, tell: *dije...dijeron*
traer—to bring: *traje...trajeron*
producir—to produce: *produje...produjeron*

3. To form the **imperfect**—*imperfecto* of regular verbs, add the following endings to the stem of the infinitive:

FOR -*AR* VERBS: -*aba, -abas, -aba, -ábamos, -abais, -aban*
FOR -*ER* AND -*IR* VERBS: -*ía, -ías, -ía, -íamos, -íais, -ían*

There are only three irregular verbs in the imperfect:

ser—to be: *era, eras, era, éramos, erais, eran*
ir—to go: *iba, ibas, iba, íbamos, ibais, iban*
ver—to see: *veía, veías, veía, veíamos, veíais, veían*

4. To form the **future**—*futuro* of regular verbs, add the following endings to the entire infinitive:

FOR -*AR, ER,* AND -*IR* VERBS: *-é, -ás, -á, -emos, -éis, -án*

5. To form the **conditional**—*potencial simple* of regular verbs, add the following endings to the entire infinitive:

FOR -*AR, ER,* AND -*IR* VERBS: *-ía, -ías, -ía, -íamos, -íais, -ían*

The same set of verbs are irregular in the future and conditional. Add the regular endings to the following stems:

tener—to have: *tendr-*
venir—to come: *vendr-*
poner—to put, place: *pondr-*
salir—to leave: *saldr-*
valer—to be worth: *valdr-*
poder—to be able: *podr-*
saber—to know: *sabr-*
haber—to have: *habr-*
caber—to fit: *cabr-*
hacer—to do, make: *har-*
decir—to say, tell: *dir-*
querer—to want: *querr-*

6. To form the **present subjunctive**—*presente de subjuntivo* of regular verbs and many irregular ones, add the following endings to the *yo* form of the present indicative after dropping the *-o:*

FOR -*AR* VERBS: *-e, -es, -e, -emos, -éis, en*
FOR -*ER* and -*IR* VERBS: *-a, -as, -a, -amos, -áis, -an*

7. To form the **past** (imperfect) **subjunctive**—*imperfecto de subjuntivo* of both regular and irregular verbs, add the following

endings to the *ellos/ellas/ustedes* (third person plural) form of the preterite after dropping the *-ron:*

FOR *-AR, -ER,* AND *-IR* VERBS: *-ra, -ras, -ra, -ramos, -rais, -ran*
OR: *-se, -ses, -se, -semos, -seis, -sen*

The *nosotros/-as* (first person plural) form has an accent on the vowel directly before the ending, e.g., *habláramos.*

• THE COMPOUND VERB FORMS •

1. To form **progressive**—*progresivo* verb forms, conjugate the verb *estar*—to be in the appropriate tense (either the present or the imperfect; see verb charts) and add the present participle. Form the present participle of most verbs by adding the following endings to the stem of the infinitive:

FOR *-AR* VERBS: *-ando*
FOR *-ER* and *-IR* VERBS: *-iendo*

2. To form **perfect**—*perfecto* verb forms, conjugate the auxiliary verb *haber*—to have in the appropriate tense (the present indicative, the imperfect, the preterite, the future, the conditional, the present subjunctive, and the past subjunctive; see verb charts) and add the past participle. Form the past participle of most verbs by adding the following endings to the stem of the infinitive:

FOR *-AR* VERBS: *-ado*
FOR *-ER* AND *-IR* VERBS: *-ido*

The irregular past participles are:

abrir—to open: *abierto*
cubrir—to cover: *cubierto*

morir—to die: *muerto*
volver—to return: *vuelto*
poner—to put, place: *puesto*
ver—to see: *visto*
escribir—to write: *escrito*
romper—to break: *roto*
decir—to say, tell: *dicho*
hacer—to do, make: *hecho*

• THE IMPERATIVE/COMMANDS •

A sample conjugation using *hablar*—to speak:

fam. sing. affirm. *habla*	pol. sing. affirm. *hable*
fam. pl. affirm. *hablad*	pol. pl. affirm. *hablen*
fam. sing. neg. *no hables*	pol. sing. neg. *no hable*
fam. pl. neg. *no habléis*	pol. pl. neg. *no hablen*

1. To form familiar (informal) singular (*tú*) affirmative commands for most verbs, use the *él/ella/usted* (third person singular) form of the present indicative.

2. To form familiar plural (*vosotros/-as*) affirmative commands for all verbs, change the *-r* of the infinitive to *-d*.

3. To form polite (formal) singular (*usted*) and plural (*ustedes*) affirmative commands and all negative commands (singular and plural, familiar and polite), use the appropriate form of the present subjunctive. Form the negative in the usual way.

4. To form first person plural (we) commands (let's...), use the subjunctive in the affirmative and the negative. In the affirmative, another option is to use *Vamos + a +* infinitive.

5. Attach reflexive, indirect, and direct object pronouns directly to the affirmative commands. For example *¡Háblame!*—Speak

to me! For *nosotros/-as* and *vosotros/-as* affirmative commands in reflexive verbs, the last letter is dropped when the reflexive pronoun is attached. For example: ¡*Lavémonos!*—Let's wash ourselves! and ¡*Lavaos!*—Wash yourselves!

In negative commands, place them before the verb in the usual manner. For example: ¡*No me hables!*—Don't speak to me!

6. There are several irregular familiar singular affirmative commands:

tener—to have: *ten*
hacer—to do, make: *haz*
venir—to come: *ven*
decir—to say, tell: *di*
poner—to put, place: *pon*
ser—to be: *sé*
salir—to leave: *sal*
ir—to go: *ve*

• IMPERSONAL VERBS •

To conjugate impersonal verbs, i.e., verbs like *gustar*—to be pleasing to, to like, and *doler*—to hurt, use the third person form of the appropriate tense, mood, etc. of the verb and the indirect object pronoun that corresponds to the person, place, or thing affected. Whether to use the singular or plural of the third person form of the verb depends on the number of the items doing the affecting. For example: *Me gusta el Señor González*——I like Mr. González (Mr. González is pleasing to me)/*Me gustan los González*—I like the Gonzálezes.

• REFLEXIVE VERBS •

To form reflexive constructions, conjugate the infinitive (without the -se) and use the reflexive pronoun that corresponds to the subject. For example:

lavarse—to wash oneself
me lavo—I wash myself

• THE PASSIVE VOICE •

There are four ways to form the passive voice—*la voz pasiva* in Spanish. Two use a form of the reflexive construction just discussed.

1. To form the reflexive passive, or passive *se,* use *se* + the third person singular or plural of the verb, depending on the number of the items being discussed. For example: *Se habla español aquí*—Spanish is spoken here, but *Se comieron las naranjas*—The oranges were eaten. This form only occurs with transitive verbs.

2. Another version, impersonal *se,* involves the use of *se* + the third person singular only of the verb. Unlike passive *se,* this construction can be used with both intransitive and transitive verbs, but is used mainly with intransitive ones. Its usage also indicates that people (but not specific individuals) are involved in the action of the verb. For example, *Se duerme muy bien en el campo*—One sleeps very well in the country.

3. When the agent (the actor) is not expressed, another possibility is to use the "impersonal they" construction. To form it, simply use the third person plural of a verb; e.g., *Dicen que es un hombre peligroso*—They say (it is said) that he is a dangerous man.

4. The true passive is formed using the appropriate conjugation of *ser* + the past participle (also called the passive participle). It is used when the agent is expressed or strongly implied. The past participle agrees with the grammatical subject. In Spanish, only direct objects (not indirect objects) may serve as the grammatical subject in the passive voice.

> subject + *ser* + past participle + *por* + agent

For example, *La cuenta fue pagada por la Señora Sánchez*—The bill was paid by Mrs. Sánchez.

• STEM-CHANGING VERBS •

There are three kinds of stem-changing verbs.

1. For verbs such as *querer*—to want and *encontrar*—to find, change *e* to *ie* and *o* to *ue* in the stems of all forms except *nosotros, -as* and *vosotros, -as* in the present indicative and present subjunctive. There are no *-ir* verbs in this category.

2. For verbs such as *sentir(se)*—to feel and *dormir*—to sleep, change *e* to *ie* and *o* to *ue* in the exact same places as in the first kind, and change *e* to *i* and *o* to *u* in the *nosotros, -as* and *vosotros, -as* forms of the present subjunctive, in the *él/ella/usted* and *ellos/ellas/ustedes* forms of the preterite, in all forms of the past subjunctive, and in the present participle. Only *-ir* verbs are in this category.

3. For verbs such as *pedir*—to request, change *e* to *i* in all places where any change occurs in the second kind. Only *-ir* verbs are in this category.

• SPELLING CHANGES •

To keep pronunciation consistent and to preserve customary spelling in Spanish, some verbs in certain tenses change their spelling. The rules are:

In verbs ending in -*car*, *c* changes to *qu* before *e* to keep the sound hard; e.g., *busqué*—I looked (from *buscar*).

In verbs ending in -*quir*, *qu* changes to *c* before *o* and *a*; e.g., *delinco*—I commit a transgression (from *delinquir*).

In verbs ending in -*zar*, *z* changes to *c* before *e*; *comencé*—I began (from *comenzar*).

In verbs ending in -*gar*, *g* changes to *gu* before *e* to keep the *g* hard; e.g., *pagué*—I paid (from *pagar*).

In verbs ending in a consonant + -*cer*/-*cir*, *c* changes to *z* before *o* and *a* to keep the sound soft; e.g., *venzo*—I conquer (from *vencer*).

In verbs ending in -*ger*/-*gir*, *g* changes to *j* before *o* and *a* to keep the sound soft; e.g., *cojo*—I catch (from *coger*).

In verbs ending in -*guir*, *gu* changes to *g* before *o* and *a* to preserve the sound; e.g., *distingo*—I distinguish (from *distinguir*).

In verbs ending in -*guar*, *gu* changes to *gü* before *e* to keep the "gw" sound; e.g., *averigüé*—I ascertained (from *averiguar*).

In verbs ending in -*eer*, the unstressed *i* between vowels becomes a *y*; e.g., *leyó*—he read (from *leer*).

In stem-changing verbs ending in -*eir*, two consecutive *i*'s become one; e.g., *rio*—he laughed (from *reír*).

In stem-changing verbs beginning with a vowel, an *h* must precede the word-initial diphthong or the initial *i* of the diphthong becomes a *y*; e.g., *huelo*—I smell (sense; from *oler*); *yerro*—I err (from *errar*).

In verbs with stems ending in *ll* or *ñ*, the *i* of the diphthongs *ie* and *ió* disappears; e.g., *bulló*—it boiled (from *bullir*).

4. English-Spanish Glossary

ABBREVIATIONS

adj.	adjective	pp.	past participle
adv.	adverb	prep.	preposition
conj.	conjunction	pres. part.	present
expl.	expletive		participle
f.	feminine	pron.	pronoun
m.	masculine	v.	verb
n.	noun		

ENGLISH	SPANISH	ENGLISH	SPANISH
A		**around** prep.	alrededor
		arms n.	los brazos
abuse v.	abusar	**arrest** v.	arrestar
accident n.	el accidente	**arrive** v.	llegar
acid n.	el ácido	**arson** n.	el incendio
across adv.	enfrente, al		premeditado
	otro lado de	**ask** v.	pedir
acquaintance n.	el conocido	**ass** n.	el culo
address n.	la dirección	**assault** n.	el asalto
admit v.	admitir	**assist** v.	atender
after prep.	después	**assign** v.	asignar
afternoon n.	la tarde, de la	**associate** v.	el compadre,
	tarde		el socio
against prep.	contra	**asshole** n.	el pendejo
ahead adv.	adelante	**attend** v.	asistir
all adj.	todo	**attorney** n.	el abogado
allergy n.	la alergia	**aunt** n.	la tía
alley n.	el callejón	**average** n.	el mediano
amphetamine n.	las anfetas	**B**	
apply v.	solicitar, pedir,		
	aplicar	**back** n.	la espalda
application n.	la solicitud	**backpack** n.	la mochila
ambulance n.	la ambulancia	**backyard** n.	el patio, el
angel dust n.	el polvo de		jardín, "la
	ángel		yarda"
angry adj.	enojado	**bad health** n.	el mal de salud
ankles n.	los tobillos	**balls** n.	los huevos, los
answer n.	la respuesta		cojones
anything pron.	algo	**bastard** n.	el cabrón, el
anyone pron.	alguien		hijo de puta
area n.	el lugar	**be** v.	ser

ENGLISH	SPANISH	ENGLISH	SPANISH
be *v.*	estar	borrow *v.*	prestar
be able to *v.*	poder	bottle *n.*	la botella
be stoned *v.*	estar en onda	boy *n.*	el niño
beard *n.*	la barba	building *n.*	el edificio
beat up *v.*	pegar	brakes *n.*	los frenos
because *conj.*	porque	brick *n.*	el ladrillo
beer *n.*	la cerveza	break *v.*	romper
before *adv.*	antes	broke *pp.*	roto
before *prep.*	antes	brother *n.*	el hermano
behind *adv.*	detrás	brown *adj.*	castaño
begin *v.*	empezar	bruise *n.*	el moretón
belch *v.*	eructar	building *n.*	el edificio
belt *n.*	el cinturón	bumper *n.*	los parachoques
below *adv.*	debajo		
between *prep.*	entre	burns *n.*	las quemaduras
bicycle *n.*	la bicicleta		
big *adj.*	grande	burn *v.*	quemar
billy club, night		bush *n.*	el coño
stick *n.*	la porra	busted *adj., pp.*	arrestado
bindle *n.*	el papelito, la bolsita	butch *n.*	el marimacho
		butcher knife *n.*	el cuchillo de carnicero
binge *n.*	la borrachera		
bitch *n.*	la chingada	butt *n.*	las nalgas, los cachetes
black *adj.*	negro		
black jack *n.*	la cachiporra	but *conj.*	pero
blade *n.*	la fila, la hoja	buy *v.*	comprar
blasted *adj.*	borracho, mamado	**C**	
bleeding *p., pr.*	sangrando	call *v.*	llamar
blonde *adj.*	rubio	can *n.*	la lata
blood pressure *n.*	la presión de la sangre	cap *n.*	la gorra
		car *n.*	el carro, la carrucha
blood type *n.*	el tipo de sangre	care *n.*	el cuidado
blouse *n.*	la blusa	carry *v.*	llevar
blow *v.*	soplar	car window *n.*	la ventanilla
blue *adj.*	azul	case *n.*	el caso
blue jeans *n.*	los vaqueros	chest *n.*	el pecho
bomb *n.*	la bomba	children *n.*	los niños
bondsman *n.*	el fiador	cigarettes *n.*	los frajos
bond *n.*	la fianza	city *n.*	la ciudad
boobs *n.*	la tetas, las chichis	clothes *n.*	la ropa
		club *n.*	el garrote, la macana
boots *n.*	las botas		
booze *n.*	el pisto	club *v.*	apalear

ENGLISH	SPANISH
clutch *n*	el embrague
coat *n.*	el abrigo
cocaine *n.*	la coca
cock *n.*	el pene
cock-sucker *n.*	el lambiscón
come *v.*	venir
copy *n.*	la copia
cooperation *n.*	la cooperación
corner *n.*	la esquina
counseling *n.*	el consejo
cousin *n.*	el primo
counterfeiting *n.*	la falsificación
crack *n.*	el crack
cramps *n.*	llos calambres
crap *n.*	la cagada
credit cards *n.*	los tarjetas de crédito
crime of passion *n.*	el crimen pasional
curfew *n.*	el toque de queda
cunt *n.*	la cabrona
curse *v.*	maldecir

D

dagger *n.*	el puñal
damned *adj.*	pinche
dark *adj.*	oscuro
dark-skinned *adj.*	moreno
darn *expl.*	híjole
daughter *n.*	la hija
dead *adj.*	muerto
deal *n.*	el dil
describe *v.*	describir
dick-head *n.*	el pendejo
die *v.*	morir
dime bag *n.*	la bolsita dea a diez
doctor *n.*	el médico
dog *n.*	el perro
doors *n.*	las puertas
down *prep.*	abajo
downers *n.*	los diablos
dress *n.*	el vestido

ENGLISH	SPANISH
drink *v.*	tomar, pistiar
drive *v.*	manejar
drive-by shooting *n.*	el desparo desde un carro
drug addict *n.*	el drogadicto
drug dealer *n.*	el traficante
drug runner *n.*	el camello
drugs *n.*	las drogas
drunk *adj.*	tomado, borracho
dumb shit *n.*	el pendejo

E

earrings *n.*	los aretes
ears *n.*	las orejas
east *n.*	este
ejaculate *v.*	correrse
elbow *n.*	el codo
embezzling *n.*	desfalco
emergency room *n.*	la sala de emergencia
emotional illness *n.*	las problemas emocionales
engine *n.*	el motor
ex-convict *n.*	el pinto
extortion *n.*	la extorsión
eyes *n.*	los ojos

F

face *n.*	la cara
fag *adj.*	joto, maricón
fall *v.*	caer
fill-in *v.*	rellenar
family *n.*	la familia
fat *adj.*	gordo
father *n.*	el padre
feet *n.*	pies
fender *n.*	los guardafangos
fine *n.*	la multa
finger fuck *v.*	meter mano
fingers *n.*	los dedos
fire *n.*	el incendio

ENGLISH	SPANISH
first degree *n.*	el primer grado
for *prep.*	por, para, a través de
fraud *n.*	el fraude
friend *n.*	el amigo
front *n.*	el frente, la fachada
fuck *expl.*	carajo, joder
fucked up *adj.*	borracho

G

gambling *n.*	el juego de apuestas
gang *n.*	la pandilla
gang members *n.*	los pandilleros
get high *v.*	agarrar onda
get laid *v.*	culear, chingar
girl *n.*	la niña
give a blow job *v.*	chupar la punta
glass *n.*	el vidrio
glasses *n.*	los lentes
glove *n.*	el guante
glove box *n.*	la cajuela
go *v.*	ir
go fuck yourself *v.*	chinga tu madre
good health *n.*	la buena salud
gram *n.*	gramo
granddaughter *n.*	la nieta
grandfather *n.*	el abuelo
grandmother *n.*	la abuela
grandson *n.*	el nieto
green *adj.*	verde
grey *adj.*	gris
gun *n.*	la pistola, el "cuete"

H

half gram *n.*	el medio gramo
hair *n.*	el pele
half ounce *n.*	la media onza

ENGLISH	SPANISH
hammer *n.*	el martillo
hands *n.*	las manos
hang-over *n.*	la mona, la resaca
hard-on *n.*	la erreción
hat *n.*	el sombrero
have *v.*	tener
he *pron.*	él
head *n.*	la cabeza
hear *v.*	oír
heart problems *n.*	las problemas de corazón
height *n.*	la altura
help *n.*	la ayuda
help *v.*	ayudar
here *adv.*	aquí
heroin *n.*	la heroína
hickey *n.*	el chupón
hip *n.*	la cadera
hit *n.*	calada
homicide *n.*	el homicidio
hood (of a car) *n.*	el capó
house *n.*	la casa
how *adv., conj.*	cómo, como
hunting knife *n.*	el cuchillo de caza
husband *n.*	el marido

I

illness *n.*	la enfermedad
informant *n.*	el chivato, la rata
inject oneself *v.*	picarse
inside *adv., prep.*	adentro, dentro de
insurance company *n.*	la compañía de seguros

J

jacket *n.*	la chaqueta
jeez *expl.*	híjole
joint *n.*	el leño, el pitillo, el porro

ENGLISH	SPANISH
K	
kick *v.*	dar patadas
kick the habit *v.*	"quiquear"
kidnapping *n.*	el secuestro
kill *v.*	matar
kilo *n.*	el kilo
kiss-ass *n.*	el lameculos
knees *n.*	las rodillas
knife *n.*	el cuchillo, la fila
know *v.*	saber
L	
labor pains *n.*	las contracciones
last *adj.*	último
last name *n.*	el apellido
lawyer *n.*	el abogado
leave *v.*	dejar
left *adv.*	a la izquierda
legs *n.*	las piernas
license plate *n.*	la placa
lid *n.*	la tapa
light *adj.*	claro
live *v.*	vivir
loaded *adj.*	borracho
look at *v.*	mirar
love *v.*	querer
luck *n.*	el suerte
M	
mail *n.*	el correo
make out *v.*	acariciar
man *n.*	el hombre
man *n., expl.*	híjole
manslaughter *n.*	el homicidio involuntario
marijuana *n.*	la grifa, la mota, la yerba
maroon *adj.*	morado
massacre *n.*	la matanza
medication *n.*	el medicamento

ENGLISH	SPANISH
mirror *n.*	el espejo
mother *n.*	la madre
mother fucker *n.*	el hijo de la chingada
moustache *n.*	el bigote
mouth *n.*	la boca
mule (drug runner) *n.*	el camello
murder *n.*	el asesinato
murderer *adj.*	el asesino
mushrooms *n.*	las sombrillas
N	
name *n.*	el nombre
neck *n.*	el cuello
necklace *n.*	el collar
need *v.*	necesitar
needle *n.*	la aguja
niece *n.*	la sobrina
neighbor *n.*	el vecino
nephew *n.*	el sobrino
nickel bag *n.*	la bolsita de a cinco
nickname *n.*	el apodo
night *n.*	la noche
north *n.*	el norte
nose *n.*	la nariz
nothing	nada
number *n.*	el número
number one (urine) *n.*	ir hacer pis
nuts *n.*	los testículos
O	
obscene call *n.*	la llamada obscena
officer (police) *n.*	el agente
old *adj.*	viejo
on the rag (to be...) *v.*	tener la regla
on top *adv.*	arriba
operating room *n.*	la sala de operaciones

ENGLISH	SPANISH	ENGLISH	SPANISH
opposite *adj.*	opuesto, al otro lado, contrario	**Q**	
		quarter ounce *n.*	el cuarto de onza
orange *adj.*	anaranjado		
ounce *n.*	la onza	queer *n.*	el homosexual
outside *adv.*	afuera	question *n.*	la pregunta
owner *n.*	el dueño	quiet *adj.*	callado
P		**R**	
pain *n.*	el dolor	recovery room *n.*	la sala de recuperación
pale *adj.*	pálido		
parents *n.*	los padres	red *adj.*	rojo
park *n.*	el parque	relatives *n.*	los parientes
park *v.*	estacionar	retarded *adj.*	retrasado mental
parole *n.*	la libertad provisional	rifle *n.*	el rifle
pass *v.*	pass	right (direction) *adv.*	a la derecha
pass out *v.*	perder el cono-cimiento	right *adv.*	derecho
passenger *n.*	el pasajero	ring *n.*	el anillo
pay *v.*	pay	roach *n.*	el colilla, cucaracha
peepee *n.*	el pene		
period *n.*	la regla	rob *v.*	robar
person *n.*	la persona	robbery *n.*	el robo a mano armada
piece (one ounce) *n.*	el cacho (una onza)	run *v.*	correr
		run over *v.*	atropellar
pills *n.*	las píldoras	**S**	
pink *adj.*	rosa		
pipe *n.*	la pipa	say *v.*	decir
place *n.*	el lugar	scar *n.*	la cicatriz
please *n.*	por favor	scared *adj.*	asustado
pocket *n.*	el bolsillo	scumbag *n.*	el huevón
pocket knife *n.*	la navaja	seats *n.*	los asientos
poisoning *n.*	el envenen-amiento	second degree *n.*	el segundo grado
police *n.*	la policía, la jura, la placa	see *v.*	ver
		senior gang member *n.*	el veterano
policy number *n.*	el número de póliza	sexual harassment *n.*	el acosamiento sexual
problem *n.*	la problema	she *pron.*	ella
purse *n.*	la bolsa	shirt *n.*	la camisa
put *v.*	poner	shit *expl.*	mierda

288

ENGLISH	SPANISH	ENGLISH	SPANISH
shit-faced *adj.*	pedo	suspect *n., adj.*	(el) sospechoso
shoes *n.*	los zapatos, "los calcos"	swallow *v.*	tragar
		syringe *n.*	la jeringa
shoot *v.*	disparar		
short *adj.*	bajo	**T**	
shot gun *n.*	la escopeta	T-shirt *n.*	la camiseta
shoulders *n.*	los hombros	take a dump *v.*	ir a cagar
sister *n.*	la hermana	tall *adj.*	also
skinny *adj.*	delgado	tattoo *n.*	el tatuaje, "la placa"
skirt *n.*	la falda		
slut *n.*	la puta	teenagers *n.*	los adolescentes
small *adj.*	pequeño		
smoke *v.*	fumar	teeth *n.*	los dientes
smuggling *n.*	el contrabando	telephone *n.*	el teléfono
snort shit *v.*	"esnifar"	thanks	gracias
socks *n.*	los calcetines	theft *n.*	el robo
solicitation *n.*	la incitación	think *v.*	pensar
someone	alguien	threat *n.*	la amenaza
son *n.*	el hijo	tire *n.*	la llanta
son of a bitch *n.*	el hijo de puta, el hijo dela chingada	tongue *n.*	la lengua
		touch *v.*	tocar
		traffic light *n.*	el semáforo
south *n.*	el sur	tranquilizer *n.*	el tranquil- izante
stepfather *n.*	el padrastro		
spaced out *adj.*	cruzado, firoláis, fumado	trespassing *n.*	la intrusión
		trip *n.*	el viaje
		trousers *n.*	los pantalones
speak *v.*	hablar	truck *n.*	la camion
speedball *n.*	el chute	trunk (of car) *n.*	el maletero
splint *n.*	el cabestrillo	turn *v.*	voltear
spoon *n.*	la cuchara	turncoat *n.*	el vendido
stab *v.*	apuñalar	**U**	
steering wheel *n.*	el volante		
stick *n.*	el palo	uncle *n.*	el tío
still	todavía	under *prep.*	debajo
stockings *adj.*	medias	understand *v.*	comprender, entender
stomach *n.*	el estomago		
stop *v.*	parar	up *prep.*	de arriba
straight forward	derecho	**V**	
strangle *v.*	estrangular		
strangulation *n.*	la estrangu- lación	vagina *n.*	la vagina
		vandalism *n.*	el vandilismo
street *n.*	la calle	vehicle *n.*	el vehículo
suicide *n.*	el suicidio		
supplier *n.*	el proveedor		

ENGLISH	SPANISH	ENGLISH	SPANISH
W		windshield *n.*	las parabrisas
		with *prep.*	con
waist *n.*	la cintura	without *prep.*	sin
waiting room *n.*	la sala de	witness *n.*	el testigo
	espera	woman *n.*	la mujer
walk *v.*	andar	work *n.*	el trabajo
wallet *n.*	la cartera	work *v.*	trabajar
weapon *n.*	la arma	working days *n.*	las días
week *n.*	la semana		laborables
weigh *v.*	peso	wound *n.*	la herida
west *n.*	el oeste	wounded *adj.*	herido
when *conj.*	cuando	wrist *n.*	la muñeca
where *conj.*	donde	write *v.*	escribir
which *pron.*	cuál		
white *adj.*	blanco	**Y**	
why *adv.*	por qúe		
wife *n.*	la mujer	year *n.*	el año
wimp *n.*	el pendejo	yellow *adj.*	amarillo
window		young man *n.*	muchacho
(of car) *n.*	la ventanilla	young person *n*	jóven
		young woman *n.*	muchacha

5. Spanish-English Glossary

SPANISH	ENGLISH	SPANISH	ENGLISH
A		acosamiento	
		sexual *n. m.*	sexual
a *prep.*	to		harassment
a la derecha *adv.*	right	adelante *adv.*	ahead
a la izquierda		admitir *v.*	to admit
adv.	left	adentro *adv.*	inside
abajo *adv.*	down	afuera *adv.*	outside
abogado *n. m.*	lawyer	agarrar onda *v.*	to get high
abrigo *n. m*	coat	agente *n. m.*	officer
abuela *n. f.*	grandmother	aguja *n. f.*	needle
abuelo *n. m.*	grandfather	alergias *n. f.*	allergies
abusar *v.*	abuse	algo *pron.*	something
adolescentes		alguien *pron.*	someone
n. m.	teenagers	alrededor *adv.*	around
acariciar *v.*	to make out	alto *adj.*	tall
accidente *n. m.*	accident	altura *n. f.*	height
ácido *n. m.*	acid	amarillo *adj.*	yellow

SPANISH	ENGLISH	SPANISH	ENGLISH
ambulancia *n. f.*	ambulance	bolsita de a	
amenaza *n. f.*	threat	diez *n. f.*	dime bag
amiga *n. f.*	friend	borrachera *n. f.*	binge
amigo *n. m.*	friend	borracho *adj.*	drunk, fucked
anaranjado			up, loaded,
adj.	orange		blasted
andar *v.*	to walk	botas *n. f.*	boots
anfetas *v.*	amphetamine	botella *n. f.*	bottle
anillo *v.*	ring	brazos *n. m*	arms
año *n. m.*	year	buena salud	
antes *adv.*	before	*n. f.*	good health
apalear *v.*	to beat		
apellido *n. m.*	last name	**C**	
apodo *n. m.*	nickname		
apuñalar *v.*	to stab	cabestrillo *n. m.*	splint
aquí *adv.*	here	cabeza *n. f.*	head
aretes *n. m.*	earrings	cabrón *adj.*	bastard
arma *n. f.*	weapon	cabrona *adj.*	cunt
arrestado *pp.*	busted	cachetes *n. m.*	butt
arrestar *v.*	to arrest	cachiporra *n. f.*	black jack
arriba *adv.*	up	cacho (una	
asalto *n. m.*	assault	onza) *n. m.*	piece (one
asesinar *v.*	to murder		ounce)
asesinato *n. m.*	murder	cadera *n. f.*	hip
asientos *n. m.*	seats	caer *v.*	fall
asistir *v.*	to attend	cagada *n. f.*	crap
asustado *adj.*	scared	cajuela *n. f.*	glove box
atender *v.*	to attend	calada *n. f.*	hit
atropellar *v.*	to run over	calambres *n. m.*	cramps
ayuda *n. f.*	help	calcetines *n. m.*	socks
ayudar *v.*	to help	callado *adj.*	quiet
azul *adj.*	blue	calle *n. f.*	street
		camello *n. m.*	mule, drug
B			runner
		camion *n. f.*	truck
bajo *adj.*	short	camisa *n. f.*	shirt
barba *n. f.*	beard	camiseta *n. f.*	T-shirt
bigote *n. m.*	moustache	capó *n. m.*	hood (of a
blanco *adj.*	white		car)
blusa *n. f.*	blouse	cara *n. f.*	face
boca *n. f.*	mouth	carajo *expl.*	fuck
bolsa *n. f.*	purse	carro *n. m.*	car
bolsillo *n. m.*	pocket	carrucha *n. f.*	car
bolsita *n. f.*	bindle	cartera *n. f.*	wallet
bolsita de a		casa *n. f.*	house
cinco *n. f.*	nickel bag	caso *n. m.*	case

SPANISH	ENGLISH
castaño adj.	brown
cerveza n. f.	beer
cicatriz n. m.	scar
cintura n. f.	waist
cinturón n. m.	belt
ciudad n. f.	city
claro adj.	light
coca n. f.	cocaine
codo n. m.	elbow
coger v.	fuck
collar n. m.	necklace
colilla n. f.	roach
cojones n. m.	balls
como adv.	how
compañía de seguros n. f.	insurance company
comprar v.	to buy
comprender v.	to understand
con prep.	with
conocer v.	to know
consejo n. m.	advice
contra prep.	against
contrabando n. m.	smuggling
contracciones n. f.	labor pains
coño n. m.	bush
cooperación n. f.	cooperation
copia n. f.	copy
correr v.	to run
correrse v.	to ejaculate
correo n. m.	mail
crack n. m.	crack
crédito n. m.	credit
crimen pasional n. m.	crime of passion
cruzado adj.	spaced out
cual pron.	which
cuando conj.	when
cucaracha n. f.	roach
cuchara n. f.	spoon
cuchillo de carnicero n. m.	butcher knife

SPANISH	ENGLISH
cuchillo de caza n. m.	hunting knife
cuchillo n. m.	knife
cuello n. m.	neck
cuete n. m.	gun
culear v.	fuck, get laid
culo n. m.	ass

CH

chaqueta n. f.	jacket
chichis n. m.	boobs
chinga tu madre expl.	go fuck yourself
chingada adj.	bitch
chingar v.	to get laid
chiva n. f.	heroin
chivato adj.	informant
chupar la punta v.	to give a blow job
chupón adj.	hickey
chute n. m.	speedball

D

dar patadas v.	to kick
debajo adv.	under
decir v.	say
dedos n. m.	fingers
dejar v.	to leave, to allow
delgado adj.	skinny
derecha adj.	right
derecho adj., adv.	straight forward
describir v.	to describe
desfalco n. m.	embezzling
después conj.	after
detrás prep.	behind
diablos n. m.	downers
días laborables n. m.	working days
dientes n. m.	teeth
direccíon n. f.	address

SPANISH	ENGLISH
disparar v.	to shoot
disparo desde un carro n. m.	drive-by shooting
dolor n. m.	pain
donde conj.	where
drogadicto n. m.	drug addict
drogas n. f.	drugs
dueño n. m.	owner

E

SPANISH	ENGLISH
edificio n. m.	building
él pron.	he
ella pron.	she
embrague n. m.	clutch
empezar v.	to begin
encima adv.	on top
enfermedad n. f.	illness
enfrente de adv.	in front, across
enojado adj.	angry
entender v.	to understand
entre prep.	between
envenenamiento n. m.	poisoning
erección n. f.	hard-on
eructar v.	to belch
escopeta n. f.	shot gun
escribir v.	to write
espalda n. f.	back
espejo n.	mirror
estacionar v.	park
estar en onda v.	to be stoned
estar v.	to be
este n. m., adj.	east, this
estómago n. m.	stomach
extorsión n. f.	extortion
estrangulación n. f.	strangulation
estrangular v.	to strangle

F

SPANISH	ENGLISH
falda n. f.	skirt
falsificación n. f.	counterfeiting
familia n. f.	family
fila n. f.	knife, blade

SPANISH	ENGLISH
firoláis adj.	spaced out
frajos n. m.	cigarettes
fraude n. m.	fraud
frenos n. m.	brakes
fumado adj.	spaced out
fumar v.	to smoke

G

SPANISH	ENGLISH
garrote n. m.	club
gordo adj.	fat
gorra n. f.	cap
gracias	thanks
gramo/medio gramo n. m.	gram/half gram
grande adj.	big
grifa n. f.	marijuana
gris adj.	grey
guante n. m.	glove
guardafangos n. m.	fender

H

SPANISH	ENGLISH
hablar v.	to speak
hacer v.	to do
herido adj.	wounded
herir v.	to wound
hermana n. f.	sister
hermano n. m.	brother
heroína n. f.	heroin
hija n. f.	daughter
hijo n. m.	son
hijo de puta expl.	bastard, son of a bitch
hijo de la chingada expl.	mother fucker, son of a bitch
híjole expl.	darn, jeez, man
hoja n. f.	blade
hombre n. m.	man
hombros n. m.	shoulders
homicidio involuntario n. m.	manslaughter

SPANISH	ENGLISH	SPANISH	ENGLISH
homicidio *n. m.*	homicide	llamar *v.*	to call
homosexual		llanta *n. f.*	tire
n. m.	queer	llegar *v.*	to arrive
huevón *n. m.*	scumbag	llevar *v.*	to carry, to
huevos *n. m.*	balls, eggs		wear

I

M

incendio *n. m.*	fire	macana *n. f.*	club
incendio		madre *n. f.*	mother
premeditado		madrina *n. f.*	godmother
n. m.	arson	mal de salud	
incitación *n. f.*	solicitation	*adj.*	bad health
intrusión *n. f.*	trespassing	maldecir *v.*	to curse
ir *v.*	to go	maletero *adj.*	trunk (of car)
ir a cagar *v.*	to take a dump	mamado *adj.*	blasted
ir a hacer pis *v.*	to do number	manejar *v.*	to drive
	one	manos *n. f.*	hands
		maricón *adj.*	fag

J

		marido *n. m.*	husband
jeringa *n. f.*	syringe	marimacho *adj.*	butch
joder *v.*	to fuck	martillo *n. m.*	hammer
joto *adj.*	fag	matanza *n. f.*	massacre
jóven *n. m.*	young person	matar *v.*	to kill
juego de		media onza *n. f.*	half ounce
apuestas *n. m.*	gambling	mediano *adj.*	average
		médico *n. m.*	doctor

K

		medias *n. f.*	stockings
kilo	kilo	medicamento	
		n. m.	medication

L

		meter mano *v.*	finger fuck
ladrillo *n. m.*	brick	mierda *n. f.,*	
lambiscón *adj.*	cock-sucker	*expl.*	shit
lameculos *adj.*	kiss-ass	mirar *v.*	to look at
lata *n. f.*	can	mochila *n. f.*	backpack
lengua *n. f.*	tongue	mona *n. f.*	hang-over
lentes *n. m.*	glasses	morado *adj.*	maroon
leño *n. m.*	joint	moreno *adj.*	dark-skinned
libertad		moretón *n. m.*	bruise
provisional		morir *v.*	to die
n. f.	parole	mota *n. f.*	marijuana
Lo siento.	I'm sorry.	motor *n. m.*	engine

LL

		muchacha *n. f.*	young woman
llamada obscena		muchacho *n. m.*	young man
n. f.	obscene call	muerto *n. m.,*	
		adj.	dead

SPANISH	ENGLISH	SPANISH	ENGLISH
mujer *n. f.*	wife, woman	papelito *n. m.*	bindle
multa *n. f.*	fine	parabrisas *n. f.*	windshield
muñeca *n. f.*	wrist	parachoques	
N		*n. m.*	bumper
		parar *v.*	to stop
nacimiento *n.*	birth	parientes *n. m.*	relatives
nada *adj., adv.*	nothing	parque *n.*	park
nalgas *n. f.*	butt	pasar *v.*	to pass
nariz *n. f.*	nose	pasajero *n. m.*	passenger
navaja *n. f.*	pocket knife	pecho *n. m.*	chest
necesitar *v.*	to need	pecoso *adj.*	freckled
negro *adj.*	black	pedir *v.*	to ask
nieta *n. f.*	grand-daughter	pedo *n. m.*	shit-faced
		pegar *v.*	to beat up
nieto *n. m.*	grandson	pelo *n. m.*	hair
niña *n. f.*	girl	pendejo *adj.*	asshole, creep, dick-head, dumb shit, wimp
niño *n. m.*	boy		
noche *n. f.*	night		
nombre *n. m.*	name		
norte *n. m.*	north	pene *n. m.*	cock, peepee
número *n. m.*	number	pensar *v.*	to think
número de		pequeño *adj.*	small
póliza *n. m.*	policy number	perder *v.*	lose
O		perder el cono-cimiento *v.*	to pass out
oeste *n. m.*	west	perro *n. m.*	dog
oír *v.*	hear	persona *n. f.*	person
ojos *n. m.*	eyes	peso *n. m.*	weigh
onza *n. f.*	ounce	picarse *v.*	inject oneself
orejas *n. f.*	ears	piernas *n. f.*	legs
orinar *v.*	to urinate	pies *n. m.*	feet
oscuro *adj.*	dark	píldoras *n. f.*	pills
P		pinche *adj.*	damned
		pinto *n. m.*	ex-convict
padrastro *n. m.*	stepfather	pipa *n. f.*	pipe
padre *n. m.*	father	pistear *v.*	drink
padres *n. m.*	parents	pisto *n. m.*	booze
padrino *n. m.*	godfather	pistola *n. f.*	gun
pagar *v.*	to pay	pitillo *n. m.*	joint
pálido *adj.*	pale	placa *n. f.*	license plate
palo *n. m.*	stick	poder *v.*	to be able to
pandilla *n. f.*	gang	polvo de	
pandilleros		ángel *n.*	angel dust
n. m.	gang members	poner *v.*	to put
pantalones *n. m.*	trousers	por *prep.*	for, through

SPANISH	ENGLISH
por favor	please
por qué	why
porque *conj.*	because
porra *n. f.*	billy club, night stick
porro *n. m.*	joint
pregunta *n. f.*	question
presión de la sangre *n. f.*	blood pressure
primer grado *adj.*	first degree
primo *n. m.*	cousin
problema *n. f.*	problem
problemas de corazón *n. f.*	heart problems
problemas emocionales *n. f.*	emotional illness
prohibido *adj., pp.*	prohibited
proveedor *n. m.*	supplier
puertas *n. f.*	doors
puñal *n. m.*	dagger
puñetazo *n. m.*	a punch with the fist
puta *n. f.*	slut

Q

quemaduras *n. f.*	burns
quemar *v.*	to burn
querer *v.*	to want, to love

R

rata *n. f.*	informant
refugio *n. m.*	shelter
regla *n. f.*	menstruation, rule, ruler
rellenar *v.*	to fill-in
resaca *n. f.*	hang-over
retrasado mental *adj.*	retarded
rifle *n. m.*	rifle
robo *n. m.*	theft

SPANISH	ENGLISH
robo a mano armada *n. m.*	robbery
rodillas *n. f.*	knees
rojo *adj.*	red
romper *v.*	to break
roto *adj.*	broken
ropa *n. f.*	clothes
rosa *adj.*	pink
rubio *adj.*	blonde

S

saber *v.*	to know
sala de emergencia *n. f.*	emergency room
sala de espera *n. f.*	waiting room
sala de opreraciones *n. f.*	operating room
sala de recuperación *n.*	recovery room
sangrando *pres. part.*	bleeding
secuestro *n. m.*	kidnapping
segundo grado *adj.*	second degree
semáforo *n. m.*	traffic light
semana *n. f.*	week
ser *v.*	to be
sin *prep.*	without
sitio *n. m.*	place
sobrina *n. f.*	niece
sobrino *n. m.*	nephew
solicitud *n. f.*	application
sombrero *n. m.*	hat
sombrillas *n. f.*	mushrooms
soplar *v.*	to blow
sospechoso *adj., n. m.*	suspect
sótano *n. m.*	basement
suerte *n.*	luck

SPANISH	ENGLISH	SPANISH	ENGLISH
suicidio *n. m.*	suicide	**V**	
sur *n. m.*	south		
T		vagina *n. f.*	vagina, cunt
		vandalismo	
tapa *n. f.*	lid	*n. m.*	vandalism
tatuaje *n. m.*	tattoo	vaqueros *n. m.*	blue jeans
teléfono *n. m*	telephone	vecino *n. m.*	neighbor
tener la regla v.	on the rag (to	vehículo *n. m.*	vehicle
	be...)	vendido *adj.*	turncoat
tener *v.*	to have	venir *v.*	to come
testículos *n. m.*	nuts	ventana *n. f.*	window
testigo *n. m.*	witness	ventanilla *n. f.*	window (of
tetas *n. f.*	boobs		car)
tía *n. f.*	aunt	ver *v.*	to see
tío *n. m.*	uncle	verde *adj.*	green
tipo de sangre		vestido *n. m.*	dress
n. m.	blood type	veterano *n. m.*	senior gang
tobillos *n. m.*	ankles		member
tocar *v.*	touch	vez *n.*	time
todavía *adv.*	still	vino *n. m.*	wine
tomado *adj.*	drunk	viajar *v.*	to travel
tomar *v.*	to drink	viaje *n. m.*	trip
toque de queda		vidrio *n. m.*	glass
n.	curfew	viejo *adj.*	old
trabajar *v.*	to work	vivir *v.*	to live
trabajo *n. m.*	work	volante *n. m.*	steering
traficante *n. m.*	drug dealer		wheel
tragar *v.*	to swallow	voltear *v.*	to turn
tranquilizante		**Y**	
n. m.	tranquilizer		
U		yerba *n. f.*	marijuana
		yo *pron.*	I
última *adj.*	last	**Z**	
un cuarto de			
onza *n. m.*	quarter ounce	zapatos *n. m.*	shoes

6. INDEX

This index lists all culture notes, grammar notes, and vocabulary in alphabetical order.

CALIFORNIA
___ California Police Officer — $35.00
___ California State Police (Highway Patrol) — $35.00
___ California Corrections Officer — $35.00
___ California Law Enforcement Career Guide — $20.00

FLORIDA
___ Florida Police Officer — $35.00
___ Florida Corrections Officer — $35.00
___ Florida Law Enforcement Career Guide — $20.00

ILLINOIS
___ Chicago Police Officer (September 1997) — $30.00

MASSACHUSETTS
___ Massachusetts Police Officer — $30.00
___ Massachusetts State Police (September 1997) — $30.00

NEW JERSEY
___ New Jersey Police Officer — $35.00
___ New Jersey State Police — $30.00
___ New Jersey Corrections Officer — $35.00
___ New Jersey Law Enforcement Career Guide — $20.00

NEW YORK
___ Suffolk County Police Officer — $30.00
___ New York City/Nassau County Police Officer — $30.00
___ New York State Police — $30.00
___ New York Corrections Officer — $30.00
___ New York Law Enforcement Career Guide — $20.00

TEXAS
___ Texas Police Officer — $35.00
___ Texas State Police — $35.00
___ Texas Corrections Officer — $35.00
___ Texas Law Enforcement Career Guide — $20.00

MIDWEST (Illinois, Indiana, Michigan, Minnesota, Ohio, Wisconsin)
___ Midwest Police Officer — $30.00
___ Midwest Firefighter — $30.00

THE SOUTH (Alabama, Arkansas, Georgia, Louisiana, Mississippi, North Carolina, South Carolina, Virginia)
___ The South Police Officer (September 1997) — $25.00
___ The South Firefighter (September 1997) — $25.00

ORDER TODAY! CALL TOLL-FREE 1-888-551-JOBS